The South Shields Poltergeist

The South Shields Poltergeist

One Family's Fight Against an Invisible Intruder

Darren W. Ritson

Foreword by
Guy Lyon Playfair
Preface by
Alan Murdie

This book is dedicated to the memory of Mark Winter, 1976–2022.
His assistance in this case was invaluable; he was a true gentleman,
a passionate investigator, and above all he was my friend.

Front cover design by Ryan Bartley

First published 2008, 2009
This edition published 2020

The History Press
97 St George's Place, Cheltenham,
Gloucestershire, GL50 3QB
www.thehistorypress.co.uk

British Library Cataloguing in Publication Data.
A catalogue record for this book is available from the British Library.

ISBN 978 0 7509 9462 0

Typesetting and origination by The History Press
Printed and bound in Great Britain by TJ Books Limited

'If events happened as alleged, it was reasoned there would be a considerable quantity of documentary, photographic and other evidence available that would be consistent with the claims made in the book. This proved to be the case – I am of the opinion the South Shields poltergeist joins a small but significant collection of spontaneous cases where credible evidence has been obtained by investigators whilst disturbances were still occurring.'

Alan Murdie LLB, Head of the Spontaneous Cases Committee for the Society for Psychical Research

'Books about poltergeist cases written by those who were there and witnessed some of the action are very rare. Investigators who witnessed as much as Mike and Darren did and manage to record a great deal of evidence are even rarer. This book is a welcome addition to the literature on the most bewildering phenomena we are ever likely to encounter.'

Guy Lyon Playfair BA,
Author of *This House is Haunted:*
An Investigation into the Enfield Poltergeist

'I am aware of many poltergeist cases, but nothing comes close to being as terrifying as the South Shields poltergeist. This case has so many disturbing events throughout the course of its stay that it surely must rank as one of the most extraordinary cases of poltergeists – ever. If you only ever read one book on poltergeists, then this must surely be it. Be prepared to have your worldly views shattered from those that say that poltergeists can't harm you; they certainly can. This is simply an astonishing book'.

Malcolm Robinson, founder of SPI and author

'From the stone throwing Guyra ghost of the Australian outback, to the Rosenheim poltergeist which allegedly plagued the electrical system of a law office, opportunities to study 'the poltergeist' in action are few. This book – whatever you may conclude from the detailed findings – is one of those rare instances in which the events were given significant observation. It demonstrates above all, the need for sceptical inquiry when such a variety of phenomena occurring becomes a 'plate-spinning' task of critical evaluation for the researchers trying to find a cause. The South Shields case is no exception. The book offers the reader a documentary-style account of the events as they unfolded, and the complexities of seemingly anomalous phenomena the investigators had to face.'

Callum E. Cooper, PhD, University of Northampton

'The Poltergeist remains a true enigma. Many consider the poltergeist to be a powerful demonstration of uncontrolled psychokinetic forces resulting from psychological angst. Others claim it to be a physical manifestation of some discarnate intelligence, one which seemingly delights at teasing and tormenting those who are unfortunate enough to encounter it. There are also those who consider the poltergeist to be entirely the result of prank, hoax or misperception.

Regardless of actual cause, those who find themselves surrounded by the poltergeist's turmoils might consider themselves to be fortunate that its disruption rarely lasts for very long. Characteristically, the poltergeist is a short-lived phenomenon, going through its entire repertoire in weeks or months before it fizzles and ceases its activities altogether. However, for those who seek to discover more about the poltergeist's nature, the short duration of the poltergeist's manifestation makes investigating such cases difficult.

All too often, by the time the investigator learns of a poltergeist case, much of the activity has already faded and they are left with only the testimony of the witnesses to consider and many unanswered questions to puzzle over. However, just occasionally, the investigators find themselves in just the right place and at just the right time. They are able to observe and document the poltergeist disturbance almost from the very first interaction and follow to its ultimate conclusion.

Over the years, many books and treatises have been written about poltergeists. But, of that considerable number, very few works exist which provide the reader with a detailed first-hand account of the perplexing, sometimes frightening and constantly changing situation that people find themselves embroiled within. The South Shields poltergeist is one of those rare examples. It is a book which documents not just the experiences of the family whose lives have become blighted by the poltergeist, but it is also an account of the struggle by the investigators to document, understand and to search for some meaning for the events they now find themselves a part of.'

Steven T Parsons, author of *Ghostology:
The Art of the Ghost Hunter

'This new updated version of this exciting page-turner digs a little deeper into the enigma of poltergeist activity. There are never two cases exactly the same but similarities and comparisons can be made in search of an answer to the sometimes terrifying experiences that some people have to endure.'

Tricia J. Robertson, psychical researcher, author, broadcaster, lecturer and former president of the Scottish Society for Psychical Research

'Undoubtedly, one of the great classic works on the poltergeist.'
Colin Wilson, philosopher, author and occultist

About the Author

Darren W. Ritson was born in March 1972 in Newcastle upon Tyne and has been fascinated with ghosts and the poltergeist phenomenon as far back as he can remember. His first real attempts of collating and documenting accounts of paranormal phenomena was in 1993–4 when he regularly corresponded with veteran UFO and ghost researcher Malcolm Robinson, who assisted Darren and steered him in the right direction. For this he will always be grateful. In later years Darren corresponded with some of the literary greats in the paranormal field such as Peter Underwood FRSA, Guy Lyon Playfair BA, Alan Murdie LLB Chairman of the Ghost Club, and the philosopher and occultist Colin Wilson. Sadly, three of the aforementioned are not with us anymore but to be a correspondent of theirs was indeed an honour and a surreal experience. Darren is still regularly in touch with Malcolm Robinson and Alan Murdie.

The poltergeist enigma always had Darren 'on the fence' so to speak, when it came to either accepting it or not, until 2006, when he was given a chance to investigate one for himself – it turned out to be one of the most intense and bewildering accounts he had ever had the fortune to encounter. And now, having seen it first hand, he is fully prepared to accept the reality of the phenomenon. Darren has also travelled the UK lecturing and giving talks about the South Shields poltergeist case, and on the poltergeist phenomenon in general.

Darren has been invited to conduct talks and lectures with some of the country's leading academic research associations into psychical research such as the Incorporated Society for Psychical Research (SPR) and The Ghost Club of Great Britain (both based in London). Further invites to lecture on the poltergeist came from Professor Nick Neave of the psychology department at Northumbria University in Newcastle upon Tyne, where for three years running he talked to first year psychology students as part of their parapsychology module, and The Scottish Society for Psychical Research (SSPR) where he addressed over two hundred psychical researchers, parapsychology students and society members at Glasgow University. Darren is also a current member of the Incorporated Society for Psychical Research after joining in 2006 in the hope that he could make a small but significant contribution to the field.

Darren has had almost twenty ghost related books published to date which include: *The Haunting of Willington Mill: In Search of Ghosts; Contagion: In The Shadow of the South Shields Poltergeist; Ghosts at Christmas; The Supernatural North; Ghost Taverns of the North East; Paranormal North East; Paranormal County Durham; Haunted Tyneside; Haunted Northumberland; Haunted Berwick; Haunted Carlisle; Haunted Durham; Haunted Newcastle* and *Newcastle East Through Time.*

Darren currently lives in Roker, in Sunderland, Tyne and Wear, after relocating there in 2018, and has a teenage daughter called Abbey. His other passions include mountain climbing, scrambling and fell-walking in the Lake District. Darren is a Black Belt in Judo, a keen wildlife and landscape photographer, a lover of travelling, and in 2015 he achieved one of his lifelong dreams and climbed Mt Fuji in Japan. Darren can be contacted at darren.ritson16@gmail.com.

Contents

Acknowledgements

The North East Ghost Research Team, for volunteering to take part in a living nightmare.

Daniel Jackson, for his services on 'Grim Saturday'.

Jill Butler, for her encouragement and advice.

Bob and Marrisse Whittaker, of Orion TV, for their help in recording some of the evidence. Stephen Swales, for his valued insight and assistance.

Dave Wood and Nicky Sewell, from PSI.

John Gledson and Andy Briggs, for their much valued help and advice.

Graphologists Dennis Duez and Dana White.★

Jon Downes, of the Centre for Fortean Zoology.

Lesley, for drawing Darren's attention to this extraordinary case.

Guy Lyon Playfair for generously agreeing to write the foreword for this book, and for his help, guidance and encouragement.

To Peter Johnson and Alan Murdie of the Society for Psychical Research for use of the Journal's book Review, and further thanks to Alan Murdie for also providing the new preface.

Author's Note

Since writing this book quite a large change has subsequently occurred in regards to its authorship. The first two editions of *The South Shields Poltergeist: One Family's Fight Against an Invisible Intruder* featured Michael J. Hallowell in its by-line, but now the observant reader may have noticed that this present and new volume has the sole author as Darren W. Ritson. This, it has to be said, is essentially down to the fact that Michael decided for reasons that were pertinent to him, that he no longer wanted to share the by-line; it is as simple as that, and it is a decision that I accept and respect.

Ill health forced Michael into retiring from paranormal research *and* writing. It must also be said that in addition, a recent change in his religious faith (around 2014) made him realise that withdrawing his name from the book and case was the correct course of action for him to take. I am more than happy to continue and promote the South Shields poltergeist book, case, and its evidence in a solo capacity, and will endeavour to push forward in an effort to assist in getting a better understanding of its nature, in whatever means possible.

The account of the Lock Street infestation will of course remain exactly the same and Michael will still feature heavily throughout the main body of the text as it is quite obvious I cannot and will not re-write its history, and nor would I want to. What was reported and documented back in 2005/06 and what was *first* published in 2008 was the truth. Michael is not edited out of the text in any way and just for the record, we *both* still categorically stand by our account of what unfolded at that time, so, in this respect, nothing has changed.

Darren W. Ritson, 2020

Some of the names in this book have been changed to protect anonymity, and are marked with an ⋆ at their first appearance.

Preface

Every decade a major poltergeist seems to erupt in Great Britain and one that lasts sufficiently long enough for investigators to arrive, observe and attempt to record events. Only a small percentage of the total number of poltergeist cases reported annually fall into this category allowing proper investigation by serious researchers so far as circumstances allow. Author Darren W. Ritson found himself in this situation in the summer of 2006 with the South Shields poltergeist, which is one of the most remarkable British poltergeist cases thus reported in the twenty-first century. It erupted in a modest house in South Shields in Tyneside, then occupied by a young couple in their twenties and their three-year-old son.

This book, first published in 2008 and now updated, provides many details obtained first-hand. It is an important study because so much material and evidence was gathered – far more than appears on these pages. Inevitably, the majority of the evidence we have on poltergeists with spontaneous cases tends to be anecdotal and after the event. In a few years, the details tend to be forgotten. In the case of haunted houses (especially haunted pubs and inns) the residents may change quickly. Domestic poltergeist outbreaks prove much the same, family life being inevitably complicated by dealing with practical day-to-day demands and issues.

These mundane matters soon eclipse what in most cases is a relatively short-lived interruption in the daily routine, and inevitably even the most amazing events get relegated to experience and family stories, forgotten with the passage of time. Therefore, a contemporary record such as this gathered by contemporary researchers on the spot is a very valuable one indeed. Much like the investigators of the classic Enfield Poltergeist of 1977–9, the original authors of The South Shields Poltergeist faced scepticism when they first published their results.

There are those who will reject any evidence of this kind if it conflicts with their beliefs, conscious or unconscious, concerning ways that physical systems should behave. This criticism was advanced by people who had little or no familiarity with the South Shields case, and certainly possessing no direct knowledge of the evidence. As the late Maurice Grosse and Guy Playfair observed (Grosse, Maurice & Playfair, Guy (1988) 'Enfield Revisited: The Evaporation of Positive Evidence' in Journal of the Society for Psychical Research. Vol 55 No.813. pp207–18): 'There are those, we have found, who are prepared to believe in psi phenomena provided they happened a long time ago and preferably in another country. The suggestion that they happened yesterday evening right here is less welcome. There are others who reject any claim for positive evidence of psi automatically, as ducks' backs repel water.'

Crucially, none of this criticism was advanced by anyone who had even attempted to engage directly with the researchers or their evidence. As the claims in this book were extraordinary, after consulting with others, I took the opportunity to inspect their evidence at first-hand, and interview the investigators at length. My conclusions being that not only were they truthful in describing and recalling their experiences, but corroboration existed, together with much additional evidence in many forms, in terms of documents, witness testimony and recordings over different media.

Accordingly, the position of those who seek to dismiss the evidence in this book without examination, bare comparison with the cardinals who (allegedly) refused to look through Galileo's telescope. Perhaps more pertinently, their position at best is no more sustainable than that of a doctor who has not examined a patient, or, indeed, any patient. Such reluctance to engage with evidence may, of course, have a psychological basis.

Speaking personally, viewing the material behind this book in its totality, from a legal perspective, I considered testimony of those who witnessed events together with the material collected, matches or exceeds the evidence accumulated in many civil and criminal proceedings. In the decade since, I have had no reason to depart from this position and events and parallels from other cases have if anything strengthened this conclusion that genuine psychokinetic incidents occurred, as the authors described them.

Thus, more than a prima facie case been presented in this book and the task now is not proof but interpretation, a matter which is still at a very early stage nearly fifteen years later. Each generation has its own poltergeists behaving in certain ways and attracting all manner of theories and hypotheses. Prior to the sixteenth century it was the angry dead. In the seventeenth century through to the mid-eighteenth century the idea of witchcraft was in vogue. Then in the nineteenth century spiritualist ideas of 'unconscious mediums' and elemental spirits or, alternatively, forces produced by living persons dubbed 'human batteries' envisaged as producing surges of electrical power.

In the twentieth century, parapsychology has supplied and concentrated upon the idea of psychokinesis from living minds, labelling it 'Recurrent Spontaneous Psychokinesis' (RSPK) pin-pointing the source of the energy as the unconscious minds of living persons, typically adolescents undergoing stress.

Yet another researcher, D. Scott Rogo, proposed in 1974 that poltergeists might be a group effort, stating: 'I have long main-tained that some poltergeists are projected by disturbed agents, while others are the outcome of a co-operative family effort.' (Rogo, Scott D., (1983) Correspondence, 'Journal of the Society for Psychical Research', Vol. 52, No. 794, pp152–3.)

The parapsychologist and psychiatrist the late Ian Stevenson went so far as to propose in an article 'Poltergeists: Are they living or dead?' that there might actually be two varieties of disturbance – relatively simple and non-complex cases attributable to the unconscious mind and those involving complex effects (such as targeted movement of objects and communications) which indicate the presence of an external intelligence. (Stevenson, Ian, (1972) 'Are Poltergeists Living or Are They Dead?' 'Journal of the American Society for Psychical Research', Vol. 66(3) pp 233–52.)

This leads to the fascinating possibility that the poltergeist at South Shields may have been shaped or influenced by the observers' beliefs at the time. If so, this might make sense in terms of the responsive nature of the phenomenon, but equally it should be noted that Darren W. Ritson has gone on to propose the thought-provoking hypothesis of an 'arch-poltergeist' as possibly behind this and other outbreaks. It is certainly an arresting idea that the victims at South Shields might have been afflicted by phenomena orchestrated by some cosmic 'arch-poltergeist', and were thus destined to suffer like Thomas Hardy's hapless heroine in *Tess of the D'Urbervilles* up until the point where 'The president of the immortals had finished his sport with Tess'. Alternatively, a case could be made that some external reservoir of energy – the nature of which must presently remain wholly opaque and mysterious – might be being drawn upon in the creation of the disturbances. But that is to run ahead of the story contained in this book. Ultimately, what this book demonstrates is that there is a real and currently unexplained force that can erupt in the material world, one which current scientific models need to be able to confront and accommodate.

It is for those who encounter poltergeists often prove far from fun or humorous, imposing a considerable personal strain not only just upon those suffering them, but also upon those who investigate, both short-term and in the long term. As D. Scott Rogo wrote: '… poltergeist (RSPK) manifestations…represent one of the most potentially horrifying experiences an individual or family may face.' (Rogo, Scott, D. (1974), 'Psychotherapy and the Poltergeist', 'Journal of the Society for Psychical Research Vol. 47, pp426–40.) This book provides a cogent illustration of this truth. Therefore, it is in my opinion, that the fact that Darren W. Ritson has been prepared to revisit these remarkable and often disturbing events again, deserves admiration and respect.

Alan Murdie
Head of the Spontaneous Cases Committee
for the Society for Psychical Research

Foreword

This remarkable book is the inside story of the invasion of a young couple's home in the north of England by an invisible intruder of the kind we call a poltergeist and the havoc, fear and panic it caused there for several months in 2006 before departing as mysteriously as it had arrived.

Many will find parts of the story hard – even impossible – to believe, and they have my sympathies; I too find poltergeist phenomena hard to believe even when I see them happen, as I have many times.

The word *poltergeist* means 'noisy ghost', which is not a very helpful definition. They are certainly noisy – they bang on walls and floors, fling things around and overturn furniture, yet are almost certainly not ghosts in the sense of spirits of specific dead people. Indeed, we really haven't a clue what they are. We don't even have a word of our own for them and have to use an archaic German one. As my late colleague Maurice Grosse, with whom I pursued the Enfield poltergeist in 1977-8, used to say, 'Anybody who says they know is a charlatan.'

There is a huge amount of evidence, much of it of a very high quality, describing cases dating back to ancient Greece and Rome – at least five hundred of them. We also know that they keep repeating themselves – we find identical phenomena reported from countries that had no contact with each other. This makes the investigator's job easier, since if they are as experienced and well informed as Mike and Darren, they will know more or less what to look for, and they will spot a fake a mile away;

People do fake poltergeists, whether in order to be re-housed by their local council (quite common, I am told) or to make large sums of money. But they have to get the detail right. When they describe a case of a kind that has never been reported before, as with the hoax known as the Amityville Horror, they do not fool a competent researcher for a minute. You may be surprised to know that nearly all the events described in this book have been reported again and again from all over the world for centuries.

There are those who just cannot take poltergeists seriously. What they are alleged to do is so obviously impossible that it simply cannot be true. Yet it is true, and we should take poltergeists seriously for at least two reasons. One is that they cause real distress to innocent people who would get immediate expert help if they had a fire, an accident, a burglary or a heart attack. There is no Emergency Poltergeist Service, however. There are only dedicated researchers like Mike and Darren who are prepared to give up a lot of their spare time – and sleep – recording the evidence as best they can, acting as volunteer social workers as well as reporters.

The other and most important reason is that the kinds of things poltergeists do force us to realise that science does not yet have all the answers. For example, solid matter cannot pass through solid matter, can it? Common sense tells us obviously not. Yet as you will read, it happened again and again throughout this case in front of several witnesses. It is in fact almost a standard part of the poltergeist repertoire. I have witnessed it myself several times. It does happen. Common sense can be wrong. Reality is not quite what you may have thought it was.

Books about poltergeist cases written by those who were there and witnessed some of the action are very rare. Investigators who witnessed as much as Mike and Darren did and who manage to record a great deal of evidence are even rarer. This book is a welcome addition to the literature on one of the most bewildering phenomena we are ever likely to come across.

Guy Lyon Playfair
Author of This House is Haunted:
the Investigation of the Enfield Poltergeist

Introduction

In one sense, it can be said that the fates conspired to bring Mike, Darren and the residents of 42 Lock Street together.

When Mike was just eight years old, he lived in Humbert Street, Jarrow. This town, which has maintained a faithful vigil over the south bank of the River Tyne for many centuries, was the home of the famous Jarrow Marchers. In October 1936, fuelled by the support of the fiery MP Ellen Wilkinson, the marchers took their grievances over unemployment and poverty all the way to Downing Street – on foot. Their courage and fortitude still inspire Jarrovians to this day.

At the other end of Humbert Street, by the second-hand bike store, there also lived a young girl of approximately the same age as Mike. One Saturday afternoon in the summer of 1965, she was roughed-up by some youngsters who lived on the other side of a nearby railway line. At least for the children of Jarrow, the line formed a physical and psychological divide between two sides of the same community. Mike, plus several friends, decided that justice should be meted out to those who were both literally and metaphorically on the wrong side of the tracks.

Later that afternoon, they raided a timber yard nearby and relieved the owner of some unseasoned staves of hard, heavy redwood. They then crossed the railway line, tracked down the offenders and dispensed a sound beating to the guilty parties. Mike and the young girl – June Peterworth* – then became friends. As a reward for his childish heroism he received an invitation to June's birthday party. Mike moved house some time later, and the two lost touch. He did remember her name, however.

Over forty years later, Mike and June's family would be reunited, albeit under the strangest of circumstances.

Most curiously, it was also an old railway line that would ultimately be responsible for bringing Mike and Darren together.

As a child', recalls Darren, 'I would ask my father to tell me ghost stories when I went to bed. One day, he told me about a little boy who used to live in our house many years ago. Tragically, he was electrocuted on the electrified railway track at the rear of the house'.

Although this is indeed a sad tale, those Darren relates it to always wonder why he refers to it as a 'ghost story'. His response is interesting:

You see, my bedroom was the same room in which the little boy had slept. On many occasions my father, downstairs, would hear footsteps walking across the floor up above. Naturally he'd yell up the stairs, telling my brother and me to get back into bed. There'd be no reply. He'd check, and always find the house in silence. My brother and I would inevitably be sound asleep in our rooms, oblivious to the spectral footfalls.

My Dad also told me another part of the story in later years, which he felt would have been too much for me to handle as a child. One night, he heard the same, eerie footsteps and came upstairs to make sure we were still in bed. As usual, we were. Puzzled, he then went into his own bedroom thinking how strange the whole thing was. At some point he looked out of the bedroom window which, incidentally, overlooked the old railway line. Through the darkness he noticed a small boy, about eight to ten years old, walking about aimlessly on the tracks. He considered it a bit late for a youngster to be out at that time, but other than that thought no more about it.

Then, weeks later, it hit him. He realised that on the night he had seen the young boy, he had also heard the mysterious footfalls across the living room ceiling, which is directly below the back bedroom overlooking the railway lines. It occurred to him that he may well have seen the ghost of the small boy who had died there.

Had the spirit of that young lad been walking around upstairs in our house, and then visited the scene of his horrific death on the railway? You can understand why he never said anything about this to me when I was young.'

Darren verified the tale's authenticity when he was older.

'It turned out to be a true story, as I found out in later years when I questioned my father about it in some depth.'

The tales Darren's father told him as a child had a profound effect on him.

'It was stories and accounts like these which made me study the paranormal and read books on this fascinating subject for years, until I decided to get involved with actual "ghost hunting"', he recalls.

Of course, the young boy seen by Darren's father may not have been a ghost at all. Perhaps he was simply a streetwise kid who had managed to convince his parents to allow him to stay out longer than he should have been, given his tender age.

Regardless, Darren's interest in ghosts had been well and truly activated, and paranormal investigation is a passion that has stayed with him throughout his entire adult life. Paranormal research is in his blood; it is part of his very essence. Darren W. Ritson is the quintessential hunter of all things insubstantial, the determined seeker of that which lies just beyond our senses.

Mike has also had several paranormal experiences. He now runs his own media business and writes about ghosts and other paranormal phenomena for a living. Both Darren and Mike later met when they became members of a local paranormal research society, and thus an enduring friendship was precipitated. Both researchers have written books about ghost-hunting.

In May 2003 Darren had begun to research his book, *Ghost Hunter: True-Life Encounters from the North East*. Early in 2006, he finally asked Mike to both review the manuscript and make the illustrations 'book ready' for sending to his publisher. Just as the task was almost completed, their lives took a dramatic and unexpected turn.

On Saturday 15 July Darren telephoned Mike and told him that a colleague had approached him and asked for some advice on behalf of a friend. Her friend's daughter, she said, was absolutely terrified to stay in the house on her own because it was haunted. She knew Darren was something of an authority on such matters, and wondered if he could help. The friend, it turned out, was none other than June Peterworth whom Mike had befriended all those years ago as a child when he lived in Jarrow. The young woman whose house was haunted was none other than June's daughter, Marianne Peterworth★.

Between them, Mike and Darren have investigated hundreds of hauntings and poltergeist infestations. Most times, it has to be said, the thrill of the chase is better than the end result. Few alleged hauntings are really paranormal; most, in fact, can be explained away quite simply. But not all; some cases present rationalists and sceptics alike with a real challenge, and the one you will read about in the following pages is no exception.

This is the true and terrifying account of a family besieged by something invisible, malevolent and intimidating; an entity of sorts that effortlessly moves heavy furniture around, breaks ornaments at will, inflicts serious slash-wounds upon people (seemingly with invisible blades), removes children from their beds without waking them, throws knives at people and, as a *piece de resistance,* occasionally scribbles death messages on a child's doodle-board. It is a creature without light, who may whisper terrible things in your ear, or if it is so moved, even communicate with you via your mobile phone. Cloaked in darkness, it wreaks havoc in the lives of all it touches.

In the pages that follow you will read of the experiences endured by Marianne and her family. You will also read of the authors' investigation into the case and their efforts to help those who had been driven to their wits' end by their unseen – and definitely unwelcome – guest.

Of course, the authors realise that many sceptics will simply refuse to believe that anything truly paranormal was taking place within this otherwise ordinary family home. To countenance the existence of quasi-corporeal entities, whatever their true nature, disturbs their worldview too much. To be honest, neither Darren nor Mike are interested in converting rabid sceptics into true believers. People will simply have to make up their own minds on the basis of the evidence.

But the authors will say this: They have no doubts whatsoever that Marianne and her kin have been, for a protracted period, frightened and terrorised by something that they cannot see, but whose presence, like a rank, foetid odour, they can easily detect. The authors have no qualms about denouncing the poltergeist that attacked Marianne and her family as evil in the purest sense of the word.

You may choose not to believe in the existence of the poltergeist phenomenon. You may, for reasons known only to yourself, put this book back upon the shelf and retreat once again into your comfortable world. The authors once lived in this world; a pleasing vista strewn with friends, wine and roses. Then, without warning, they were forced to look into the very heart of darkness. This is their story.

Darren W. Ritson & Michael J. Hallowell
February 2007

CHAPTER ONE

Contact

On 19 June 2006, Darren Ritson was informed by a colleague, Lesley, about an alleged haunting at a house in South Tyneside. He was told that the owners of this house were 'at their wits' end' because of the 'ghostly goings-on' that had been occurring there over the preceding months.

The following day, after being told that they wanted help with this matter, Darren contacted the homeowner's mother, June Peterworth, and asked her if she was prepared to talk to him about it. On the basis of that brief conversation, he then sent June an e-mail which read as follows:

Hi June, its Darren here, the paranormal investigator.

I was just wondering if you could give me an in-depth idea of the things that have been going on at your daughter's house. If you could write down in detail what has been happening and what you have experienced, that would be great.

Of course, I would love to talk to your daughter, to hear her experiences and get some more background information. An investigation of the property would be a good idea, too. We have a few night-vision video cameras and other tools of the ghost-hunting trade we could use in an effort to catch something on film. If what I hear from Lesley [Darren's colleague]

is right, it sounds too good to be true from an investigator's point of view; however, for the family at the focus of the alleged haunting it is a different story and we would try to help in whatever way we can.
Darren.

Some time later, Darren received a welcome reply from June:

Hi Darren, I will try and list as much as possible from what she has told me and what I experienced myself last night – she is very frightened at what's happening and is willing to get any help possible. She is more than happy for you to go to her house at any time and talk to her or do whatever you need to do – I will get back to you with the list of occurrences. Thanks, June.

Darren forwarded his reply to June immediately:

Thanks June. I could start the ball rolling by phoning up Marianne tonight to arrange a time when I can visit her at her home. Darren.

More from June:

Darren
She is going to the spiritualist church tonight, and she may be stopping at my house as her partner is out all night and she is too afraid to stay at home on her own. You can catch her on her mobile. June.

After giving the matter some thought, Darren – whose obsession with detail could shame both Holmes and Watson – decided that he still wanted to elicit further information about the case before contacting Marianne directly. He again e-mailed her mother in an effort to find out more.

One of the difficulties in researching poltergeist infestations is that the experients often formulate a fixed view of what the problem is very early on in the investigation. These perceptions may seem logical on the surface, but are often wildly incorrect and made on the basis of cultural and spiritual ideas prevalent in the locale where the 'haunting' is taking place. For instance, a poltergeist is almost universally perceived as a disturbed or angry spirit. Indeed, the word *poltergeist* is derived from the German and translates literally as 'boisterous ghost' or 'knocking ghost'. While the visible symptoms of a poltergeist investigation may appear to back such a conclusion strongly investigators know that there is another, far more likely cause that needs to be given serious consideration. This will be discussed further in this volume, but Darren was already aware that those who experience poltergeist activity directly, because of their deeply-ingrained beliefs, will subconsciously edit their experiences to match their perceptions. It is often better, therefore, to accumulate the initial evidence from third parties who may have no preconceived opinions, or who have not had time to formulate any ideas about the cause of the phenomena taking place.

Thanks June.

What is the spiritualist church going to do? Are they offering her help? If so, this may be the best 'port of call'. If they are a reputable spiritual group they may be able to make the activity cease. If they don't, I know someone who may be able to help. Whatever the scenario, I would like to investigate in the hope we can prove one way or another that something odd is going on, and of course help your daughter. However, the chances are that the activity will cease as quickly as it all began; but when? That's another question. Darren.

June replied:

Darren,

She's going to the open circle, which is where a lot of the mediums that have been to her house go to - I am not sure what they are going to do; they just keep telling her what spirits are there and pass on messages. They have said they can't force them to go and that it would stop soon.

I suggest you would be better off talking to my daughter as she could give you a lot more information. She has been saying that she has had something in her house for months now and things have escalated in the past couple of weeks.

I'll pull together a list of things at lunchtime for you. June.

As these correspondences show, when Darren began to liaise with June Peterworth she had already endured some strange experiences herself while visiting her daughter's home. Obviously, then, the focal point of the phenomenon, geographically speaking, was the best place to start.

June gave Darren her daughter's telephone number and told him that he could phone her at any time. June had already informed her daughter about Darren, and Marianne had made it clear that she would welcome any possible assistance.

June told Darren that the bizarre phenomena taking place in Marianne's home had began several months earlier. However, over the last few weeks, things had escalated dramatically. Marianne was now so scared that she would rarely sleep in the house alone when her partner was working nightshift.

June Peterworth, by nature a sceptical person, didn't formerly believe in ghosts. When her daughter had first informed her of what was happening, she laughed it off and told Marianne that she must have been imagining things, or was at least mistaken. Then, as the weeks passed by and the strange activity escalated, she began to change her mind. Mainly, this change was precipitated by first-hand experience of the phenomena that had already terrified her daughter and her boyfriend, Marc Karlsonn★.

As stated earlier, Darren had urged June to write down in detail what she had personally experienced at her daughter's house along with a list of any other phenomena that had, to her knowledge, taken place there. What follows is a transcript of her hand-written notes.

Things that have happened over the months:
- Shower has been mysteriously turned on.
- Robert★ (3 yrs old) has seen a lady in his bedroom and has talked to her.

- General noises and bumps have been heard when no one is around etc.

More recently (last couple of weeks):
- A cup fell from the worktop into bin next to Marianne and her dad – twice.
- The blinds keep being taken down in Robert's room.
- Robert has seen a little boy called Sam and plays with him in his room.
- Marianne and Marc (her boyfriend) have heard a voice on the baby monitor telling Robert that he was going to fall out of bed.
- A vase on stair landing keeps moving from one side to another.
- Coats are thrown up the stairs.
- A chair has been wedged up to the door in Robert's room.
- Robert's table and chair found on the landing.
- Marianne and her dad were standing at back door when a cup from Robert's room landed in the garden and smashed – the window was closed and the blind was down.
- Robert's rocking horse keeps getting moved and turned upside down.
- Ornaments keep getting moved.

Last night (19th June 2006) I went to Marianne's house for the first time since all this has happened in the last couple of weeks. We all went to Robert's room while he got ready for bed. We were there for about 10 minutes, then we all went downstairs together while Robert had his supper. After approximately 20 minutes we all went back upstairs together into Robert's room when we noticed his chair had gone – it was in Marianne's room and the door was shut. I had stood in the doorway before we went downstairs and the door was definitely open.

Darren's first thought when he reviewed June's notes was that this might indeed be a genuine case of poltergeist infestation. Many of the 'symptoms' mentioned above are classic examples of what investigators often refer to as 'polt-presence'. What intrigued Darren, however, was that on one occasion a cup from the child's bedroom had apparently passed through one closed window and a set of drawn blinds before smashing to smithereens in the garden below. Even in poltergeist cases, incidents of solid matter passing through solid matter are quite rare. They are not, however, unknown. In one well-attested case in 1977, a child who was the poltergeist 'focus' levitated up into the air and passed through an adjoining wall into a neighbour's house, taking a book with her. The book remained in the neighbour's house after the focus was mysteriously returned to her room, where she was later found by investigators.

At 3.30pm, on 20 June, Darren phoned Marianne for an informal chat. They discussed the 'strange happenings' in detail, and Marianne agreed to write down, in depth, everything that had occurred to date for research purposes. Darren also asked her if she would keep a record of any other phenomena or strange events that happened between the end of the phone call (4pm) and when he next made contact with her.

June again contacted Darren on Friday 14 July,

Hi Darren,

Marianne has asked me to contact you as she is still having problems. It started again over a week ago and things are getting worse – she had a priest in on Monday and things seemed to quieten down, but last night things got really bad and they all left the house to stay at mine. Things are getting quite scary and sinister for them, furniture is moving in front on them, things are getting thrown at them, things thrown down stairs at them and much more. Marianne has asked if you can ring her as soon as possible if you don't mind. Thanks, June.

That afternoon Darren again telephoned Marianne, and it was clear that she was becoming increasingly distressed. To his knowledge, she had already sought help from two sources; a local spiritualist 'circle' and a priest. This in itself was indicative of the fact that, to Marianne at least, the problem was becoming serious and some form of extra-familial help was needed.

For about forty-five minutes, Marianne reiterated what her mother had told Darren in her last e-mail; a priest had indeed visited the house to perform 'a blessing'. This was followed by a short lull, after which the activity started up once more – with a vengeance. It is common for such rituals to cause a short cessation of symptoms. Unfortunately, it is also common for them to start up again, usually after ten to fourteen days, with renewed ferocity.

Marianne then told him about some of the other incidents that had occurred since they last spoke. Marianne's son, Robert, had a rocking horse that usually stood in his bedroom. One evening, to their horror, Marianne's brother Ian★ found the horse hanging from the loft hatch by its reins. It was subsequently put in the garden and left overnight, only to be found *inside* the house the following morning. It was then destroyed.

Robert also possessed a cuddly toy; specifically a large, tan-coloured rabbit with a white face and feet. On one occasion, Ian found the rabbit sitting in a blue, plastic bucket chair at the top of the stairs. The chair also belonged to Robert and, like the rabbit, was always kept in the toddler's room. Chillingly, the rabbit had in its hand a razor-sharp blade from a box-cutter. One could be forgiven for thinking that whoever – or whatever – was behind these bizarre incidents was trying to send some sort of message to Marianne and her family, and it certainly wasn't pleasant.

Like many children of his age, Robert had a burgeoning collection of toy cars. Mike has found that, for reasons not quite clear, poltergeists seem to have an unusual fascination with miniature or toy vehicles. On one occasion, he was called in by a married couple who were repeatedly subjected to a whole range of 'polt' symptoms. During the initial interview, a commotion broke out in the couple's loft. Neither was prepared to venture up the ladder into the roof space, but Mike did. In the loft was a large, cardboard box filled with a collection of remote control cars which the husband had kept since his childhood. He takes up the story;

There were approximately ten to twelve cars in the box, all covered with a thick layer of dust. Every single vehicle was in motion, their wheels spinning as fast as their electric motors would let them. Some had lights which were flashing on and off constantly. I detached the battery cover from one car and found it empty. Regardless, the wheels were still spinning frantically and the lights continued to flash. I detached a battery cover from a second car. There were two AA batteries inside, but they were badly corroded and highly unlikely to be generating any electricity. Suddenly the activity stopped. At the same instant, all the wheels stopped spinning and the lights all went out. It was as if nothing had ever happened.

Marianne told Darren that, on a number of occasions, she had been hit in the back by toy cars, sometimes as she walked down the stairs. She also said that she had several times been 'hit on the back by an invisible force', but when she turned around nothing was there.

Boyfriend Marc had on occasion been pushed over, and large objects such as stepladders and bed frames had fallen on him while they were propped up against a wall.

On one occasion, a set of large stepladders fell over, as if pushed by an invisible pair of hands. Marc had instinctively raised an arm to protect himself. The ladders caught him on the shoulder, causing pain and bruising which lasted for several days. This was both unusual and disturbing. Poltergeists often intimidate and frighten people – it actually seems to be part of their *modus operandi* – but they usually don't cause physical harm. Later, both Darren and Mike would feel uneasy at this development, as it indicated that the entity they were dealing with was either of a type they had never encountered before, or at least one of unusual strength and ability. This assessment turned out to be essentially correct, but the authors later realised that they had massively underestimated both the power and the cunning of this particular polt.

It was the following day when Darren telephoned Mike and told him about this new case for the first time. Darren asked if Mike would be prepared to visit the house with him. Mike laughed and quipped, 'Is the Pope Catholic?' 'Live' polt cases are not common, and it is a rare opportunity that presents itself for investigators to experience such things first-hand. Mike wouldn't pass up a chance like that for the world.

CHAPTER TWO

Full English

For some time, Darren and Mike have engaged in an extremely constructive ritual that they both hope to enjoy for many years to come. Every few weeks, normally on a Saturday morning, they meet in The Market Cafe in Market Square, South Shields, to discuss the latest news and events in the world of paranormal activity. Often, Mike will solicit from Darren information about the latter's current investigations and write them up in his *WraithScape* column in the borough's newspaper, the *Shields Gazette*. The *Gazette* is Britain's oldest provincial newspaper, and *WraithScape* is probably the longest-running weekly column of its kind in the UK. Every Thursday, Mike entertains readers with tales of ghosts, UFOs, psychic phenomena and sea monsters. Both Mike and Darren feel that it's important to inform the public about paranormal activity. They call it 'consciousness-raising'.

On Monday, 17 July, Mike and Darren met up for breakfast. Mike arrived first, and ordered two cups of tea. Darren, he knew, wouldn't be long. When Darren did arrive, he had with him a large hold-all filled with all the tricks of the ghost-hunting trade. These included a digital video camera and a pair of motion sensors. Mike, in a smaller bag, had a digital camera and his treasured Olympus digital sound recorder. He also had with him the more conventional accoutrements of the professional journalist, such as a pen and notebook.

It was only 9am, but the day was already proving to be uncomfortably hot. The country was basking in the midst of a heat-wave, and neither Darren nor Mike cared for it too much. They both hate the heat passionately, and carefully selected a table away from the large, plate-glass windows so that they could enjoy as much shade as possible.

Within the hour, both investigators would visit the troubled dwelling, but first they needed to formulate a strategy and assess the meagre amount of evidence they had accumulated so far. Most of it had been drawn from the oral and written testimonies of Marianne and her mother, June.

Darren takes an extremely 'evidential' perspective towards paranormal research. His primary goal is to gather evidence, accumulate data. Mike is more 'experiential'. He isn't so much interested in the recipe of a paranormal event as he is in its flavour. Darren will gather data, Mike will listen to his senses and inner instinct. Perhaps that's why they work so well together as a team; they complement each other.

Darren had brought with him a copy of some further diary notes made by June Peterworth. In them, she detailed the ongoing litany of strange experiences that were disturbing her daughter so deeply. He handed them to Mike and asked him what he thought.

Mike, who had already seen a typed transcript of the notes, looked over them again for a minute or two.

'Well, if all this is accurate then it seems pretty much like a classic polt case to me. There's only one thing that bothers me, Darren: as you know, in polt cases there is almost always present a young, pubescent female under stress. Marianne is too old, and I see no mention of a younger sister, visiting cousin, or whatever. That's odd. Darren agreed, and they both made a mental note to raise this with Marianne during their visit. At this juncture, a word of explanation would probably be appropriate.

For reasons that will become clearer later, in the vast majority of polt cases the infested home almost always plays host to a female of teenage years who is unhappy to one degree or another. Typically, the girl will have at least begun – if not actually completed – the first stages of puberty, including menstruation, but will be under the age of seventeen. She will also be under great stress. This may be because she is being bullied, struggling with schoolwork or perhaps having to witness discord between parents within the familial home.

It is not always necessary for the youngster to be living at the infected premises. She may simply be a regular visitor there. A typical scenario involves a young female who regularly visits her older, married sister. When she is absent, all will be quiet. When she is present, all manner of polt-like symptoms may manifest themselves. As we shall see, this peculiar phenomenon may provide potent clues regarding the true nature of the poltergeist enigma.

Mike mopped up a smudge of egg yolk with a triangle of toast and asked Darren just what he thought they should try and achieve from the forthcoming visit.

'We don't want to go in there with size nine boots, Darren. The family is obviously upset, and I think we're going to have to be particularly tactful.'

Again, Darren agreed.

'Maybe we should just talk at first; you know, get to know them . . . put them at ease.'

'Do you think we'll get to carry out any hard research?'

'Maybe', replied Darren. 'We'll just have to play it by ear. I've brought my gear along just in case.'

'Ever the optimist, eh?'

'We can live in hope', said Darren with a grin. 'I'll tell you what, Mike; it would be terrific if we actually got the chance to witness some activity first-hand.'

'Yeah, if only', Replied Mike. 'Small chance though, eh?' 'Yeah. Still, you never know . . .'

Mike and Darren left the cafe and walked across Market Square. Suddenly, a penetrating two-tone siren broke forth from Darren's bag. The delicately-calibrated motion sensors had been activated. Darren quickly pulled on the zip, reached inside and deactivated them.

'I hate it when that happens', he said sheepishly.

'Don't worry, my lips are sealed', said Mike, After all, you paid for the breakfasts.'

Meanwhile, several miles away, Marianne and her boyfriend Marc Karlsonn were sitting in the living room of their home, wondering what was causing the terrific banging and clashing noises in the bedrooms up above. There was, after all, no one up there.

At least, there was no one up there they could see.

CHAPTER THREE

Shivers

Marianne's home is a terraced house in Lock Street* on the outskirts of a fairly modern estate within the Borough of South Tyneside. It bears none of the stereotypical hallmarks one normally associates with haunted dwellings. There are no gloomy cellars or darkened stairwells, no suits of armour in the hall or sinister-looking portraits hanging on the walls. The rooms are bright, airy and furnished accordingly. To all intents and purposes, it is a typical family home.

Often, when one enters a polt-infested home, there is an aura or atmosphere that hits you like a steam train just as you cross the threshold. This feeling is hard to describe, but well-known to investigators. Typical symptoms include a deep sense of unease, a knotted feeling in the stomach and tightness around the chest. Neither Darren nor Mike felt anything like this. The atmosphere in the home seemed relaxed. Even Marianne and Marc seemed at ease, which was surprising. Could it be that the problem was not as great as they were making out? Later this unwarranted assumption would be completely dispelled. The problem was serious indeed; Marianne and Marc were simply coping with it extremely well.

Once they had been ushered into the living room, Mike cast his eyes around, scrutinising every detail. Seasoned investigators will look for anything and everything that may provide clues as to the nature of an unusual phenomenon. A shelf filled with books on the paranormal may well indicate a predisposition on the part of the experients towards the study of strange phenomena. Religious artefacts such as crosses and menorahs will provide clues as to how the witnesses may perceive the phenomena they are actually experiencing.

Often, an allegedly polt-infested home may just be presenting a set of mundane symptoms that are being misinterpreted. Some types of heating systems are notorious for causing creaks, groans and bangs as they warm up and cool down. The malevolent spirit in the bathroom may simply be an airlock in a pipe, and calling for a plumber may be far more appropriate than calling for a priest.

In this case, there was nothing untoward or unusual about either the exterior or interior of the household apart from the nauseating, inescapable heat which was slowly roasting the entire country alive. Marianne brought both Darren and Mike a large glass of ice-cold water, which was truly appreciated.

Once the formal introductions were out of the way, Mike made a quick mental assessment of Marianne and Marc. They were friendly, pleasant and open. Marc was the quieter of the two – quite reserved, in fact – but still very co-operative. There was absolutely nothing about their initial demeanour that made either of the two investigators suspicious. Nevertheless, fraud is a word that hangs over every poltergeist investigation like a dark cloud, and witnesses who seem both honest and genuine can often turn out to be cunning, manipulative liars. In many cases, there is no malice behind the deception. The witnesses simply feel compelled to draw attention to themselves to fulfil an inner need. Sometimes, however, greed is the motivating factor. Mike and Darren have known cases where people have claimed to have a poltergeist in their home because they believe that doing so will encourage TV producers, newspaper editors and filmmakers to throw buckets of cash at them. This is rarely the case, of course. Sometimes even experienced investigators can be fooled for a while, but most often the deceit is apparent from the beginning.

Mike was asked to investigate an alleged poltergeist infestation several years ago. From the moment he met the supposed witnesses, a middle-aged married couple, he was suspicious.

At one point during the initial conversation, Mike tested out the husband.

'I know this might sound crazy, but have you ever seen luminous smoke coming out of the plug-hole in your bath? It's just that in virtually every genuine poltergeist case you get this mist or smoke rising up out of the bath drain. Sometimes it will even make shapes, and take on the appearance of a loved one who has just passed over into the spirit world.'

'Oh, yes' replied the man immediately. 'You know, I think we saw that just the other day, didn't we, Agnes? In fact, I could swear it took the shape of my dead mother.'

Mike scolded the couple for wasting his time and told them never to contact him again. Someone had told them that he would pay experients £50 for every story he wrote up in his *WraithScape* column, which was totally untrue. The only reward correspondents to Mike's column get is the satisfaction of seeing their story in print.

Oftentimes, investigators feel guilty about treating experients with suspicion in the early days of an enquiry, but there is really no alternative. Before an investigation can be carried out in earnest, fraud and deception on the part of the alleged witnesses needs to be eliminated as effectively as possible.

In fraudulent cases, the so-called experients will often try to impress investigators from the outset by creating polt-like phenomena by trickery. Seasoned researchers will, therefore, constantly monitor the movements of the witnesses during the entire span of an investigation. Still, we can all be fooled; but the old maxim holds true that you can't fool all of the people all the time. Both Marianne and Marc seemed genuine enough, but the investigators just needed to be sure.

At Darren's request, Marianne had kept a meticulous log of every seemingly paranormal incident that had taken place within her home. Like June's log, it made fascinating reading. Some of the information in Marianne's log confirmed incidents mentioned earlier either by June in written correspondence and/or by Marianne during telephone conversations with Darren.

Monday 3 July 2006

11.00am: A white figure was seen in the bedroom.

11.30am: Marianne was poked in the back at the top of the stairs.

Tuesday 4 July 2006

(No activity)

Wednesday 5 July 2006

8.00pm: The wooden rocking horse was found hanging from the loft hatch by the reins.

Thursday 6 July 2006

(No activity)

Friday 7 July 2006

(No activity)

Saturday 8 July 2006

9.00pm: a set of ladders was pushed over on the stairway and a child's chair was found at the top of the stairs.

Sunday 9 July 2006

10.00am: Child's chair was found on landing.

10.15am: Rocking horse was found on landing.

10.30am: Toy cars were found on landing and in bedroom 1.

11.00am: Rocking horse was moved again from its place in bedroom 2.

Until 12.00 midday: Cars, blocks and the like were moved and thrown around.

12.00 midday: A prayer on bedroom door was found to be scribbled on with red crayon. The red crayon was then thrown at Marianne's brother and then the toy Noddy figure was thrown at Marianne's back. A toy block was then caught on mobile phone video falling from the ceiling (possibly the loft) but then it was deleted somehow.

1.00pm: Small toys and badges were then found in the loft.

1.10pm: The rocking horse was moved on to the landing again.

1.15pm: More toys were found scattered on the landing and the ladders fell over on the stairwell again.

1. 30 – 6.00pm: The house was empty but on return the bed had been moved, as had the chest of drawers, the rocking horse had been moved yet again into another bedroom. The items were moved back into place.

6.10pm: The rocking horse was found yet again on the landing and moved back and forth from the landing and the bedroom every time it was moved back by Marianne.

7.00pm: A message saying 'DIE' was found on Robert's doodle-board.

8.00 – 11.00pm: Toys were repeatedly thrown around upstairs and two toys were thrown at Marianne and Marc. The chests of drawers were once again moved around. After the horse moved again Marc then put it in the garden.

Monday 10 July 2006

2.00am: Toy rabbit was found on landing.

3.00am: The family dog was heard growling at the bedroom 2 door and a chair moved from the floor onto the table in the same bedroom. The cat downstairs was heard hissing and crying.

7.00am: The rocking horse, which had been placed outside in the garden, had been found inside the house near the kitchen door.

7.30am: Another chair found on the landing.

10.30am: The priest came to visit and bless the house and there was no activity until Thursday 13 July 2006.

Thursday 13 July 2006

9.30pm: The big toy rabbit was found sitting in a child's chair with a razor blade between its hand and body at the top of the stairs.

9.40pm: Some of the toys in bedroom 2 were thrown at Marianne.

9.45pm: The chairs in the downstairs dinning room were seen moving around, one also moved when Marianne was sitting on it.

10.15pm: Chest of drawers moved again in bedroom 2 and toys were thrown around again.

10.30pm: the chairs in the dinning room moved again.

10.40pm: Chest of drawers tipped on Robert's bed when he was in it.

11.00pm: We left the house to stay at parents. As we left an old bed frame fell on us in the garden.

Friday 14 July 2006

On our return to the house we found the doodle-board with the letters

'CU CU CU' written upon it. 8.00am: We found the loft hatch had been moved. No more activity happened that day.

Marianne is to be commended for keeping such a meticulous log, particularly under such trying circumstances. If the events she related were indeed true then there seemed to be little room for doubt; something very strange indeed was occurring in her household. The question was what?

During the rest of the interview, Mike questioned both Marianne and Marc about a number of things. He wanted to know about their lives in general. What did they do for a living, for instance? Marianne, it transpired, was a supervisor in a residential home while Marc worked in the catering industry. Mike also asked them if they'd had spiritual, psychic or paranormal encounters before. Both admitted that during their lives, stretching back to childhood, they had had a handful of 'strange experiences'. This is valuable information for a researcher, because it helps investigators to determine which incidents are 'person-centred' – that is, focused on the individual experient – and which are 'place-centred' or focused on the building or environment.

At this point, Darren tactfully asked the couple if they would mind if some preliminary investigations were carried out there and then. The couple had no objections whatsoever. In fact, the sense of relief emanating from both Marianne and Marc was almost palpable. They were desperate for something to be done that would not only explain what was happening but also, hopefully, make it stop.

Darren left the living room at this point and went upstairs to set up some equipment. Mike, meanwhile, continued with the preliminary interview.

About five minutes after Darren left the room, Mike experienced what he believes was his first paranormal experience in the investigation. He was sitting on a black leather sofa which was on the east wall of the living room, facing the large window on the west wall. The temperature in the room was consistently hot and muggy due to the heat wave. Suddenly, and without any warning, the temperature around Mike plummeted. Within seconds, he felt icy cold and began to shiver. He mentioned this to Marianne and Marc, both of whom immediately stated that they had experienced exactly the same thing, although not in that particular part of the room.

Mike shouted for Darren and asked him if he had brought his digital thermometer with him. Darren answered in the affirmative, and said he'd try and find it among his other equipment and return to the living room with it as soon as possible. He did so within two minutes, but by then it was too late. The temperature had risen again just as suddenly as it had dropped and, despite Darren's best efforts, no anomalous temperature fluctuations could be detected.

'I've experienced temperature drops or 'cold spots' on investigations before', Mike said later, 'but nothing as dramatic as that. It was like falling into a lake of ice water. If either Marianne or Marc faked that, then I'd love to know how they did it.'

This was a phrase that Mike would come to repeat many times during the course of the investigation.

Darren, who had gone back upstairs to finish setting up his equipment, entered the living room once again.

'Okay', he said enthusiastically, 'We're all set.'

Just minutes later the two investigators would, without warning, be thrown into the centre of a protracted paranormal maelstrom.

CHAPTER FOUR

Nuts and Bolts

Marianne, Marc, Darren and Mike walked in file from the living room into the small hallway. Marianne hesitated momentarily and said, 'Would . . . would you two mind going up first? I'm a bit nervous.'

Darren and Mike obliged. Marianne had commented earlier that the landing at the top of the stairwell was one of the locations in the house where she always had an uneasy feeling.

As they walked up the stairs, Mike fully expected to sense something malignant, but nothing happened. When they reached the landing the atmosphere was calm, relaxed even. If there was a polt hiding there, it was hiding itself well.

To the left was the toilet. Directly ahead was the bathroom. To the right was a recess. By entering the recess and turning right again, the investigators would enter the couple's bedroom. By entering the recess and walking straight ahead, they would find themselves in young Robert's bedroom, which was, according to Marianne and Marc, the focal point for most of the paranormal activity on the first floor of their home.

On entering Robert's room, the investigators were met by a blaze of colour. Vivid blues and yellows predominated in the colour scheme, giving the room a light, cheerful ambience. The floor and shelves were littered with dozens of toys; a veritable paradise for a young child. Again, not a single thing presented itself to indicate that there was anything untoward transpiring in this outwardly happy home.

Darren unzipped his hold-all and removed yet more equipment, including the motion sensors and his digital video camera. He quickly got to work. The motion sensors were placed in the doorway, one on each side of the step.

'Remember these are here when you enter and leave the room', he warned. 'If you don't step over the beam you'll trigger the sensors and set the alarm off.'

Both Darren and Mike forgot to do this repeatedly. Mike was the worst offender, triggering the sensors at least half-a-dozen times. This was the source of much merriment among the other three, and helped diffuse some of the underlying tension that Marianne and Marc, despite their best efforts, were still feeling.

There were two small kiddie-sized chairs in Robert's room. One was a rather old-fashioned wooden chair with a slatted back. The chair had been painted vivid red at some point, although it was now rather chipped. Darren placed the chair in the centre of the room and carefully set his camera on the seat. The lens was pointing to the northerly wall with the westerly, window-bearing wall to his left.

A lot of stuff happens in here', commented Marc. 'Sometimes it just goes crazy.'

'Who knows', replied Mike, 'something might happen today if we get lucky'.

Mike recalled later though that he didn't feel lucky:

'The atmosphere just seemed too relaxed. Normally when a polt starts to play you get a build-up; it's almost like static electricity, only a little more subtle. There's an underlying tension that rubs at your bones – gently at first, and then it gets stronger. In this case there was nothing . . . nothing at all.'

In the north-west corner of the room stood a child's desk finished in white melamine. Just in front of the desk was one of Robert's favourite toys; a miniature 'workbench' complete with plastic wrenches, screwdrivers and hammers. Here, Robert could pretend to be a joiner, a plumber, a car mechanic or anything else his little heart desired. Beside the workbench lay a number of large, vivid-yellow, plastic nuts and bolts. Their chunky design enabled them to be grasped easily in the small hands of a child and screwed together. Although they didn't realise it at the time, something in Robert's room – undetected by any of them up to this juncture – had already turned its attention to this innocuous-looking plaything.

Mike was standing by the door on the east wall which led into the room. To his left stood Marianne and Marc. Marc was standing just in front of Marianne; a seemingly trivial detail, but one which would prove to be of crucial importance later. Darren was stooped over the small chair in the centre of the room, facing north, and adjusting the settings on his camera. Mike distinctly recalls that he had all three of his companions in full view when the entity sprung into action.

Something in the north-westerly corner of the room had attracted Mike's attention. Whatever it was, it had been of such a subtle nature that, later, he was unable to state with any clarity exactly what it had been. Was it a slight movement, a delicate shimmer of light? Mike could not then and cannot now articulate just what it was that pulled at him. All he can say is that something barely perceptible happened near Robert's junior workbench, but it was just enough to make him take notice.

Suddenly, without warning, there was a definite movement near the workbench. For a fleeting second Mike was aware of something akin to a small object crossing his field of vision. Again, he could not say exactly what it had been; merely that it was 'an impression' of something traversing the room from the vicinity of the workbench to the south-east corner where Marc and Marianne were standing.

'It was barely noticeable, to be honest', said Mike, 'but I definitely saw something. Whatever it was, it was so small and travelled so fast I couldn't focus upon it.'

An instant later, there was a loud crack. Marianne suddenly grabbed her right buttock with her right hand and exclaimed, 'Ow! God! Did you *see* that? It hit my hip!'

At the same time, something hit the floor behind her. Everyone turned and stared at the floor behind Marianne and Marc. There, in full view, was a yellow, plastic nut that had, seconds earlier, been lying beside the junior workbench on the other side of the room.

Almost immediately, Darren and Mike tried to put together a workable scenario regarding what had just transpired. Someone – or something – had apparently thrown the nut with great force from the north-westerly corner of Robert's bedroom. It had travelled to the south-easterly corner where both Marc and Marianne were standing. It had bypassed them, however, and struck a wooden door behind them which led into a small, recessed cupboard. This, they believe, was responsible for the loud 'crack' which they'd heard. The nut had travelled with such velocity that it then bounced off the door and hit Marianne on the buttock before eventually dropping to the floor.

Mike grabbed his camera and photographed the object where it lay.

The mixture of emotions in that little room was quite intriguing. Marianne looked shocked, scared even. Marc looked both confused and bemused. Darren and Mike, on the contrary, were ecstatic. Nothing pleases investigators more than when they witness paranormal activity first-hand.

Both Mike and Darren apologised to the couple, and explained that they took no pleasure in seeing them distressed. It was simply that, from an investigator's point of view, a golden opportunity had presented itself.

'Bear in mind', said Darren, 'that the more we see the more likely we are to be able to work out exactly what's going on here; and that means we're far more likely to be able to help you.'

Marc and Marianne agreed.

As they stood and discussed this rather dramatic turn-up for the books, Mike pointed out one or two interesting details. Firstly, Darren, Marc and Marianne had all been clearly in Mike's view when the incident occurred. None of them had moved a muscle, so it was unlikely that one of them had surreptitiously thrown the nut in an effort to deceive the investigators.

Secondly, it was also unlikely that either Marc or Marianne had concealed the nut in their hand and then flicked it towards the door with their thumb. It would, in theory, be possible to do this with a minimum of movement, but the facts speak against it. Marianne was standing approximately 2ft from the cupboard door. For the nut to bounce off the door and strike her forcibly on the buttock – she visibly winced, and admitted later that it had 'stung' her – it must have been thrown with considerable force; far more force than one could muster simply with a deft flick of the wrist.

It is also important to note that Marc was standing in front of Marianne. Had Marc been responsible for throwing the nut backwards towards the cupboard door he simply could not have done so without Marianne noticing. Sceptics may say that both Marianne *and* Marc could have been engaged in a joint effort to deceive the investigators, but neither Mike nor Darren can give this idea any credibility.

'You only have to see Marianne's reactions – her facial expressions – when the phenomena occur to realise that she is genuinely bemused and frightened', said Mike.

'In any case, if Marianne and Marc are making this up, then so must all the other witnesses who have seen and heard things even when both Marianne and Marc have been absent from the house. These include Marianne's mother, father and brother.'

Once those in the bedroom had regained their composure, the researchers made a suggestion. The entity had on several occasions left messages on Robert's 'doodle-boards', of which there were two.

The boards are essentially plastic-coated rectangles, in a frame, with a reactive layer underneath. When you write on the board with a stylus, the plastic cover adheres to the subsurface and turns black. When the user has finished writing or drawing, they simply slide a separator from left to right by means of a small handle and the board returns to normal.

The entity had left a number of messages, some rather cryptic, on the doodle-boards, including 'DIE', 'CU, CU, CU', 'BEY BEY' [which may possibly mean 'Bye-Bye'] and *'GIVE IT A CHANCE'*. Could it be enticed to write more if the researchers actually started the conversation going?

Mike picked up the first doodle-board and wrote a question upon it. *'HOW OLD ARE YOU?'* Picking up the second board he wrote, *'WHAT IS YOUR NAME?'* He then placed the two boards on Robert's bed, propped up against the wall. Each question had a space underneath where the entity could, if it felt so disposed, scribble an answer. Darren pointed his video camera at the doodle-boards while Mike activated his digital sound recorder and placed it on Robert's desk. Darren checked his camera yet again, and the researchers suggested that if a poltergeist was present they might be able to flush it out further by actually leaving it alone for a while. All four then left the room and went downstairs, but not before Mike had blundered through the beam emanating from the motion sensors and set off the alarm.

'I can't believe how lucky we've been to see that', said Mike.

Absolutely', replied Darren. As an afterthought he then added, 'Sorry Marianne ... we just can't help getting excited'.

It wouldn't be long before the researchers would have a lot more to be excited about.

CHAPTER FIVE

Petulance

Downstairs in the kitchen, Marianne, Marc, Darren and Mike gathered around the dining table.

'I'm glad you both saw that, you know', said Marianne, as she lit up a cigarette. At least now you *know* . . . '

Reluctant though Mike and Darren were, they had to broach the subject of fraud once again as there were still some unanswered questions. When dealing with experients who are on the brink of nervous exhaustion, one has to be extremely careful. It's like walking on eggshells. One wrong word and your witness can fly off the handle -assuming, perhaps with some justification, that you are accusing them of faking the entire experience.

Mike began by asking Marianne whether anything ever happened when Marc wasn't there.

'No ... I think Marc's always around when things happen', she replied. 'Well, nine times out of ten, anyway . . .'

As you can imagine, this set alarm bells ringing in the heads of both Darren and Mike. If trickery was involved, then Marc could well be the culprit. Initially this line of thinking didn't really go anywhere, although it would be the subject of considerable debate later on. Firstly, a review of Marianne's incident log demonstrated that her memory was at fault – a common occurrence with stressed-out poltergeist experients. There *had* been a number of incidents where Marc had either not been at home or, for some other reason, could seemingly not have been responsible for them.

On one occasion, for example, Marianne was taking a shower in the bathroom while her brother Ian was using the toilet in the adjacent room. Suddenly, a series of terrific bangs sounded upon the bathroom door, scaring the living daylights out of Marianne. Before she could catch her breath, a series of similar bangs resounded on the door of the adjacent toilet where Ian was sitting.

'Where was Marc when this happened?' asked Mike.

'He was sitting downstairs watching the TV.'

Of course, Darren and Mike had to consider the possibility that Marc could easily have crept up the stairs, banged on both doors quickly and then raced back downstairs again. This was possible, but unlikely. It would only have taken Ian a split-second to open the toilet door, and he could have easily seen Marc running down the stairs. Marc, just possibly, could have turned the corner onto the next landing in time, but the risk of getting caught would have been very high indeed. Marianne, who may have been out of the bath by that time for all Marc knew, could easily have seen Marc fleeing down the stairs had she opened the bathroom door quickly enough. The bathroom door looks directly down the first flight of stairs from the upper landing to the middle landing of the stairwell.

In addition to this, something else happened at the same time which effectively ruled out Marc as the perpetrator of a hoax. Just after Marianne heard the loud bangs on the bathroom door, she saw a container of talcum powder tip over, as if pushed, and empty its contents on the floor. She was the only person in the bathroom at the time, and was not standing anywhere near the drum of talc.

'There was absolutely no way it could have fallen over by itself, Marianne added. 'I saw it just tip over with my own eyes. It was weird.'

Theoretically, Marc could have been responsible for banging on the doors, but he could hardly have been responsible for pushing the talcum powder over. Mike asked Marianne if the bathroom door had been locked, and she answered in the affirmative.

On another occasion, Marianne and her father were standing at the back door when a ceramic mug, which had been left standing on a chest of drawers in Robert's room, came hurtling through the bedroom window. It then – its trajectory dictated by the force of gravity – careered earthwards and smashed into a thousand pieces on the path where Marianne and her father were standing. Bizarrely, it left the closed bedroom window intact.

Mike asked Marianne where Marc had been at this time.

Again, watching TV downstairs', she said.

Once again, Darren and Mike had to consider the possibility that Marc could have sneaked upstairs, thrown the mug from Robert's window and then quickly run back downstairs to pretend he'd never left the TV lounge.

This idea doesn't fit either. Firstly, it's impossible to open the window in Robert's room without making a noise. The back garden of the house does not face a main road, and is exceedingly quiet. It just isn't possible to open a bedroom window without attracting the attention of anyone standing in the garden directly below. The window also has blinds, which make a lot of noise when they are opened or moved. Marianne confirmed that before and immediately after the mug hit the ground the blinds were in the closed position.

Secondly, even if someone did manage to open the window without attracting attention and throw a mug out, the instinctive reaction of any witnesses would be to look up as soon as it hit the pavement. The perpetrator would have to shut the window extremely quickly and in perfect silence. Mike has examined both the window and the garden and concluded that such a trick would be virtually impossible.

'Besides', added Marianne, 'when the mug hit the path, Marc came to the living room window within a couple of seconds to see what had happened. There's just no way he could have run down the stairs that quickly. In fact, he couldn't have even got *up* the stairs ... he'd just walked away from my father and I into the living room.'

According to Marc's version of events, he left Marianne and her Dad at the back door which leads into the garden, walked through the dining room and entered the adjacent living room. Before he'd even had time to sit down and resume watching TV, he heard a loud crash outside. He walked straight over to the window and looked out. There he saw Marianne and her father staring at the remains of the mug on the path. The two accounts dovetail perfectly, and it's hard to see how Marc could have hoaxed the incident.

The idea that the entire phenomenon surrounding the Lock Street home had been faked just didn't seem to add up. Every single experient had witnessed eerie things happen when alone as well as when in the company of others. At worst, it was theoretically possible that Marc or Marianne may have been exaggerating the nature or extent of the problem, but they certainly weren't making it up altogether.

Before the researchers knew it, twenty minutes had passed, so they decided to venture into Robert's bedroom once more. Darren, Marianne and Marc carefully avoided the motion sensors at the door. Mike blundered straight through and set them off again.

Nothing seemed out of place. Mike half-considered playing back the recording he'd just made, but as it was over twenty minutes long, decided against the idea. He opted to listen to it later when he got home.

The doodle-boards remained untouched. However, within minutes of entering the room the invisible entity again made its presence felt, but this time much more strongly.

To entice the entity to 'show its hand' Mike and Darren decided to try a different tactic during their second stint in the room. Instead of simply sitting or standing quietly, they directly issued it with a challenge. After switching on both the camera and digital sound recorder they loudly announced that they frankly didn't believe the entity was capable of moving anything at all. It had simply tricked them, they announced, for if it had *really* been able to move anything then it would have done so again just to prove the point. By being mildly insulting to the entity, they hoped to elicit a reaction. On this occasion, the tactic failed miserably

Ah well, so much for that', said Mike dejectedly. 'We'll have to try Plan B.'

Marianne looked at Mike curiously.

'What's Plan B?' she asked.

'Well, that's where we just sit around and chat, and try *not* to think about what we're really doing here', said Mike. 'We just sit and talk about anything – anything *except* what's going on just now in your house. Sometimes these things are more likely to show up when you're not trying too hard. Sometimes, the harder you concentrate on trying to get something to happen the less likely it is to occur.'

Plan B worked a treat. At first the entity just limbered up with a few gentle exercises; the odd creak here, a gentle knocking noise there. Then it got into its stride and petulantly threw a pencil eraser onto the floor.

At this juncture, Marianne and Marc sat down upon their son's bed. They weren't there too long before Marianne shrieked and leaped up to a standing position, quickly followed by Marc who looked genuinely shaken.

Sitting on the bed was a vivid-orange coloured, rubber ball. To the couple's consternation, it had suddenly appeared betwixt them, nestling between Marianne's left thigh and Marc's right. The sudden sensation of something moving between them had caused an immediate reaction. Seconds later they were standing shaking in the centre of the room, staring at the bed and the shiny rubber which was sitting comfortably on top of the quilt. Enigmatically, the ball also felt hot to the touch.

'I'm impressed', said Mike, as he took more pictures. But the entity was far from finished.

It then turned its attention once more to the yellow nut from the junior workbench. Marc had picked the nut up from the floor where it had fallen and placed it on top of a chest of drawers. Suddenly, the nut flew off and landed in a cardboard box nearby. No one was anywhere near the chest of drawers, or the nut which sat on top of it at the time. Marc walked across the room, looking distinctly uneasy, and leant against another chest of drawers by the bedroom door. Behind him was a small toy which, ironically, bore a logo from the 1984 film *Ghostbusters* starring Dan Aykroyd. Suddenly the toy slid off the top of the drawers and deposited itself in a trash can down below. Because Marc was standing right next to the chest of drawers, it is theoretically possible that he could have either pushed it or accidentally knocked it, but the researchers don't think so.

Mike and Darren suggested that they depart the room once again. This time they left two new messages on the doodle-boards. The first message read, 'THANK YOU FOR PLAYING. HOW OLD ARE YOU?' The second message asked, 'THANK YOU. WHAT DO YOU WANT TO DO NOW?' Darren reset his camera and the room was vacated.

Twenty minutes later Marianne, Marc and the two researchers returned. Nothing was out of place, the messages on the doodle-board remained unanswered and the entity did not manifest itself further within Robert's bedroom.

As the researchers left the room for the last time, they collected their equipment. Marc left the bedroom first, and pointed out to Marianne, Mike and Darren that a night light, which had been plugged into a socket on the landing, had been removed and was now sitting on the floor. As Marc left the room maybe one or two seconds ahead of anyone else, it is just possible that he could have quickly removed the night light from the socket and placed it on the ground. Again, to attempt such a deception would have been extremely risky – Marc knew that the investigators were literally right behind him as they all left the room, and it was therefore unlikely that trickery had been a factor. In addition, Marianne confirmed that the night light *had* been in the socket when they all entered the room.

Back at the dining table, Mike and Darren quizzed Marianne about some of the incidents that had really disturbed her. There were two or three that had upset her deeply. The doodle-board message which had simply said, 'DIE' had frightened her, obviously. What was this? A prophecy? A threat? And to whom was it addressed?

The second incident that chilled Marianne to the bone was when her brother Ian had found the stuffed rabbit in the chair at the top of the stairwell with the box-cutter blade in its hand. It was difficult to escape the conclusion that there was something darkly symbolic about this act, and the thought was not lost on Marianne.

Finally, Marianne recalled the time when her brother had found Robert's rocking horse hanging by its reins from the loft hatch. It is hard to comprehend the impact such a bizarre sight must have had upon them. Their reaction was sheer terror, and it was this incident in particular that dissuaded them both from staying in the house alone when the other was absent.

Darren and Mike did their best to reassure Marianne and Marc that the situation was unlikely to drag on for months or years. Intimidating though poltergeist infestation is, it normally has a relatively short shelf-life. Most poltergeists burn themselves out after six to eight weeks. What worried the researchers a little was the fact that *this* polt had been flexing its psychic muscles for seven months now, and its influence and power seemed to be getting stronger by the day. Nevertheless, the researchers assured the couple that they would not cut and run. Whatever happened, they'd see it through till the end and would not give up until the situation had been rectified. For this, Marc and Marianne seemed extremely grateful.

Just then, Marianne's brother Ian arrived. The researchers were formally introduced to him for the first time and, from, the outset, were impressed by his seeming openness and sincerity. Before Darren and Mike left, they took the opportunity to quiz Ian about his own experiences. He had a number to relate. Significantly, several of these incidents occurred when Ian was alone in the house with his nephew, Robert.

As they were running late and didn't want to impinge on the couple's time any longer, the researchers made to leave. Darren told Marianne and Marc that they would be in touch after a few days.

As they walked away from the house, Mike asked Darren what his impressions were.

'To be honest, I'm not really sure. *Something* is going on there. We just need to think about this for a while.'

Later, Darren and Mike arranged to meet on Friday 21 July for another 'Full English' at the Market Cafe. Both researchers would have had time to assess the evidence they'd accumulated by then and, hopefully, come up with some assessment as to what exactly was going on within the house on Lock Street. Hopefully, they'd also be able to present Marc and Marianne with a game plan for dealing with it.

CHAPTER SIX

Noises

When Mike got home that evening, he was physically and mentally exhausted. He ate and then decided to sleep for a while, but suddenly remembered the recording he'd made in Robert's bedroom. Even though he simply wanted to close his eyes and rest, he couldn't resist the temptation to listen to the recording in the hope that he'd picked something up. He removed the digital recorder from his bag, sat down on the sofa and switched it on. Then he pressed the play button, closed his eyes and lay back.

Within two minutes or so, the need for sleep became almost irresistible and he began to drift off. However, before he entered the Land of Nod completely something strange happened. At exactly 4 minutes and 30 seconds into the tape, he was jolted back into full consciousness by a bizarre noise. He rewound the recording and played it again. Suddenly, the need for sleep plummeted down his list of priorities. The recorder *had* picked something up.

The noise was clear, sharp and easy to hear. It was not, however, so easy to define. At first, it sounded like a glass marble bouncing on a hard surface before eventually coming to rest. By the third replay he was beginning to wonder if the sound was that of a coin spinning before coming to a standstill. When his wife Jackie listened to it later, she offered another interpretation which impressed Mike greatly.

'You know what it sounds like to me, Mike? Let me tell you. Can you remember when the kids were little there was a wooden cot in their room with vertical dowels on the side to stop them falling out of bed when they were asleep? It sounds to me like someone running a piece of wood – a pencil, maybe – along the dowels.'

Jackie asked if there was a cot in Robert's room. Mike told her there wasn't, but he had to agree that her interpretation of the sound could well be accurate.

Mike, now wide awake, continued to listen to the tape. At exactly 5 minutes and 30 seconds, he heard an almost identical noise to the first. At 7 minutes and 52 seconds there was a sharp bang followed by a snapping sound and a crack. To Mike the *bang* was devoid of interpretation, but the *snap* and the *crack* sounded for all the world like a small missile of some kind being fired from a catapult or slingshot.

At 8 minutes and 5 seconds, Mike heard a sharp, singular *snap* again. At 8 minutes and 12 seconds, there was another, different noise. It was impossible to define exactly, but sounded like a small, hard object bouncing off several hard surfaces before coming to land in a container. This interpretation is based upon the fact that the last, sharp *clank* has an echo to it, suggesting that the object, whatever it was, had come to rest in a receptacle of some sort.

At 9 minutes and 2 seconds, one can hear two faint but distinct footsteps walking across the carpeted floor of the bedroom. The sound, combined with the length of time in between each footfall, led Mike to believe that the noise had been made by an adult.

At 10 minutes and 2 seconds, Mike heard a faint, barely percep-tible *bang*. Then, at 10 minutes and 32 seconds, there is a duller but louder noise; a *thud*. This is repeated, although slightly louder, at 10 minutes and 35 seconds.

At 12 minutes and 44 seconds, Mike heard two rapid *knocks*. He later commented that it sounded like a small, hollow receptacle being tapped upon a hard surface.

At 13 minutes and 47 seconds, Mike heard a loud, sharp sound that sounded mechanical in nature. Not normally lost for words, he later conjectured that it sounded something like a *snap, clank* and *ping* combined. When Darren heard the tape later, he did admit that this might have been the sound of his own sound recorder switching itself off.

At 13 minutes and 49 seconds into the tape, there was another sharp, singular knocking noise. At 15 minutes exactly there was also a faint bang, followed at 15 minutes and 10 seconds by a distinct *cough*. At this juncture, the recorder began to pick up an increasing level of background noise from downstairs.

Mike and Darren both have deep, naturally loud voices, and, about five minutes before they went back upstairs and re-entered the bedroom, they stood up and walked towards the living room door. They had intended to walk straight into the hallway, but again became engrossed in conversation with Marc and Marianne. Nevertheless, their closer proximity to the living room door allowed their voices, although still faint, to become distinctly clearer on the recorder upstairs. Oddly, from that moment onwards, the anomalous noises in the bedroom stopped completely. Mike later wondered if the entity in the bedroom, whatever it was, had heard their voices getting louder and, assuming that the researchers were about to come back up the stairs, quite literally went into hiding. This was merely an assumption, but it later proved to be highly significant when both Mike and Darren tried to piece together just what was going on in this ordinary, and yet simultaneously extraordinary, home.

CHAPTER SEVEN

Bloop, Bloop, Bloop . . .

It took Darren a while to find the time to analyse the video footage from the investigators' first trip to the house on Lock Street, but when he did, the results proved interesting. The camera had been running simultaneously with Mike's digital sound recorder, so one would have imagined that both devices would have picked up the same anomalous noises. In most respects this was indeed the case, but not all.

Darren made two separate recordings. On the first, there are a number of sounds that are absent on Mike's recording. For example, sixteen minutes into the tape one can distinctly hear a strange electronic noise – *bloop, bloop, bloop, bloop* – which sounds similar to a battery operated child's toy of some kind. Two minutes later, there are two sharp knocks, followed by a pause and then another two knocks.

At one point the camera picked up a visual anomaly; a strange, white light moving across the cupboard door in Robert's room. This would also prove to be significant at a later stage in the investigation.

Shortly afterwards, a distinct and easily identifiable sound can be heard; two notes being plucked on a guitar. There was, of course, no guitar in the room with strings – only a toy guitar without strings, which had been substituted with a series of plastic buttons.

Darren's second recording was made when the two doodle-board messages were left on the bed by the investigators. Because of the angle Darren's camera was pointing at it did not pick up the yellow, plastic nut that was thrown across the room and which ricocheted unceremoniously off Marianne's backside.

Later, after the room was vacated and subjected to 'lock-off, a succession of bangs, thumps, knocks and other anomalous noises could be heard, interspersed with what clearly sound like footsteps.

'Something or someone was messing around in that room after we locked it off, Darren commented after reviewing the tapes. 'There's just no doubt about it.'

CHAPTER EIGHT

Interpretations & Perspectives

Bizarre though it may seem, accumulating the evidence and data during a poltergeist investigation is not the most difficult task. By far the biggest challenge to investigators is the interpretation of that data, and from the very outset there are a number of huge hurdles in the way that can frustrate the most tenacious of researchers.

There are a lot of self-professed paranormal investigators out there who are 'on the job' for all the wrong reasons. Some enjoy dressing up in paramilitary uniforms and adorning themselves with all sorts of strange-looking gizmos and gadgets. Others give themselves grandiose titles, and still others will claim to have detected the spirit of every dead rock star and film actor under the sun. Some, sadly, do it just for the money. These – and we have to be blunt here – bumbling glory-seekers are a pain in the backside to serious researchers. Sadly, they can also confuse genuine experients by proffering ridiculous answers to their questions.

Mike recalls one instance where a middle-aged lady was undergoing a mild but nevertheless disturbing poltergeist infestation. He was asked by the woman's son to investigate and perhaps offer some reassurance, but the woman had already been visited by 'an investigation unit' who, after a few short minutes, told the woman that they knew *exactly* what was going on in her house.

The poltergeist, they informed her, was actually the spirit of her dead husband. He was very angry with her for 'not grieving enough' after his demise, and that was why he was moving things around and making frightening noises. The 'unit' offered to 'move him into the light' so that he couldn't attack her any more. This had to be done quickly because, according to one leading light in this motley crew, he was 'getting angrier every day', and if he wasn't stopped he 'might end up killing' her.

Mike did his best to reassure the woman that what she'd been told was nonsense, but the damage had been done. She became terrified of talking to Mike in case 'he' [her dead husband] was watching and became even angrier with her.

Not much chance of getting any data there, then.

Researchers also have to contend with their own beliefs and prejudices. Mike has Native American heritage and takes the cultural and spiritual side of Indian life very seriously. He admits 'looking at the world through Indian eyes', and will therefore interpret evidence in accord with his spiritual and cultural leanings. What he will not do, however, is alter the data or use it selectively to fit his beliefs.

'There are', says Mike, 'a number of questions that good researchers must ask during the investigative process. Can the accumulated data be harmonised? Does the data enable conclusions to be drawn, and are those conclusions workable? If the researchers feel able to offer help to the experients, is the help or advice they offer workable and dictated by the known facts? In short, does the advice offered make sense when examined alongside the accumulated data?'

Mike also gets extremely exasperated at amateur researchers who allow their own spiritual and cultural views to interfere too much in the investigative process:

'Every day I hear of investigators who supposedly contact the spirits of the dead and then attempt to 'move them on to the light'.'

'Look, I'm *not* saying that there isn't a place for this sort of activity, but we need to tread very carefully. In my estimation, the majority – although not the overwhelming majority – of people involved in this 'soul rescue' or 'spirit rescue' business are either fraudulent or deluded. They'll blithely walk into someone's home and come out with some baloney like, 'Oh, there are seventeen spirits in here . . . one is an old man wearing a uniform, there's another of a young girl with a twisted arm . . . and I'm picking up the spirit of a Cocker Spaniel called Fido . . .'

'Who are we to say that we have the right to move a spirit 'into the light'? How do we know what sort of spirit we're dealing with? How do we know that they're not *meant* to be here for a fixed duration of time, and that by 'moving them on' we're not upsetting a higher spiritual agenda?'

Mike spent several days mulling over the evidence the researchers had gleaned from their first visit to the Lock Street house, trying earnestly to determine exactly what sort of entity – or entities – they were dealing with. He eventually came to two possible conclusions. The first hypothesis was that the family was being subjected to a poltergeist attack, plain and simple, and that all the symptoms could be traced back to a singular phenomenon. The second was that there were possibly two phenomena at work, radically different in nature but producing broadly similar symptoms. To understand why he reached this position it is necessary to know something about the nature of the poltergeist phenomenon and what precipitates it.

There is a general belief, at least in Europe and the USA, that a poltergeist is basically a disruptive spirit; a disembodied personality who at one time was alive in the flesh but who now, after death, spends his or her time frightening the living daylights out of the living. Probe a little deeper and those who go along with this idea will tell you that the spirit probably belonged to someone who, in this life, had an extremely disturbed personality. They may have been mentally ill, violent, psychotic or delusional. After death, so the theory goes, this disembodied personality becomes more confused than ever, perhaps not even realising that they're dead. Angry because they can no longer interact with the physical world by conventional means, their frustration and aggression grows. Eventually they will settle in a house – perhaps the one in which they previously lived –

or take over the will of a still-living person. That, allegedly, is when the fun starts. Filled with hate, the poltergeist will then wreak vengeance on humanity by doing the very things that poltergeists are good at; throwing things around, moving objects, making loud noises and generally causing havoc.

Mike is the first to admit that this hypothesis appears to have, on the surface at least, much to support it. Poltergeist phenomena certainly appear to be precipitated by someone or something that has intelligence and sentience. If a poltergeist is not sentient, has no intelligence and cannot be described as 'living' in any meaningful sense, how on earth could it leave intimidating messages on a doodle-board, throw objects at specific individuals instead of in random directions and otherwise behave as if it was possessed by a sense of purpose? There is an ostensibly plausible answer to this question, and we will examine it presently. However, it is an answer that Mike would come to give far less credence to as the investigation steadily progressed.

First, though, we need to carry out a behavioural analysis of the entity or entities present in the Lock Street house, as this may shed some vital clues as to 'the nature of the beast', so to speak.

Fortunately, at the beginning of the investigation, Darren had the presence of mind to ask Marianne to keep a detailed log of all seemingly paranormal incidents that took place within her home. The first part of the log appeared in Chapter 3. What follows is the second part of Marianne's log dated from 17 July, the day of Darren and Mike's initial visit. By studying this first-hand account we can see exactly what the entity was getting up to when it was busy. The activity erupted seriously almost as soon as the researchers had left the house.

Monday 17 July 2006

2.35pm: The waste bin in [Robert's] bedroom was moved.

3.15pm: While Marc was in the toilet, the door slammed shut and locked him in.

5.45pm: The talc bottle which stood on the shelf in the bathroom was pushed over. Marianne was in the bathroom on her own. Also, when she was in the bathroom a tremendous bang was heard on the door; on looking out no one was there. A plastic toy was then found at the top of the stairs.

5.55pm: Robert's toy tractor was pushed off the chest of drawers.

7.30pm: A toy lion was thrown from Robert's bedroom into the garden, again without the window being open.

8.30pm: Marianne found 3 building blocks on her bedroom windowsill which were not there previously.

8.50pm: Another toy was found on the windowsill in the bedroom and the blinds in there were moving. The window was closed. An umbrella was found hanging on the handle of Robert's closet door. We found Robert moved from his bed, with his quilt wrapped around him, stuffed under the table in his room. His eyes were wide open.

8.55pm: A crayon was thrown from Robert's bedroom window into the garden. The window was closed, and a walkie-talkie was found on the windowsill.

9.05pm: Another crayon was thrown into the garden.

Tuesday 18 July 2006

8.50am: A speaker from a hi-fi was moved in Marianne's bedroom.

2.20pm: While tidying up the bedrooms, various toys were thrown around the room hitting the walls, windows and Marianne. A big wooden train hit Marc on the head. Toy nuts and screws appeared from nowhere and flew across the room. Lego blocks were thrown out of the bedroom window (closed) and a piece of wood from the laundry basket vanished without a trace. Two chairs were then turned upside down and left on the landing upstairs.

3.00pm: The toilet door was difficult to push open while in the toilet. It was as though someone was pushing back the door from the other side.

3.15pm: Two large bangs were heard in the sitting room downstairs and Robert's bed was moved halfway across his room.

4.55pm: Robert's moneybox was pushed off the windowsill and smashed to smithereens, scattering the money everywhere.

5.00pm: The waste bin in [Robert's] bedroom was pushed over.

5.00pm–6.00pm: The house was empty, but on return the waste bin, chair and storage unit in Robert's room had been moved from their positions.

6.05pm: a table with some drinks on it was thrown over, subsequently breaking one of the table legs. A toy was then thrown across the room.

6.30pm: The waste bin in [Robert's] bedroom moved yet again.

7.30pm: A large box, waste bin, chair and storage unit all moved in Robert's bedroom. Robert then said he saw a man in the room.

7.45pm: Robert said the man was now sitting on the sofa in the living room and Marianne could clearly see an indentation in the chair.

7.50pm: Robert returned to his bedroom but was afraid because he said the man was floating above his bed. Later he said the man was lying on his bed and then felt the quilt being pulled off. A tin of body spray was then thrown down the stairs.

Wednesday 19 July 2006

No activity reported until 11.50pm when the chair was found in the bedroom on top of the storage unit [in Robert's room].

Thursday 20 July 2006

11.00am: Toys were being thrown at Marianne and Marc in the bedroom.

11.15am: A large box and the chest of drawers were moved [in Robert's room], and a chair was put on top of the other chest of drawers. The storage unit was dismantled.

11.30am: A toy was thrown down the stairs. No one was upstairs at the time.

11.50am: The kitchen door flew open and no one was on the other side.

12.00pm: Robert said he saw the man in the cupboard downstairs. The cupboard door then opened after we closed it.

12.20pm: The fuses in the cupboard (where Robert had seen the man, and the same cupboard where the door had just opened) tripped.

They came back on after 3 seconds.

12.25pm: A juice bottle that had just been filled up was found empty in Robert's bedroom. No one had drunk it.

12.27pm: Two small magnets appeared from nowhere, dropping from the living room ceiling and bouncing along the floor.

12.40pm: Bed, box and drawers were heard moving in the [Robert's] bedroom upstairs. When looking upstairs, they were all found out of place. No one was upstairs at the time.

12.41pm: We then found two chairs had been stacked on top of one another on top of the table in the bedroom.

12.50pm: A large box was pushed over onto the floor after it was left on the chest of drawers. It made such a noise, as it was full of stuff. The vacuum cleaner in Marianne's bedroom was seen shaking. Then a battery on the floor rolled towards Marc when he was on the top of the stairs. 1.15pm–5.00pm: The house was empty.

5.00pm: The chest of drawers [from Robert's room] was pulled out onto the landing on the top of the stairs and the large box full of stuff was moved from one bedroom to another.

5.10pm: While in the bedroom, two toys were thrown at Marianne and Marc.

5.20pm: The door leading into the kitchen opened three times on its own, and some missing dog-food was found in one of the cupboards in the kitchen.

Let us now piece together just what the researchers were able to determine about whomever or whatever was causing the diverse phenomena within the Lock Street house.

Moving Objects

Firstly, we can see that the entity had a propensity for moving objects, often without any obvious rationale behind the actions. Boxes, toys, household implements and articles, personal possessions ... all these things and more had on occasion been translocated by the entity. Perhaps the most startling example of this occurred on Wednesday 5 July, when Robert's rocking horse was found hanging by its reins from the loft hatch at the top of the stairwell.

The entity also seems to have had a fixation with specific objects other than the rocking horse. On numerous occasions, it moved two small chairs belonging to Robert which are normally situated in his bedroom. It also demonstrated a propensity for shifting heavy items of furniture. Two chests of drawers, again situated in Robert's room, were also moved on numerous occasions. Sometimes the entity would place an item of furniture strategically against the door leading to Robert's bedroom, on the inside, as if trying to prevent those who lived in the house gaining access.

Most often, the objects would be moved without the family members actually witnessing the translocation taking place, but on occasion witnesses would be present.

The entity also seems to have had a predisposition for throwing smaller objects around, usually (but not exclusively) toys belonging to Robert. Favourite missiles seem to have been toy cars and building blocks. Significantly, the missiles would be thrown when the witnesses had their backs turned. In virtually all poltergeist cases, witnesses never actually see the objects start to move. Rather, when their attention is diverted, the entity will throw a small object at them. The target area is usually the back of the experient, somewhere between the neck and the buttocks.

Occasionally the witnesses will see the object while it is in flight, travelling towards them just before impact, but never do they actually see the object *begin* to move from its previous stationary position. Why this 'rule' of paranormal activity is so consistently adhered to by poltergeists is still a mystery.

Physical Contact

The entity was not averse to making physical contact with Marianne, Marc or other experients, although this was not its most obvious type of activity. On Monday 3 July, for example, Marianne was 'poked in the back' by the entity at the top of the stairwell. On another occasion Marc was actually 'pushed over', again on the stairwell. Disturbingly, this seemed to indicate that the entity, whatever its nature, could exercise at will a degree of strength which was, at the very least, equal to that of a fully-grown man. It's hitherto reluctance to cause serious physical harm to the experients within the household could well be interpreted as merely a lack of desire, then, and not a lack of ability. Perhaps the entity *could* have caused serious injury or worse to Marianne and Marc if it wished to, but had chosen, for reasons best known to itself, to refrain.

This sort of behaviour, it must be said, was perfectly typical of the poltergeist phenomenon. Poltergeists are certainly not models of propriety and good manners, but instances in which serious physical harm has been meted out to witnesses are rare. Even in cases where physical attacks upon experients have been carried out, there has often been a degree of doubt as to whether the phenomenon was truly that of a poltergeist or some other type of paranormal activity altogether. The researchers would later find, to their utter dismay, that the Lock Street polt certainly could mete out physical harm to experients when it wanted to, and in the most terrible of ways.

Another possibility the researchers had to consider was that the typical poltergeist entity was, unbeknown to investigators, bound by a set of spiritual and/or physical laws which restrained its behaviour. Perhaps there was a law of physics – or maybe even a divinely instituted commandment, who knows – which usually prevented the poltergeist from seriously injuring those in its presence. When a poltergeist got angry and attacked someone, was there something which, in effect, said, 'Thus far and no further'? It would be reassuring to think that this was indeed the case, but Mike was doubtful.

As detailed in an earlier chapter, on 8 July, 2006, Marc *was* physically hurt, although not seriously, when the entity pushed over a set of stepladders at the top of the stairwell. It has been suggested that poltergeists may, like humans, sometimes injure people unintentionally. Perhaps, the researchers thought, when the polt pushed the stepladders over it had merely meant to frighten Marc, and not harm him. Nevertheless, a degree of physical injury had been sustained, albeit minor. This meant that, at best, poltergeists may only have been prevented from *deliberately* harming experients, still leaving open the possibility that they may have been harmed unintentionally or accidentally.

Other incidents that took place within the home often left one feeling that a dearth of physical injuries to the experients had been due more to good luck than anything else.

On Thursday 13 July, Marianne and Marc entered Robert's bedroom and found a chest of drawers unceremoniously dumped upon Robert's bed when he was sleeping in it. Fortunately, he was unharmed.

After a further series of incidents that evening, both Marianne and Marc decided they'd had enough. They telephoned Marianne's mum, June, and asked if they could spend the evening there. At precisely 11pm, they left via the rear entrance to the house. As they did so, the entity decided to push over a large bed frame, which was propped up against the wall of the house awaiting collection. The bed frame fell upon the family as they walked down the path, but luckily they weren't injured. This told the investigators something else about this particular poltergeist; regardless of the extent to which it was capable, and/or allowed to mete out physical harm to witnesses, it certainly had no inherent regard for their safety. Had the injury to Marc's arm been unintentional, and had it precipitated some degree of guilt within the entity, one would imagine that it would thereafter have modified its behaviour to prevent such a thing happening again. Not so. Recklessly throwing a heavy bed frame at a child and its parents hardly characterises restraint, remorse or a caring nature. This was an entity which seemed to be perfectly capable of injuring those in its presence. It had hitherto refrained from doing so, but the evidence suggested that it had no concern for the well-being of the family. The fact that they had, up to that juncture, remained largely unscathed seems to have been down to good fortune rather than good management.

The entity within the household also on occasion turned its attention to young Robert, as we shall soon see, although it did not harm him physically.

Researchers know that poltergeists often exhibit strange behaviour patterns that in humans would probably be characterised as an Obsessive Compulsive Disorder. Poltergeists have an obsession with neatness and tidiness, for instance. They will often 'tidy up' household items and artefacts in the strangest of ways. Mike once investigated a poltergeist infestation at a well-known public house, wherein the polt would remove randomly scattered disinfectant blocks from the trough of the gent's urinal and arrange them in neat geometric patterns on the tiled floor. In another case, the polt would take all the canned food from the larder and arrange the tins in rather spectacular pyramid formations on the kitchen workbench.

Conversely, it must be said, poltergeists often seem to take great delight in turning a neat and orderly room into something that resembles a bombsite, so neither Mike or Darren would recommend hiring a bored polt as a domestic help. Unfortunately, the polt that infested the house at Lock Street seemed quite happy to wreak havoc but did very little tidying up.

Poltergeists also have a fascination with beds and bedding. They just love to whip the bedclothes from slumbering individuals, or even just tug at them to cause annoyance. They will sometimes even sit upon a bed, causing terrified witnesses to see a sudden indentation form even though the polt is actually invisible. They also have a distinguished track record of physically removing people from their beds – particularly children. On at least two occasions, this has happened to young Robert.

Late in the evening of 17 July, when the terrified family finally decided to vacate their home to stay with Marianne's mother June, Marc and Marianne went upstairs to wake up Robert so that they could get him dressed. To their horror, the child was no longer in bed. Rather, he was lying on the floor tightly wrapped in his bed quilt. What disturbed them, however, was the fact that a plastic table had been placed on top of Robert, thereby making it impossible for him to move even had he wanted to. The couple knew that Robert was unlikely to have moved this table by himself, let alone manoeuvred it over his small frame in this manner.

Naturally in a state of panic, Marianne and Marc quickly removed the table and checked to see if Robert was alright. Marianne described to the researchers what happened next.

> I was worried sick. I just wanted to know what this thing was and why it was doing this. The first thing I noticed was that Robert was tightly wrapped in the quilt; so tight it made it impossible for him to move. He couldn't have managed to get the quilt wrapped around him in that manner. Someone else would have to have done that.
>
> After we moved the table I turned Robert over to make sure he was alright. He was asleep, but the weird thing was that his eyes were wide open. It was as if he was in some sort of trance and it took me a while to get him out of it. That was the point where Marc and I thought, 'that's it – we're getting out of here'.

This incident introduced another disturbing thought. Marianne had found her son in a strange, trance-like state and it is difficult not to conclude that the entity that seemed to be toying with this poor family was in some way responsible.

The next day the family returned, and the polt was there waiting for them. As Marc ascended the now-dreaded stairwell, it hit him over the head with a large, toy train. *Welcome home.*

Whatever the reason, we can be thankful that poltergeists do not normally cause serious harm to their victims, although this rule of thumb would eventually prove to be of little comfort to the family in Lock Street.

Intimidation

Although poltergeists do not typically harm their victims – at least physically – they certainly seem to have a penchant for intimidating and scaring them. Legendary in ghost-hunting circles is the story known as 'The Amherst Incident'.

In 1878, there lived in Amherst, Nova Scotia, one Daniel Teed, a shoemaker, and his wife Olive. Also in the same house lived

Daniel's sister-in-law, Esther Cox. Esther was highly spoken of by all who knew her and respected as a 'truth-loving woman'.

On Wednesday 4 September of that year, Esther was lying in bed with her sister, Jennie, when they heard a strange scraping noise emanating from underneath the bed. The two young women pulled a pasteboard box from underneath the bed, in which they thought a mouse had ingratiated itself. As the girls removed the lid the box jumped at least one foot in the air, turned itself over and promptly fell back down to the ground. When the same thing happened a second time they both fled the room screaming.

Although their tale was greeted by older family members with guffaws of laughter, those within the Teed home didn't see the funny side of things for long. Soon, all manner of terrifying occurrences took place, many of them very similar indeed to what had recently transpired within Marianne's home.

Perhaps the most terrible incident in the whole affair occurred when, in front of witnesses, the entity scratched in the wall above Esther's bed the chilling words, 'ESTHER COX YOU ARE MINE TO KILL'. The parallels between this and the message left upon Robert Peterworth's doodle-board – 'DIE' are so obvious they do not warrant further commentary.

Poltergeists, whatever they are, seem to thrive on instilling a sense of morbid dread within their victims. Death messages, objects being thrown, eerie noises and the translocation of furniture seem almost calculated to frighten those who witness these things. Why, then, would poltergeists go to so much trouble to frighten people and yet almost always stop short of doing them serious physical harm? At least one extremely plausible solution has been put forward to explain this enigma.

It has long been recognised that human beings can both generate and detect what may best be described as 'emotional atmospheres'. Just about everyone reading this book will, at some time, have walked into a room containing two or more people and detected an unpleasant or negative 'feeling'. The expression, 'You could have cut the atmosphere with a knife' is often used in situations like this.

Now it may be that the unwary visitor is able to detect subtle signs that point to an argument having just taken place before they arrived; the body language and facial expressions of those in the room could be powerful indicators, for instance. Without anything being said, you just know by the way your hosts are acting that they aren't exactly bosom buddies at that juncture in time.

Yet, we know that this isn't the whole story. When two individuals in a confined space have a violent disagreement with each other, we all know that the entire room seems to fill with an awful, negative energy that is almost palpable. This is why we all so readily use expressions such as, 'there was a terrible atmosphere in that office', or 'the mood in that room was just awful'. It is as if the negative feelings and emotions within the combatants have the ability to radiate outwards and fill the entire space.

There is a theory about poltergeists that dovetails very well with this notion. Some suggest that fear, like many other emotions, is actually a form of energy which, like light and heat, radiates outwards until it is blocked by a physical object such as a wall. Despite the fact that 'spiritual energy' is a concept much overworked by some, as we shall see, those who endorse this theory believe that this is why a room or other clearly-partitioned space can become 'filled' with different 'atmospheres' depending upon the mood of those within.

Now if it is true that fear is a form of energy, then we have to consider seriously the notion that poltergeists may feed on it and even rely on it to sustain their very strange mode of existence. Just as plants can't exist without water and animals can't survive without food, poltergeists may need to 'tap in' to unconventional energy sources – such as powerful emotional discharges – to sustain themselves. This, then, could well explain why poltergeists seem to go to such extreme lengths to generate feelings of fear and dread within humans. When humans become scared, they generate fear and the poltergeist can feed. Causing people to become frightened so that they can feed on the emotional discharge that follows is, quite possibly, the poltergeist's equivalent of charging up a car battery.

This theory also explains why poltergeists usually demonstrate little interest in causing physical harm to people. It is the *fear* of being attacked which precipitates the awful sense of dread the poltergeist dines upon with relish, not the act itself.

Not all forms of poltergeist attack are presented as unsubtly as the message left for Esther Cox, or the one scribbled upon young Robert's doodle-board.

On Wednesday 5 July, Marianne decided that she needed to do something; take the initiative and attempt to fight the invisible entity that was wrecking her life. She wrote out a short, heartfelt prayer and attached it to the back of Robert's bedroom door. Later, when she re-entered the room, she found that the entity had scribbled over the prayer violently with one of Robert's red wax crayons. It was as if the polt was saying, 'Your God can't help you now!'

In a similar vein, we may return to the incident involving the large, furry rabbit toy that was found sitting in a chair at the top of the stairs with a box-cutter blade in its hand. There is something horribly sinister about this scenario, and yet no one was injured, no one was cut, no one carted off to hospital. The only thing that happened was that Marianne and Marc became very, very frightened.

It seems that the Lock Street polt could feed on the fear generated by animals, too. At 3am on Monday 10 July, the family's pet dog, Bounder, was found growling and snarling just outside of Robert's bedroom door. Midnight the cat had been affected too; the couple on one occasion found it crying and hissing downstairs as if severely traumatised.

Incidents such as this make it almost irresistible to conclude that the primary focus of this entity was to instil fear, dread and terror into its victims. Once this was achieved, it could feed.

Control

Another, although less discussed, phenomenon connected with poltergeist activity is the entity's seeming desire to exercise varying degrees of control over its victims. This may just be another tactic used to intimidate and frighten experients, but it is interesting nonetheless.

On a number of occasions, Marianne and Marc found that the dining room chairs they were sitting on would move without any effort from themselves, as if an unseen pair of hands was pulling at the chair. On another occasion, Marc stood up to fetch something from the kitchen. When he returned he went to sit back down on the chair. Without warning, it was unceremoniously yanked from underneath him. Marc just managed to avoid falling to the floor. Of course, this could simply be viewed as one of the mischievous pranks that poltergeists are famous for, but there is also in such instances a subtle, subliminal message; *I can control where you sit and where you stand. I can control what you do.*

On Monday 17 July, just after Darren and Mike had departed following their first visit, Marc went upstairs to use the toilet. As soon as he entered the closet, the door slammed shut behind him and the lock was activated. No matter how hard he tried, he was unable to release the lock and free himself. After a short while he tried again and, to his relief, the door opened.

The following day Marc was again in the toilet when the polt struck. He attempted to leave the toilet by pushing the door, which opens onto the landing. The door partially opened, but not enough to allow Marc to exit the toilet. No matter how hard he pushed, the door wouldn't budge. 'It was', he said later, 'as if someone was pushing the door from the other side'.

Marianne, alerted by Marc's shouts, ascended the stairs and tried to pull the door open from the outside. It moved, but only an inch or two for a fleeting moment before moving back again.

'It was like being in a tug of war', she said.

Trying to be tactful, the researchers asked Marianne if Marc could have been pulling on the door from the other side 'for a joke'.

'No', she said categorically. I could see through the door and both of Marc's hands were nowhere near the handle when I was trying to pull the door open.'

In addition to incidents like this, the poltergeist had, as detailed previously, occasionally manoeuvred items of furniture – a chair

on one occasion, a chest of drawers on another – up against doors
to prevent the couple gaining access to a particular room. Again,
it is hard to avoid the conclusion that the entity was trying to
intimidate the experients further by exercising control over them
in a way which is calculated to annoy, frighten and upset.

Destruction

In many poltergeist cases, the entity seems to enjoy moving
things around, throwing objects hither and thither and generally making a nuisance of itself. However, polts will often stop
short of physically breaking anything. Cups may be thrown to
the floor with great fury, but, on examination, are found to be
perfectly intact. In one case investigated by Mike, a lady repeatedly heard a huge crashing noise emanating from her kitchen.
The sound, to this experient, was unmistakable; it was that of
her kitchen crockery being scattered from its home on a Welsh
dresser and thrown to the floor. However, whenever she entered
the kitchen everything would be in place without so much as a
cracked saucer to be seen.

Unfortunately, not all polts are like this. Some have displayed a
worrisome ability to cause physical damage, seemingly whenever
they feel like it. This was certainly the case in the Lock Street
house. Cups and mugs were thrown out of windows, and, on
one occasion, Robert's ceramic, football-shaped money-box was
pushed from a window-ledge in his bedroom onto a chair below.
The receptacle was smashed into tiny pieces.

The only conclusion that can be reached, Mike suggests, is that
poltergeists are able to cause physical damage if they want to; it's
just that, mercifully, they *choose* not to – most of the time at least.

Communication

Poltergeists are not opposed to communicating with their victims, but they tend to do so very much on their own terms. It

must also be said that messages from your typical polt are rarely of the 'sweetness and light' variety. Usually they are curt, negative and intimidating. There are exceptions to this rule, of course, as we shall see presently. Examining these messages may provide some clues as to both the nature and intent of the entity in question, although we need to avoid developing a disposition of unbridled optimism.

Poltergeists do not normally engage in direct oral communication with their victims. When such communication does occur, it is usually one-sided; the poltergeist will speak, but rarely respond to questions. Again, there have been notable exceptions recorded in the annals of paranormal research, but generally, the principle holds true. Poltergeists may tell you things, but they rarely seem interested in anything you may have to say.

On one occasion, Marc and a friend of Marianne's were sitting in the living room when Marianne herself was descending the stairwell. At that precise moment, the polt whispered 'Bitch!' in Marc's ear. This was also heard by Marianne's friend.

Polts seem to favour the written word as a means of communication. They have been known to write upon walls, trace characters in the moisture upon steamed-up windows, scribble missives on bits of paper and, would you believe, even send the odd e-mail or two. No one can accuse the thoroughly modern poltergeist of lagging behind the times when it wants to get its point across.

Occasionally, poltergeists will utilise the telephone when communicating, although on reflection 'communicating' may not always be an accurate description. Sometimes they will dial out from a phone the same number repeatedly. There was a quite famous case in Germany where a polt kept dialling the speaking clock from the office of a local businessman. He received a staggeringly high bill, but appealed against it successfully. The telecommunications company waived the entire amount when he proved that it had been physically impossible to dial the speaking clock – or any other number, come to that – so many times in one day. The polt was actually dialling faster than the number could be entered.

Marc had one such telephonic experience with the polt. One evening he was at his mother's house when his mobile phone rang. The caller display indicated that he was being phoned by someone at the home he shared with Marianne and Robert. When he answered, the line went dead. Bizarrely, there had been no one in their home at the time, except for the playful polt, of course. This would certainly not be the last time it would use the telephone to harass its victims, as we shall see.

Still talking on the technological front, there is one other incident that needs to be mentioned at this juncture. On one occasion, both Marianne and Marc were in the living room when they heard a voice on the baby monitor say, 'Robert, you're going to fall out of bed!'

The couple raced up the stairs, but no one was in the room except Robert, who was sound asleep.

The poltergeist had also left several written messages on Robert's doodle-board, as discussed earlier. In the early days of the infestation a message was left simply saying, 'BEY-BEY'. Marianne speculated, probably correctly, that this was probably meant to be, 'BYE-BYE', as if the polt was politely bidding them farewell when they were forced to leave the house temporarily due to its incessant antics.

Later, when they were once again driven from their home due to the polt's handiwork, they returned to find the letters, 'CU, CU, CU' scribbled on one of Robert's doodle-boards. Again, Marianne speculated that the letters were an abbreviation for 'See you . . . see you ... see you'. The repetition of the letters three times could be interpreted as three individual farewell messages for Marianne, Marc and little Robert.

On Sunday 9 July, a far darker message was left for the family, or possibly one individual within it. It simply said, in true polt fashion, 'DIE'.

On another occasion, the polt, in an unusually philosophical mood, asked the family to 'GIVE IT A CHANCE'. Was the polt asking the family to exercise a degree of tolerance towards its antics? Or was it referring to something else altogether? No one knows.

Appearances

Finally, we will examine one of the most intriguing questions of all; did the polt that had taken up residence within the Lock Street home have a physical shape, size and appearance? Polts normally don't show themselves, but they have been known to do so when the fancy takes them.

The first appearance of the entity – or perhaps we should say something anomalous that may or may not have been the entity – occurred before the investigators were on the case. Robert claimed that he had seen 'a lady' in his bedroom and had actually had a conversation with her. Just what was said we do not know, but the incident was significant enough for the toddler to mention it to his mother. It would be easy – too easy – at this juncture to make some sort of categorical statement that the lady and the polt were obviously one and the same; but we must tread carefully. Shortly afterwards, Robert claimed that he had been visited on a number of occasions by yet another anomalous personage; this time it was a young boy whom he referred to as 'Sam' or 'Sammy'. Robert blithely told Marianne and Marc that he and Sammy often played together in his room.

On Monday 3 July, things became even more complicated. Marianne and Marc both saw a 'white figure' fleetingly in Robert's room. One could be forgiven for thinking that their home – or particularly Robert's bit of it – was becoming like a busy interchange for all sorts of paranormal waifs and strays.

At 7.30pm on Tuesday 18 July, the polt got to work in Robert's bedroom and moved several items of furniture around. These included a large box, a storage unit, a trash can and a chair. After the polt had finished rearranging the fixtures and fittings, Robert claimed to have seen 'a man' in the room. Wisely, Marianne decided to take Robert downstairs until 'the man' had vacated the premises.

Fifteen minutes later, Robert pointed excitedly to a point in the room near the sofa and, exclaimed, 'Look! It's the man!'

We may presume that this was the same man that the youngster had seen fifteen minutes earlier in his room, but we can't be absolutely certain. Nevertheless, *something* was in the room, because Marianne watched incredulously as a deep indentation formed on the seat cushion of the sofa. The 'invisible' man had taken a pew.

Trying to stay one step ahead of the ephemeral visitor, Marianne decided to return Robert to his room. Everything was fine until they opened the door, at which point Robert shouted, 'Mam! There's the man again ... he's floating above the bed!'

You just can't fox a good polt.

Eventually, Marianne managed to settle Robert down for the night, but 'the man' had no intention of retiring for the evening just yet. Robert complained that at one point the man actually lay down on his bed, and, in true polt fashion, tried to pull the quilt off Robert as he attempted to go to sleep.

Fed up, Marianne muttered a few choice words for the benefit of Robert's tormentor. In return, it threw an aerosol of body spray at her as she descended the stairs.

Two days later, 'the man' returned. This time he ensconced himself in a cupboard downstairs where a much-startled Robert stumbled upon him. Presumably irritated at being interrupted, the man started to open and shut the cupboard door repeatedly.

Robert later described the man as being tall, with straight black hair, and wearing a long, black coat. He also sported a beard and a Homburg-like hat.

A 'lady', a 'man', a 'white figure', a young boy called Sammy ... what are we to make of this strange coterie of quasi-corporeal personages? There are, Mike thinks, only two possible explanations. Firstly, there may simply have been one entity in the household that had the ability to present itself in a variety of different forms; a woman one minute, a young boy the next, and so on. On the other hand, it is possible that there may have been a number of different entities that had taken up residence there simultaneously. Further analysis of the data would be needed before any firm conclusions could be drawn. Mike's initial feeling, however, was that the latter hypothesis was the more likely of the two. Darren's perspective was somewhat different.

Although Darren agreed with Mike to a certain extent, he felt that there were other factors to consider.

Both Darren and Mike agreed wholeheartedly that there was indeed a poltergeist active at Lock Street. Darren also agreed with Mike that there may have been a second entity present, although they differed on what the nature of that second entity was likely to be.

Mike had already discussed with Darren, Marc and Marianne the 'multiple entity' hypothesis, and had pointed out an obvious difficulty. If there *were* two or more separate entities operating at the same time, it may prove exceedingly difficult to determine which entity was responsible for each symptom of the infestation. It may prove exceedingly hard to draw a line between the two – or three, as the case may be.

As Darren pointed out, Robert had indeed seen an apparition of a child and referred to him as 'Sam' or 'Sammy'. Neither researcher could ultimately decide exactly what the polt was doing or what Sam was doing at any given juncture.

Darren noted that a lot of previously recorded data, collected during investigations into numerous famous cases, showed that poltergeists often have 'accompanying apparitions'. His thought was that this may be the explanation for 'Sammy'. Mike felt that Sammy may have been another type of paranormal phenomenon altogether; specifically, what he has come to refer to as a 'quasi-corporeal companion'. This will be investigated more thoroughly in a later chapter.

Darren understood Mike's line of thinking, but commented, 'There have certainly been other apparitions witnessed at the house, particularly 'the man', and I tend to think that the other personalities are conventional apparitions and not necessarily quasi-corporeal companions. I think that these apparitions are attached to this particular poltergeist. In other words, the poltergeist and the apparitions are all rolled into one; they are one phenomenon, and not two.'

Both Darren's and Mike's hypotheses would be well tested in the days that followed, and both researchers would be forced to reappraise their understanding of the poltergeist phenomenon. That reappraisal would lead them to some very disturbing conclusions.

CHAPTER NINE

The Nature of the Beast

Darren also had some further thoughts on the nature of the poltergeist:

> As Mike has said, the word *poltergeist* derives from two German words; *polter,* meaning to knock, rap or generally be boisterous, and *geist,* meaning 'ghost'. To refer to poltergeists as 'boisterous ghosts' is, I think, something of an understatement. Incidentally, the word *poltergeist* is not used much by German-speakers these days. Generally, the term *ein spuk* is used in Germany, while English-speakers still tend to use the older *poltergeist*. Whatever you call the phenomenon, if you've ever experienced genuine poltergeist activity there is no doubt that it leaves you shaken up and very frightened indeed.

Darren should know, as he had a first-hand experience of true polt activity while on holiday in Dieppe, France, in 1986.

Although it was a single, isolated incident, it will stay with him for the rest of his life and it is something he will never forget.

> At the age of thirteen I visited Dieppe with my school for a week, and I stayed in a huge, old mansion which had been converted into a residential centre. It was situated off a winding country road and was hidden deep behind a copse of trees. It

had rooms converted into dormitories, and the whole place had a very religious feel to it. There were crucifixes on nearly all of the walls, and portraits of Christ were in abundance. There were approximately six dormitories in the building. The largest slept about twenty-five, and the smallest about five or six. I was in one of the small rooms with one of my school friends and four pupils from another school.

It all started during the last day when we smuggled some fresh orange juice up the stairs and into the dorm. We were not allowed to take food or drink into the bedrooms, and I spilled nearly half the carton onto the wooden floor. Instead of mopping it all up, as I should have done, I had one of my dorm colleagues help me lift up my bedside cabinet – it took two of us to carry it – and place it over the stain we had left in the middle of the floor.

We weren't thinking about what would happen if the teacher came in to the dormitory; despite the fact that his first question would have been to ask why my bedside cabinet was in the middle of the floor. Anyway, it stayed there for the rest of the day.

Night-time came and we went to our beds. It wasn't long before we were all out for the count. Throughout the night I was repeatedly woken by a slow, continuous knocking sound. I remember opening my eyes and thinking to myself, 'What on earth is that?' The noise seemed to be coming from within the room itself.

As I turned and peered into the darkness of the room I could see the bedside cabinet that we'd moved earlier into the middle of the floor. It was slowly rocking from side to side. I watched this for about twenty seconds. It would balance on one side of its base, then come to rest normally, then tip at an angle and rest on the other side of its base. It continued to rock back and forth like this, continually creating a knocking sound as it came to rest on the floor. No one was next to it, yet it kept on rocking and balancing perfectly. I couldn't believe what I was seeing, so I slid my legs off the side of the bed (the bottom bunk) and put my feet on the floor. The cabinet was still rocking. I wiped my eyes in utter disbelief, and then lunged forward to take a closer look.

For the rest of my life I will never forget what happened next. As I leant forward, the cabinet seemed to throw itself violently across the dormitory, scattering my belongings everywhere. Simultaneously there was a huge crash that nearly burst my eardrums. Needless to say I ran for the light switch, crying in absolute terror, while the rest of my dormitory colleagues woke up with a fright saying, 'What on earth was that?'

I was hysterical, and my friends were also shocked to find the cabinet almost wrecked and my belongings strewn all over the place. We left the light on for the rest of the night. Needless to say, we did not get any more sleep. In fact, we sat up together and chatted until breakfast. Later, we packed our suitcases and left. Thankfully, it had been our last night in France, and it was just as well as I couldn't have stayed another night in that room.

So, what was it that so abruptly woke us from our sleep that night? As with the other ghosts and hauntings there are no definite answers, only speculations.'

In Harry Price's 1945 book, *Poltergeist over England* the author puts forward the theory that poltergeist disturbances are caused by evil or demonic spirits, imps and elementals who are malicious in intent and out to cause misery and suffering to those whose homes are infested by them. This explains, at least in part, why many people are terrified at the idea of having a poltergeist in their home. What we must remember is that when Harry Price was trying to understand the nature of poltergeists this is *exactly* how they must have appeared to him. They really did seem to be a manifestation of invisible forces that cause mayhem and absolute terror. They were very much misunderstood, and it was only natural to assume these infestations were actually the work of evil spirits or demons.

But at least it was Harry Price who got the ball rolling and tried to begin to understand what they might be. Price was determined to find out why these infestations occurred, and for this we must thank him.

Since Price's investigation into poltergeists in the 1930s and 1940s, we have come a long way scientifically. With our greater knowledge, we now have a better understanding of our minds, our bodies and the world we live in. Significantly, we also have a deeper understanding of the *subconscious* mind.

Nowadays, new and impressive theories have come into existence as to what poltergeists may actually be. However, unlikely as it may seem, we must accept that the poltergeist may just be exactly what the German term describes it as; a *loud or boisterous ghost,* whether it be a place-centred haunting or attached in some way to a human 'focus'.

'Nine times out of ten the typical poltergeist has a human focus. In almost every case, the focus is a young female who has either gone through, or is going through, puberty. Few poltergeist foci are older than nineteen years of age.'

There are rare exceptions to the general rule that the typical poltergeist focus will be a pubescent or post-pubescent teenager. Ultimately, this proved to be the case at 42 Lock Street.

Regarding the nature of the poltergeist, there is nowadays an alternative to the 'demon' idea, which has gained much greater acceptance. Most researchers now believe that the poltergeist is not a ghost or demon at all, but an energy emanating from the telekinetic (TK) or psychokinetic (PK) mind of a disturbed adolescent child.

The terms telekinesis and psychokinesis both relate to the ability of humans to move objects remotely while using nothing more than the power of the mind. However, researchers now commonly refer to a similar process which is termed *recurrent spontaneous psychokinesis* (RSPK). In TK and PK, the subject is fully aware of what their mind is doing and can often exercise a significant degree of control over their abilities. In RSPK, however, objects are moved – and sometimes even thrown about – when the person or 'focus' responsible *is totally unaware of their actions.*

One version of the RSPK theory goes like this:

Sometimes, growing youngsters may be subjected to some kind of trauma. They may be abused at home, bullied at school, ravaged by serious illness or critically injured in an accident. Any intense degree of trauma produces 'blowback' or negative results that may manifest themselves immediately or, in many cases, years later. Traumatised children may bottle up their negative emotions and anger to an extraordinary degree. This 'bottling up' process can only be sustained for so long; then, 'something has to give', so to speak.

Normally, teenagers may give vent to pent-up emotions and feelings by throwing a temper tantrum, playing aggressive sports or engaging in some of the adrenalin-inducing lunacy for which the under-20s are famous. If such common outlets are available, then much pent-up negative emotion can be dispelled there and then. However, in extreme cases such individuals may not be able to release their emotions and anger. Perhaps they live in an environment where normal (and for 'normal' please don't read 'sensible') teenage outlets for stress are culturally or socially unacceptable. Perhaps the trauma they suffered, particularly in cases of severe illness or accident, was just too much to cope with.

Many believers in RSPK are of the opinion that repressed and suppressed emotions can sometimes precipitate a build-up of psychic energy. For some reason, when such a person reaches puberty, and particularly if they are female, that energy can be released in the form of RSPK. Just *how* that energy is released may give us an important clue regarding the nature of the poltergeist phenomenon.

Imagine that a young teenager who was subjected to an extraordinary degree of trauma as a child suddenly releases a huge amount of this stored psychic energy; call it having a subconscious, psychic temper tantrum if you will. The person releasing this psychic energy may be totally unaware of the process. Now imagine that, subconsciously, they can still exercise a degree of control over this energy even after it has been released or 'externalised'. The person in question may subconsciously utilise this energy as a mechanism for releasing all that pent-up emotion and stress, but merely *releasing* the accumulation of psychic energy may not be enough; they have to *do* something with it. How better to utilise it than to psychically precipitate the stress-releasing actions that, culturally, socially or for some other reason, they have been hitherto unable to carry out physically? The subject may subconsciously utilise this discharge of psychic energy to move or break physical objects and generally 'pay back' the world at large for the fact that they were made to suffer so unjustly earlier in their youth.

At this juncture, it is vitally important to understand that the 'focus' in this process is in no way to blame for what happens. They are not engaging in this form of covert psychic warfare consciously. In fact, they are as much a victim as those around them when the action starts.

In short, what the authors suggest is that some individuals may, without realising it, release large amounts of psychic energy which they then subconsciously use to create the very symptoms associated with poltergeist activity. This is not a new hypothesis, but it has a growing body of supporters. Mike believes that a careful analysis of all the evidence points strongly to the RSPK theory being the most likely explanation for the poltergeist phenomenon.

If the RSPK hypothesis is correct, then the poltergeist may not normally be a sentient entity which enjoys an independent existence. Rather, it may be a form of negative energy which is being manipulated subconsciously by a previously-traumatised person; an *innocent* person who is totally unaware of what they are doing. This theory, while attractive, may need to be modified somewhat, as we shall see.

Of course, the RSPK hypothesis is only an idea which is as yet unproven by science. However, with every passing year science is making new discoveries concerning just how potent and powerful the human mind actually is. We really should not be surprised if the subconscious can cause as yet unknown forms of energy to a) leave the body, and b) thereafter manifest themselves in ways that, due to our impoverished level of understanding, seem truly bizarre or frightening.

There are, of course, a number of serious questions that need to be addressed in regards to the RSPK hypothesis.

The primary question asked by many people is, 'If a poltergeist is merely a form of energy and has no inherent consciousness, how can it act as if it is both highly aware and intelligent?'

A typical poltergeist, for instance, will often leave written messages that refer directly to people living in the household it has infested. These messages may also make direct reference to events and circumstances the victims are well aware of, and may even be given in response to questions posed by a victim to a polt. These answers are usually articulate, coherent and logically structured. How could a non-sentient form of energy possibly achieve this?

The answer is not that difficult to work out. Remember, although poltergeist energy may normally have no consciousness in and of itself, it is being directed and controlled, albeit subconsciously, by a human being who *does* possess all the faculties that a poltergeist lacks.

Imagine, by way of an analogy, that it were possible to resurrect into the twenty-first century a person who died in the seventeenth century, before the advent of the technological revolution. Imagine further that this person – we'll call him 'Jake' – is at some point introduced to a TV. In the seventeenth century, Jake would have had no concept of television or the power of electricity that makes televisual broadcasting possible.

Let's pretend that when Jake sits down in front of a TV for the first time he sees something that we all take for granted; a news broadcast. In front of him, he sees a strange box. Inside the box, he sees a man who is speaking. Likely Jake will be forced to conclude that the man is really inside the box, but his head will be flooded with questions. The box is so small; how could a fully-grown man fit inside it? Are his body and legs squashed beneath him, or is he a demon whose body only exists from the shoulders upwards? Why does the man seem so strange, sporting a rather 'flat' physiognomy? Jake can only interpret the evidence as far as his understanding of the world and the physical laws it operates by allow him to. Despite his confusion, Jake will be forced to conclude that the man inside the box, no matter how bizarre his appearance, is actually alive and sentient. After all, Jake can see him talking and moving in a way that only living, conscious creatures can.

Of course, we know that what Jake is actually seeing is not a living human being, but rather a series of dots on a screen. The ability to see a newsreader on TV, keeping us up-to-date with world affairs, is the culmination of numerous scientific discoveries over the years. Intelligent, creative human beings over the decades have found ingenious ways to both harness and manipulate electricity. The intelligence of the inventor is 'behind' the use of electricity as a means of transmitting televisual images. Therefore, although electricity has no intelligence or consciousness, it can be given the *appearance* of intelligence and consciousness when it is manipulated by a sentient creature who *does* possesses those qualities.

The poltergeist is no different. When the 'focus' of the poltergeist subconsciously manipulates poltergeist energy, they imbue it with qualities and characteristics of their own. The intelligence lies not within the polt, but within the person who is subconsciously manipulating the polt energy. When a polt writes a message for its victim on a piece of paper it is not necessarily displaying intelligence, just as the image of a newsreader on TV displays no intelligence either. What we are seeing, in both scenarios, is the *appearance* of intelligence, not intelligence itself. The 'intelligence' of the man on TV lies not on the screen, but back in the TV studio many miles away. Similarly, the intelligence of the polt lies behind the scenes in the cerebrum of the focus, not in the visible display of polt symptoms.

In the light of the above, why then, in this volume, do the authors sometimes speak of poltergeists as if they were actually living, sentient creatures? Mike comments:

Sometimes it's just a literary device. Because poltergeists act as if they were sentient and superficially behave as if they possessed awareness, it's easier to talk about them in those terms. However, we mustn't forget that although the poltergeist may possess no intelligence or sentience in and of itself, there *is* a sentience and intelligence controlling it behind the scenes; that of the unwitting focus.

In terms of how the poltergeist acts and behaves, the source or location of the guiding intelligence is of little consequence. Poltergeist is as poltergeist does, you could say. However, when we come to consider how we should deal with a poltergeist infestation the difference is crucial.

Further, in the later stages of the investigation Darren and I were forced to rethink our understanding of the poltergeist phenomenon. This also had an influence on our understanding of the relationship between the polt-energy, sentience and self-awareness. This, in turn, greatly influenced our decision to refer to the polt as a person and not just a form of externalised energy.

This is something that the authors will return to in later chapters. However, it must be said at this point that the researchers would eventually be forced to confront a very disturbing possibility. Although, at least in the early stages, a polt may only mimic the appearance of intelligence, is it possible that at some point it may become so powerful that it can effectively disengage from its host and take upon itself the sentience and consciousness hitherto denied it? Under certain circumstances, can a poltergeist eventually separate from its human focus and live its own, separate, conscious existence, perhaps even developing its own personality and idiosyncrasies?

Another question concerns the nature of polt activity. Why, in many cases, does the polt energy attack the focus – the very source of its existence – as vehemently as others who happen to be in the vicinity? Some researchers have suggested that there are very deep emotional and psychological forces at work here, and that the focus may want to punish his or herself to some degree. Mike isn't sure whether enough evidence exists to justify this hypothesis, but he comments:

Paranormal research is not yet an exact science. Whereas conventional researchers 'work with what they know', researchers into the paranormal are almost working exclusively with what they *don't* know. Paranormal activity of all kinds seems to share a common characteristic; it is unpredictable and almost impossible to precipitate to order. When a chemist mixes two known chemicals together, he or she can say with the utmost

confidence what the result will be. When paranormal researchers enter a haunted house they can do little except wait to see
if anything happens. Chemical reactions can be produced to
order; ghosts and the like cannot.

Seasoned paranormal researchers never claim to have all the
answers. They will humbly admit that they are working in a darkened room, not a sunlit vista. For every hypothesis that is put
forward to explain the poltergeist phenomenon, data will exist
somewhere that appears to contradict it.

Why do polts so often bite the hand that feeds them, attacking
the focus that unwittingly gives them life? We do not know, but
we can speculate.

In the world of paranormal research, particularly those aspects
of it strongly influenced by New Age spiritual concepts, there is
much talk about 'energy'. Energy is the current buzz-word, the
flavour-of-the-month concept. Visit any New Age spiritual con-
vocation and you will hear the word 'energy' repeated with both
unbridled enthusiasm and cavalier abandon.

'You can feel the energy in this place', they will say. 'The energy
in here is very negative/positive', they will declare.

'That person drains my psychic energy', they will moan.

'Let me raise your energy to a higher vibration by working on
your chakras', they will offer.

And so it goes on. In some New Age circles – although certainly not all, we must point out – 'energy' is the psychic 'Staff
of Life'.

Mike has attended hundreds of New Age gatherings of all per-
suasions. Whenever he hears the word 'energy' uttered – which is
usually every few minutes – he will often take the opportunity to
ask the person concerned exactly what they're talking about. Just
what do the proponents of New Age spirituality mean when they
talk about 'energy'?

He is yet to receive a truly meaningful answer.

Most people who talk about 'working with spiritual energies',
'dispelling negative energy' or 'raising their energy to a higher

vibration' really haven't a clue what they're talking about. Ask them what the word energy means, and you'll almost certainly be met with a pitiful dearth of understanding.

I've had Tarot readers tell me that the 'energy' they 'work with' is 'a strong spiritual feeling'. Healers have told me that it's a 'divine essence' that they can 'channel into patients' and those who claim to channel 'alien intelligences' have informed me that the energy they work with is 'the collective mind of the Ascended Masters'.

I don't wish to be offensive, but my feeling is that those who use the term 'energy' in such a cavalier way really *haven't* a clue what they're talking about. 'Energy', it seems, can mean anything they want it to.'

One dictionary describes energy as, 'The inherent power to act ... the power to work'. This is a simple but accurate definition. The authors are not against the idea that human beings may have, lying latently within them, energies as yet unknown to science and have said so earlier in this book. However, we need to be careful that we don't make our concept of *energy* so loose that it can mean virtually anything, rendering the definition of the word essentially meaningless.

There is a great deal of circumstantial evidence that poltergeist foci do indeed have within them some form of energy or power that has been precipitated by stress or trauma, and that this energy can, under some circumstances, be externalised or 'let loose' and manipulated by the focus subconsciously to create poltergeist-like phenomena. Many poltergeist foci have reported that the symptoms of polt infestation inevitably get worse when their stress levels rise, and, conversely, diminish or disappear altogether when they become more relaxed and at peace with themselves. Mike has helped numerous experients deal with poltergeist infestation, and his first line of attack is to identify the focus, discover why they are under stress, and finally work with them to eliminate the cause of that stress. In almost every case, the infestation disappears within the space of 7-14 days.

If the presence of stress or upset within the focus makes the polt stronger, then it is logical to assume that the entity is more comfortable in a stress-filled environment or in the presence of a stress-filled person. It is as if the polt *feeds* upon the stress being generated both within and from the focus, drawing strength from it. Naturally, then, when the stress-levels within the focus start to diminish the poltergeist is not going to be happy with the situation. To perpetuate its own existence it must maintain an environment in which it can grow and flourish. From the poltergeist's point of view, then, it has a vested interest in maintaining or even raising the levels of stress and anxiety within those who share its 'home'. In effect, it is creating its own 'psychic larder' that it can dip into whenever it is hungry.

There is another peculiarity of polt infestation that supports this argument powerfully. It has long been known that poltergeists, despite their propensity for causing a sense of dread and terror within their victims, rarely attack them physically. We have already seen how the evidence does *not* support the idea that poltergeists can't harm their victims; they can, but simply choose not to most of the time. Why would a poltergeist go to such lengths to frighten people and yet rarely cause them harm?

Mike spent a number of years in the police service and, on occasion, had to deal with victims of assault including acts of domestic violence. On many occasions, the assailant was known to the victim and had threatened them with violence before the actual assault took place.

In terms of fear, the worst period for the victim was prior to the assault when the threats had been made but not yet carried out. The targeted person would be sick with worry, terrified to leave the house in case the aggressor 'caught up with them'. The stress that such a situation can cause to the mind and the body is horrific. The fear of impending physical violence is one of the most awful burdens a human being can endure.

Strangely, when the physical attack is actually carried out it can bring about a sense of release in the victim. The deed has been done, and all the victim has to do now is recover from the physical injuries. The physical assault may have been deeply unpleasant, but at least the victim has survived. The aggressor has, in his or her own twisted mind, achieved their objective and now redressed whatever perceived slight it was that made them carry out the attack. Although the victim may be bruised or worse, at least that sick, gnawing fear has been put to bed and they can at last get on with their life.

There are two logical reasons, then, why poltergeists rarely attack or injure their victims physically. Firstly, physical injury may cause the victim to be removed from the environment –perhaps even to hospital if the damage is serious enough. In the worst-case scenario, the victim could even be killed. Now although poltergeists are 'person-centred' as opposed to 'place-centred', they seem to function far more efficiently in the home environment of their host. Therefore, although they may not need to stay at home to feed, they certainly prefer it that way. Although leaving one's home permanently is almost always futile when trying to escape a poltergeist, a temporary relocation for a few days seems to disorientate the polt and give the experients a short but welcome respite. The removal of the victim from their home, then, may temporarily cut off the poltergeist from its food source or at least make feeding difficult. Thus, the polt has a vested interest in keeping the victim in a reasonable state of good health and, if possible, within their own home.

The second reason that poltergeists usually refrain from physically injuring their victims is that such an attack would not serve the polt's purpose. If anything, it may even work against it. The polt knows that its victim is most afraid when the *fear* of being physically and/or psychologically assaulted is present. The poltergeist can feed most efficiently when its victims are kept in a constant state of high tension, waiting morbidly for 'the next thing' to happen. The poltergeist may draw no pleasure or benefit from physically harming the experients; only from frightening them. So, that is exactly what it almost always does.

In the case of the Lock Street family, it did it exceedingly well. However, it later turned on one of the householders with unbridled ferocity and demonstrated that causing severe physical injury is certainly not beyond its ability.

Of course, much of this is still just a hypothesis. However, there are other characteristics of polt infestation which support it very strongly. If the poltergeist feeds on fear, then fear is the very emotion that it needs to generate in its victims to sustain itself. It can be no coincidence, then, that the generation of fear and anxiety within its victims is the *primary activity* of the typical polt.

The polt will leave threatening messages, throw objects at its victims, frighten them with loud and unexpected noises and, on occasion, engage in far more sinister activities. The Lock Street family know this only too well. Leaving Robert's large, fluffy bunny rabbit sitting in a chair on the landing with a box-cutter blade in its hand is a chilling example of polt intimidation. After such an attack, the fear and stress levels within the experients will go up considerably, thus allowing the polt to dine sumptuously. This is precisely why the poltergeist 'bites the hand that feeds it'; for only by attacking the focus that unwittingly gave it life can it generate the fear energy it feeds on so voraciously.

Another problematical area involves the relationship between the poltergeist and the sustenance it needs to survive. If the polt is actually a form of energy, and so too is the fear it feeds upon, does this mean that, in some bizarre way, one form of psychic energy is feeding off another? This notion hardly sits well with orthodox scientific doctrine. Energy *is* power, and does not need to 'feed' in this way. It may well be, then, that when the latent polt-energy is externalised by the experient it changes its nature. Perhaps in some way that we do not quite understand, it becomes 'embodied', taking on an existence of its own. The researchers would almost irresistibly be forced to this conclusion in the closing stages of their investigation.

The study of the paranormal is not, as we have said, an exact science. There are features of poltergeist infestations that remain baffling to the most learned of investigators. However, the RSPK theory is the one that, for the most part, fits the known facts.

As Darren has commented:

The symptoms of poltergeist infestation can be some-what terrifying. To see things being violently thrown around, without anyone seemingly being there to do it, is a harrowing experience.

The RSPK theory is an absolutely fascinating one, and if it was proven to be valid – that the cause of a poltergeist is not really a ghost or spirit – it still leaves us with powerful evidence of psychic power and the ability to do fantastic things with the subconscious mind.

CHAPTER TEN

Smudging

On Friday 21 July, Darren and Mike met once again for breakfast in the Market Cafe. Dining upon another Full English would be the first ritual they would carry out that day. Another, of much greater significance, would follow later.

The purpose of the meeting was to re-assess the evidence that the two researchers had accumulated so far, and see if any further insight could be gained into the exact nature of the problem facing the Lock Street family.

Mike told Darren that he had a working hypothesis; essentially the same one he had voiced earlier.

Mike expressed the opinion that there were two separate phenomena taking place in the household simultaneously. Like Darren, he believed that the family's home was infested by a poltergeist. However, as detailed previously, he also believed that the second entity was far different. As the food upon the researchers' plates disappeared steadily, Mike told Darren what had drawn him to this conclusion.

In June 2006, Mike had been asked to give a lecture at a conference on paranormal phenomena. His chosen subject – a favourite – was 'Quasi-Corporeal Companions', or 'QCCs'. For the benefit of the reader, it will be necessary to take a slight detour at this juncture and explain just what this strange phenomenon entails.

Many young children have what their parents call 'imaginary friends' whom they play with. Mike had two when he was a toddler: a bossy little madam called Elizabeth and a scruffy but loveable urchin called Maureen. To Mike these 'imaginary' play-mates were very, very real. Mike has written a book about the phenomenon, and has interviewed experients from no less than five different continents.

Mike's conclusion is that these 'imaginary' friends are not really imaginary at all; which is why he prefers to use the term 'quasi-corporeal companions'. They are, he vouches, sentient creatures who have the ability to appear and disappear at will. Like other paranormal entities, they seem to live by a set of 'rules' – which to we humans may at times seem baffling – come in a number of dif-ferent 'types' and engage in behaviour patterns that are sometimes reasonably predictable.

Mike, after examining the evidence, concluded that the second entity in the Lock Street dwelling was a quasi-corporeal compan-ion or 'QCC.

The first thing I noticed was the types of phenomena that were manifesting themselves in the house. Just about everything that was happening was consistent with typical poltergeist phenom-ena – except for one room; Robert's bedroom.

Throughout the rest of the house there have been cold spots, coins dropping to the floor with a clatter, chairs being moved while experients were sitting on them … just the sort of intimidating behaviour that polts like to engage in. However, in Robert's room it was different.

There were some sorts of activity in his room which on the surface were polt-like, but in reality were subtly different. Until the latter stages of the infestation, everything that took place in that room had a distinct child-like quality about it. Even when the entity in that room threw things around, they were almost always toys, and they always had a low trajectory – as if they were being thrown by a small child who was standing no more than three feet in height or even sitting down on the floor.

And there's another thing: The phenomena that took place in the bedroom sometimes seemed like displays of childish petulance, but were hardly ever sinister. Everything truly sinister seemed to take place outside of that room; until the later stages, that is.

Darren wasn't convinced.

'But what about the message it left on the doodle-board; 'DIE'?'

Mike admitted that it was hard to explain away, but he made a suggestion.

'Look, kids sometimes say stupid things. How many youngsters will say to their playmates, 'I'm going to kill you!'? They don't really mean it. Kids just don't have the same sense of propriety that most adults possess. True, it looks like a typical polt threat, but it could also be something that a young child would write in a temper tantrum.

'I can't be sure, Darren, but there's something different about the phenomenon in that room that makes me think it may have a different origin to those occurring in the rest of the house.'

Darren and Mike finished their tea and then departed for Lock Street.

When they arrived, the weather was cooler than it had been on their first visit. As they entered, Marianne lost no time in showing Mike a picture she'd taken with the camera facility on her mobile phone.

'Can you remember the last time you were here, Mike? You asked me if I could change a £5 note. Can you remember that I took five £1 coins from the money-box in Robert's room? Well, the next day the pot was smashed to smithereens! It was knocked off the window-ledge onto Robert's chair. Look ... I took a picture with my phone.'

Marianne flipped open the cover of her mobile phone, pressed a series of buttons on the keypad and presented the screen to Mike. He could see a picture of Robert's red, wooden bedroom chair. On the seat were the shattered remains of his money pot and a large collection of coins.

'Oh', said Marianne, 'There's something else. I forgot to give you a copy of the other film I took with my phone ... of the dining room chair moving.'

Using the bluetooth facility on her phone, Marianne sent Mike a short video. Although the quality of the picture wasn't perfect, you could clearly see a dining chair seemingly moving independently of any human assistance. Further, a leather jacket hanging over the back of the chair appeared to be moving of its own accord too. At the point on the footage where the chair moved, a clearly terrified Marianne could be heard screaming, 'Oh my God!' Marc, who sounded equally horrified, similarly exclaimed, 'Oh God!'

Shortly thereafter, the investigators and Marianne, accompanied by Marc and Marianne's brother Ian, gathered around the dining room table. Mike then explained how, from his perspective, the problem should best be handled.

As far as I can see, you have two options', said Mike. 'Option one is that I can try and do something to reduce the intensity of the infestation, to take down the frequency of the phenomena to an acceptable level – or at least a level that you can cope with.'

Marianne looked puzzled.

'What's the second option?'

'It's simple; you do nothing at all'.

Both Marianne and Marc now looked more bemused than ever.

'Let me explain. As I've told you, I have Native American heritage and I follow Indian spirituality very seriously. We call our spiritual path 'The Medicine Way', medicine meaning 'spirit'. There's a ritual we sometimes carry out called 'smudging'. Depending on how and where I carry the ritual out, there's a possibility that I can restrict the activities of the poltergeist to some degree. However, my advice would not be to have the smudging ritual done at this stage. Personally, I think you should go for option two and do absolutely nothing at all.'

'But I don't understand', replied Marianne. 'If you can do something to help, why would it be better to do nothing?'

'Well, it's like this. Smudging is a ritual that's designed to achieve a specific goal; in this case to reduce the activity of the poltergeist. The problem is that because there may be more than one phenomenon at work here, we don't know which entity is responsible for each specific symptom. We also don't know where the territorial boundaries lie; which rooms the polt is active in, exactly which areas the QCC operates in, and so on. If I carry out a smudging ritual in a particular area of the house, I can't be sure exactly what type of entity operates there. Hence, if the ritual is not the correct one for dealing with that particular problem, it may not work.'

'But I thought you did know', said Marianne. 'Earlier you said that the – what did you call it ... quasi-corporeal companion? – was in the bedroom and the polt was active throughout the rest of the house.'

'That's my feeling, but we can't be absolutely certain at this point. Until we are certain, I don't think that a smudging ritual would be the best way forward.'

Marc interjected at this point.

'You said the second option was to do nothing; how would that help?'

'Well, the fact is that the average poltergeist has a very short shelf-life. They don't last very long, normally about six to eight weeks. My feeling is that it's probably reaching its peak around now, and if you can just ride the storm for a little while longer it will just die off without you actually doing anything.'

Marianne wasn't convinced.

'You say they normally last just a few weeks. This all started just before Christmas, and it's July now'.

Mike thought for a moment, and then replied.

'Look, you can't be very precise about this sort of thing. On the surface, it does look as if your polt has lasted far longer than we'd normally expect. On the other hand, if I'm right about you having a second entity in your home – a quasi-corporeal companion – then that changes things. They have been known to last far longer than your average polt. It's like I said, we still haven't sussed out the exact dynamics here.'

Marianne stared into space for a while, obviously weighing up the two options.

'What would you say if I told you that I'd still like you to try option one?'

'I'd understand fully. I can see that you're at the end of your tether here. If you tell me that you just can't stand it any more and that you just don't have the stamina to sit it out, I'd understand completely and I wouldn't take offence. If you want me to carry out the smudging, then I'll do it.'

'I want you to', said Marianne without hesitation. 'I just can't take this any more. I've tried to ignore it, like you said when you came the first time, but it's hard. I'm frightened, Mike.'

Mike opened his bag and removed from it a smaller, multicoloured cloth bag with a cotton shoulder strap. The bag had a flap, which was fastened down with a toggle fashioned from a small piece of birch wood. This was Mike's 'medicine bag', in which he kept a bewildering array of shells, stones, feathers, herbs and other artefacts. To non-Indians they probably look more like junk, but to Native American 'medicine' people they possess great significance.

'Okay; the first thing we have to do is decide which area of the house we want to work the ritual in.'

Both Darren and Marianne felt that the landing at the top of the stairwell would be the best choice. The upper landing was an area where much of the paranormal activity took place. Interestingly, both the polt and the QCC – if such it was – seemed to present themselves here. The polt certainly operated on the landing, for this was where Robert's rocking horse was found hanging from the loft hatch, and it was also the place where the rabbit was found sitting holding the box-cutter blade. Quasi-corporeal companions never carry out stunts like this. It had to be the polt.

However, the landing was also directly adjacent to Robert's bedroom, and Mike said he couldn't rule out the possibility that the QCC could occasionally leave the room and venture onto the landing itself.

There was some circumstantial evidence to support this view. Both Marianne and Marc had reported having small toys – normally model cars – thrown at them as they descended the stairs from the landing. This was not typical activity for the poltergeist in *their* home, but it *was* typical of the phenomena which had taken place in Robert's bedroom. The entity in the bedroom often threw cars and other toys at the couple when they were putting Robert to bed. It seemed that the upper landing, then, could be one area where the two entities operated simultaneously. This, Mike agreed, made it the logical place to carry out the ritual.

'There's only one thing I would ask', said Mike. 'When I carry out the ritual I want everybody to stand on the first landing half-way up the stairwell. You can watch me carry out the smudging at the top of the stairwell on the second landing.' Marianne wanted to know why.

'We still don't know exactly what we're dealing with, and the polt might become extremely angry when it realises what's going on.'

'Will it attack us?' asked Marc.

'Well', said Mike. 'It may not actually attack anybody, but if it does it will attack me. That's why I don't want anyone standing around me when I smudge.'

'Okay', Mike added, 'Let's do it, then. But first we need to have another look in Robert's room.'

In the room, Mike sat down on Robert's small, wooden chair. The others stood around; Ian, Marc and Marianne looking a little apprehensive. Mike placed his shoulder bag on the floor, and, almost immediately, the entity in the room – Sammy or the polt – started to make its presence felt. The strap on Mike's bag started to move, as if being jerked violently by invisible hands.

'He – or it – is still here, then', said Mike.

Darren switched on his camera, but by the time he was ready to film the bag strap had stopped moving. Undaunted, he started to film randomly around the bedroom.

Later, when analysing the tape, the investigators could hear what sounded like a bell ringing. Darren felt it could possibly have been a telephone ring-tone, but it was dissimilar to the telephone in the house.

At one point, Darren's camera pans around and focuses on Mike as he is re-doing his Indian ponytail. Once again, a mysterious white light can be seen caressing the wall behind him.

After wrapping up the evidence-gathering aspect of the second visit, the two investigators then left the room, followed by Ian, Marianne and Marc. Darren and the three others descended to the lower landing. Just a few steps further up the stairwell, on the upper landing, stood Mike. The strap from his medicine bag was draped over his left shoulder, while the bag itself hung by his right side.

Mike opened the bag and removed two items. The first was a large, flat shell. The second was a traditional 'smudging stick'. The stick was a cigar-shaped bundle of herbs – sweet-grass and sage – bound together with blue cord.

Mike removed a cigarette lighter from his trouser pocket and showed it to the others.

'See this? It's an ancient Indian cigarette lighter – very traditional!'

Everyone laughed, albeit nervously, at his attempt to lighten the mood.

Mike flicked the lighter wheel and a small, orange flame burst forth. He held it to the end of the smudging stick. At first, nothing happened, and then a plume of thick, white smoke rose towards the ceiling.

'Okay', said Mike, 'Now we can begin.'

Mike faced what Indians call 'the Four Directions' – East, South, West and North – and uttered some prayers.

'Now for the Seven Directions', he whispered.

Once again he prayed to the cardinal compass points, but then he held the smudging stick aloft.

'To the Above', he muttered, followed by a short prayer in a language that his observers couldn't understand.

Then Mike crouched down and held the smudging stick just above the floor, whispering, 'To the Below'.

Finally he held the stick next to his heart and, with his free hand, wafted the incense smoke towards him.

'To the Within', he added, before concluding with another prayer.

'There . . . it's done.'

At no time did the polt attempt to interfere with the ritual or in any other way disrupt the proceedings.

After the smudging was concluded, Marianne mentioned that things were still disappearing from the house, but that many of the items were being found in the loft. She asked if someone would check the roof space. In particular, she wanted them to look for a piece of wood that Marc had wanted to use in a DIY job, but which had maddeningly disappeared. A blue, plastic box cover was also missing. As Darren was busy collecting up his equipment, Mike volunteered. Using a chair to stand on he removed the loft hatch cover and peered into the darkness aided only by a small torch. There was no wood, no box cover. Nothing in the loft looked out of place at all. Mike took several pictures. When he examined them later there was nothing unusual. He replaced the loft cover and stepped down from the chair. Later, just before they left, Darren had to replace the loft cover again. Someone – or something – had moved it.

That evening the polt made only one, brief appearance. Approximately one hour after the researchers left, it moved a vacuum cleaner which had been standing in Marianne's bedroom onto the first landing half way down the stairwell.

The following day was also unusually quiet. Marianne had a small toy thrown at her while standing in her bedroom, which made Mike wonder if the QCC which seemingly inhabited Robert's room had access to her room too.

On the Sunday Mike telephoned Marianne to see how things were going.

'I hope we've turned a corner', she said. 'Whatever you did in that ritual seems to have worked in some way. The odd thing is still happening, but it's not threatening or intimidating now. It's different. It doesn't scare us so much.'

What the researchers didn't know was that several days after Mike completed his smudging ritual Marc was put under a degree of emotional stress by a set of circumstances that it is not necessary to divulge in this book. Almost at the same time, the polt started to act up again with renewed vigour.

On Monday 24 July, Marc's credit card went missing. He searched high and low for it, but to no avail. Later, as he ascended the stairs, he found it. It was standing vertically on edge, upon a stair, as if held in an upright position by invisible fingers.

The following day Marianne's travel pass went missing. It too turned up later on the stairwell. Alongside it was a lottery scratch card that had gone missing three weeks earlier.

That evening, which was unusually hot and clammy, little Robert was happily playing in his bedroom. Marianne and Marc were also present. In the corner of the room a children's TV programme played through, seemingly unwatched.

Suddenly, Marianne became aware of something extremely odd. Strange flashes of white light seemed to be flickering around the room. Sensing that the polt – or something paranormal, at least – may be active she removed her mobile phone from her pocket and switched on the video camera facility. Marc grabbed his mobile and did the same.

As both Marc and Marianne switched on their phones, Robert clambered upon the bed and lay down. He looked hot, which was not unusual considering the soaring temperature. Britain was still basking in an intense heat-wave.

Not wanting to alarm Robert, Marc tried to maintain an air of normality in the room. At the beginning of the footage, extracted later from Marianne's phone, Marc can be heard talking. He sounds nervous, out of breath even, although it's obvious that for Robert's benefit he is trying to sound relaxed.

'Marianne, would you like to go and get some dinner?'

This, the authors think, was probably an attempt by Marc to remove Robert from the room, without alarming him, by getting his mother to take him downstairs for something to eat.

Just then, Robert turns his head slightly to the right and seems to stare across the room.

'He's said 'yes.''

Realising that Robert is apparently referring to someone in the room, albeit invisibly, Marc hesitates slightly and then replies, '. . . has he?'

At that point Robert seems to point directly towards the cupboard door in the corner of the room and, smiling, seems to say, 'Yes . . . he . . . *yes* . . .'

At this point, the clip ends.

After Mike returned home he decided to download onto his computer the two video clips that Marianne had sent to his phone. He made a fresh pot of coffee, washed, and then got to work.

First, he inserted into one of his computer's USB ports the wireless 'dongle' that could pick up multimedia files remotely. Then he activated the connection between his phone and his PC and prepared to download the clips. It was at this point, as the files were transferring, that he noticed something odd. Three files, not two, were sitting on the desktop of his PC. Files one and two were the clips of the moving chair and the lights in Robert's room. The third file was different and had an unrecognisable grey and black icon. What puzzled Mike even more was that the file had no name – there was just the strange grey and black icon.

Regardless, Mike took the risk and double-clicked on the icon with his mouse. The file opened in QuickTime, a multimedia player. The screen was perfectly white, but in the centre, in large black letters, were the words, *HA HA*. Mike tried to save the file onto his desktop with a name, but before he had time to complete the operation, the media player shut down and the file disappeared from the desktop altogether. He could find no copy of the file on his phone, and none on his computer.

Had the file actually been on his phone to start with, or had it simply appeared alongside the transferred movie clips on his computer? The researchers don't know.

Was the entity toying with Mike? He thinks so, and found the idea that it could interfere with both his mobile phone and his computer unnerving.

CHAPTER ELEVEN

Battle Lines

On Friday 28 July, Mike rose just before dawn and washed. He quietly opened the back door that led into the garden and stepped into the already warming air. Still, the heat wasn't too bad – yet.

Mike's medicine bag was draped over his shoulder. From it, he removed his smudging shell and a small wrap of hide. In the twilight, he could just see well enough to undo the thong that bound it together. Inside was a small pinch of incense that had been prepared to a unique formula.

As he whispered some prayers, Mike took from his pocket a cigarette lighter. The *click* of the ignition broke the silence of the night, while the flame pierced the dark comfortingly.

As the incense ignited, it hissed and spluttered. The sweet aroma of copal filled the air, carried northwards on the breeze. Mike was glad that the smoke went north; the Grandfather Spirits were trying to tell him something.

'Today will be the day – today will be the day it begins.'

Mike looked up at the heavens and raised the smudging shell aloft in his right hand.

'Migwetch!' he acknowledged. *'Thank you.'*

Later that morning, Mike made his way down to South Shields town centre for the now familiar rendezvous at the Market Cafe.

He'd arranged to meet Darren there at 12.30pm. He was early, and took the opportunity to wander around the legendary South Shields flea market that draws visitors from all over the region. He couldn't help but smile when he glanced upon a copy of *The Exorcist* in a box full of old video tapes.

'Only a quid!' said the stallholder enthusiastically.

'Nah', said Mike. 'I prefer the real thing, thanks.'

The sun was still beating down mercilessly. Mike hated the heat, always had. He decided to take shelter in the cafe even if Darren wasn't there yet, so he made his way through the throng of people searching for bargains and crossed the road. Just as he did so, his mobile phone beeped to indicate he'd received a multimedia message. It was from Marianne: *Got some things to tell u. I have been talking to Sammy thru the picture board. Tell u about it when u get here.*

Attached to the message were some photographs of the doodle-boards which, if genuine, seemed to contain messages written by the entity. Further, these messages seemed to have been left in direct response to questions vocalised by Marianne while she was in Robert's room.

Mike had urged her to send him copies of any picture, video or audio evidence by multimedia phone message or by e-mail as soon as possible, as the entity had already proved that it was capable of deleting information that it presumably didn't want them to see. The footage of the strange, torpedo-shaped lights that both Marc and Marianne had filmed zooming around Robert's room is a good example. Marc had filmed some of the most spectacular phenomena, but within the hour, all trace of the footage had mysteriously been erased from his phone. Marianne had the presence of mind to send Mike her footage, which was fortuitous as it too was erased from her phone thirty minutes later.

Things were certainly hotting up, it seemed. If Mike had understood Marianne's message correctly, a reasonably successful means of communication seemed to have been established between herself and the entity in her son's bedroom. Mike realised that this sort of communication could be a risky business and needed to be handled very carefully indeed; nevertheless, it did boost the researchers' chances of establishing just what sort of phenomenon they were dealing with.

Inside the Market Cafe, Mike glanced around but there was no sign of Darren. He ordered a coffee and sat down.

Within minutes, Darren arrived, and he was not alone. He was accompanied by another investigator who was also called Darren – Darren Olley.

'Hi, Mike . . . Hope you don't mind me bringing Darren along. I just thought it might be a good idea to get a second opinion.'

Mike had no problem with that at all. He'd met Darren Olley previously and welcomed his potential insight into the case.

Because it was market day, the cafe was getting really busy and it was difficult to find three seats together. The trio decided to skip coffee and head directly to Lock Street. Well, almost directly. Darren Olley was famished and desperate for something to eat. Darren and Mike took shade under an overhead walkway on the north side of the square, while Darren Olley queued at a mobile burger stand for sustenance. Mike played back the bedroom footage that Marianne had sent to his phone earlier, plus the images he'd just received that morning. Irritatingly the intense sunlight obscured the screen so badly that it made it almost impossible for Darren to see anything clearly.

'When I get home I'll download these onto my computer and have a better look at them. Meanwhile, any feelings about this afternoon?'

Darren paused thoughtfully and said, 'Actually, I do. Not so much thoughts as a gut instinct'. And what's that?'

'To be honest, Mike, I just get this feeling that something is going to happen. Maybe I'm wrong, but ... I can just *feel* it.'

Although Darren is very much more technically-minded than Mike – Darren analyses phenomena while Mike tends to experience and interact with them – Mike has come to trust Darren's instinctual urges and intuitive hypotheses. Darren has a good nose for the truth, and Mike has learned that when his friend gets a 'feeling in his water' it's normally pretty accurate.

'You could be right', answered Mike. 'Its reaching a climax now, I think . . . it's coming to its peak. To be honest, Darren, I'm glad for the family. They're being very courageous in the way they're handling this, but I don't know how much more they can take.

'You know how these things go, though; once they peak like this they normally die out pretty soon afterwards. Like you though, I have my reasons for thinking that today could be very significant.'

'Darren agreed, but saw a problem from an investigative point of view.

'I feel torn, in a way. One half of me wants this thing to end for the sake of the family, and yet the researcher in me wants it to continue so we can gather more data.'

Mike laughed. 'I know what you mean. Still, if you're right about today we may get all the data we need.'

Darren Olley returned from the burger van with a giant carton of fries and something meaty in half a stottie bun. Darren pinched a fry apologetically, before pinching a second and a third.

Aw ... I wish I'd got some now.'

The trio headed off for a nearby taxi rank. Meanwhile, the entity was already beginning to set the pecking order for the day ahead. Soon, it would begin to establish to everyone aware of its presence that it – and it alone – was Top Dog, and that it would brook no interference from anyone as it went about its business. Later, it would also prove the researchers' theory that it was 'reaching its peak' to be woefully premature.

CHAPTER TWELVE

Paranormal Pen-Friends

When the investigators arrived at Lock Street, Darren introduced Darren Olley to Marianne, Marc and Ian. Mike was delighted to find June, Marianne's mum, in the living room. It was over forty years since he and his friends had defended her honour against a gang of ruffians.

'Let's hope it's not another forty years before we meet again!' Mike joked.

June had been sceptical at first. She had harboured no ideas about malicious deception, but wondered if practical jokes, misunderstandings and maybe even a mild touch of paranoia had all conspired together to make her daughter think her house was 'haunted'.

June's scepticism didn't last long. Once she'd had personal experience of the polt first-hand she knew with a certainty that something truly extraordinary was going on. Like her daughter, she simply wanted to know what.

'It sounds like you've been having fun!' quipped Darren Olley.

'It's been amazing, really . . .' said Marianne. Darren interrupted.

'Marianne, I hate to stop you in mid-flow but we need to get this on tape. I'm going to set up the motion sensors on the landing, put the camera in the bedroom, have a quick look around and then come back. If you can just hang on to your story till I return I'd appreciate it.'

Darren went upstairs with his kit bag, along with Darren Olley. Meanwhile, Mike talked to the family members and reassured them that this situation was not going to last forever. Then he turned to June.

'June, I can tell you without a shadow of a doubt that your daughter and her partner are not imagining this. If anyone who knows about this situation claims that it's a hoax or simply all being imagined, please give them a personal message from me; they're talking *bollocks*.'

'You don't have to convince me now!' June replied. 'I *know* there's something going on.'

When the two Darrens came back downstairs, the researchers formally taped Marianne's account of what had transpired since their last visit. Referring to detailed hand-written notes, she recalled every last instance of paranormal activity.

That morning the entity had got to work early. At exactly 8.30am, the alarm on Marianne's phone rang as she lay in bed. She pressed the 'snooze' button and replaced the phone on the nearby bedside cabinet. Five minutes later, she was startled to hear knocking on her bedroom door. It was June. She'd obviously decided to pay them an early visit, but how had she gotten in the house?

'The back door was open so I just let myself in', she explained. Marc and Marianne were both adamant that they'd locked the door before going to bed the previous evening. Marianne told her mother that she'd be with her in a moment. She got out of bed and dressed hurriedly. Instinctively she reached for her mobile phone on the bedside cabinet, but it had disappeared. She scoured the room with her eyes and eventually located the errant mobile. It was sitting on top of the wardrobe. Bemused, she went downstairs to join her mother.

At 9am, Marianne again went into her bedroom and momentarily placed her phone on the bed. Within seconds, it had disappeared, only to reappear on the landing outside of the room.

At 9.30am precisely, after June had left, Marianne was sitting in the living room. Her mobile phone was on the arm-rest of the sofa. Again, while she was momentarily distracted, it disappeared. Marianne, using another phone, tried to ring her mobile on the basis that when it rang she'd be able to locate it quite easily. There was no answer. As the entity seemed to have a penchant for leaving things at the top of the stairs, Marianne decided that the upper landing would be as good a place as any to begin her search. Sure enough, the phone was there.

'The weird thing was that on the screen was the box asking for my security code. This only happens when you first switch the phone on. I knew then that the phone had been switched off and then switched on again. It must have been switched off when I tried to ring it, and that's why I couldn't hear the ring tone. But who switched it on again?'

Who indeed.

At 9.40am both Marc and Marianne placed their mobile phones on the kitchen worktop and retired to the living room. Almost as soon as they had sat down, the kitchen door flew open. The couple went to investigate and, to their dismay, found that both phones were missing. Ironically, it was Marianne's reaction to the repeated translocation of the phones that ultimately helped the investigators immensely in their research.

To put it bluntly, Marianne just 'blew her top'. She'd had just about enough of this ridiculous charade and wasn't going to put up with it any longer.

What follows is Marianne's account in her own words:

Whatever it was, it was really acting itself and I was fed up. I was standing in the kitchen and I shouted, 'Look you have to *stop* this!'

Then we decided to go into Robert's bedroom and say something similar in there. We went up the stairs and Marc was the first one to try and make contact with it. He said, 'If this is you, Sammy, you have to stop it now. If you frighten us you might bring other things into the house, and if you do that we won't be able to stay here. If we move, *you* won't be able to stay here or see Robert any more.'

Just then we heard what sounded like a thump coming from the cupboard in the corner of the room. Then the cupboard door shot open. I looked over, and inside the cupboard I saw one of Robert's doodle-boards lying on the floor. I went over and picked it up.'

At this juncture Marianne was amazed to see that 'Sammy' had apparently left a message for them. It simply said, *I AM SORRY.*

Again, the researchers were lucky that Marianne had found the presence of mind to capture proof of the incident. She fled downstairs as quickly as she could and found her phone had been returned to its resting place on the kitchen worktop. She raced back upstairs and quickly activated the camera facility. Then she snapped a photograph of the message, worried perhaps that it would disappear as magically as it had appeared.

At this point Marianne wondered if she dared push her luck and try to get Sammy to leave another message. She picked up the doodle-board and erased the message on it before replacing it in the cupboard. Then, sitting down next to Marc on the bed, she spoke.

'We know you like being here, Sammy, and we know you like Robert, but you must stop being naughty. You mustn't throw things around – you should put things back where you find them.'

The couple waited for a minute or two and then Marc opened the cupboard door gingerly. He picked up the doodle-board and held it up so Marianne could see it. There was another message. 'Sammy' had simply written, *OK.*

Once again the message was photographed and then erased. The doodle-board was placed back in the cupboard and Marianne considered what she should say to Sammy next.

'Sammy, we aren't here to harm you. We only want to help.'

This time Marianne went to the cupboard and removed the doodle-board. Sammy had seemingly written, rather touchingly *I LOVE ROBBERT.* His spelling wasn't too hot, but the thought was there.

Marianne handed the board to Marc, who photographed it and then erased it before putting it back in its now familiar position in the cupboard.

Marianne said, 'If you love Robert please don't throw things around, because you'll frighten him and then he won't want to play with you'.

The next message left by Sammy was extraordinary in a number of respects. It said, *OK MAM BUT THE* . . . and there the text stopped. The word 'THE' was then followed by what appeared to be a crude drawing of an animal. Almost immediately the couple concluded that the picture was probably meant to represent their pet dog, Bounder. Had Sammy meant to say, *OKAY MAM BUT WHAT ABOUT THE DOG?* and for some reason substituted the word DOG with a pictogram meaning the same thing?

Of course, the most startling aspect of the message was the fact that Sammy addressed Marianne as 'MAM'; a Geordie colloquialism for 'mum' or 'mother'.

The point of the message seemed to be that Sammy wanted to be on good terms with Robert, but had a problem with Bounder, the dog.

'I think he's afraid of the dog', said Marc, 'but we can't be sure. Maybe we should ask him.'

Yet again the message was erased and the board put back in the cupboard after a picture was taken. For the time being, Marianne decided to play along with 'Sammy's' perception that she was actually his mother.

'Sammy, this is your mam. We don't understand what you meant by your last message.'

Sammy replied, *BAD DOG.*

This certainly seemed to indicate that Sammy really did have a problem with Bounder, the family pet. However, Marc still needed to be sure.

Marc wiped the board clean after Marianne snapped a picture of the message. Marianne then replaced it in the cupboard.

Once again she asked Sammy, 'Is it the dog you're frightened of?'

There was a faint *thump* from within the cupboard, but when Marianne opened the door the doodle-board did not seem to have been moved. But there was a message on it: *YES.*

Strangely, it had been written upside down. Marianne photographed the board and then carefully erased the message.

Having satisfied themselves that Sammy definitely didn't like Bounder, Marianne and Marc decided to change the subject. Marianne again spoke to Sammy. 'Sammy, Mike and Darren are coming here later. They don't want to do you any harm; they only want to talk to you. They want to help you, Sammy. Will you talk to them?' *NO.*

Another photograph.

'But Sammy, they only want to help you. They aren't coming to trick you or anything – they just want to talk. Will that be okay?'

At this juncture, Marc and Marianne had to leave the room and attend to something downstairs. Not long after they'd entered the kitchen the couple heard a loud bang from the upper floor.

As they ascended the stairwell everything seemed in order. An initial perusal of Robert's room indicated that everything was in place there, too. Marianne decided to check the cupboard to see if Sammy had left another message. He had. In answer to Marianne's second plea for Sammy to talk to the researchers, he'd made his feelings quite clear:

NO NO NO NO NO
NO NO NO NO NO
NO NO NO NO NO

Bizarrely, after leaving this terse and strident message, Sammy then seemed to want to lighten the mood because he drew a quite artistic sketch of a butterfly at the bottom of the board.

Just why Sammy didn't want to talk to the researchers is a mystery, but there are several obvious possibilities. From the outset, Darren and Mike had made it clear that, although they truly appreciated the opportunity to investigate such an active case, their primary objective was to help the family find some resolution due to the catastrophic effect it was having on their well-being. Was Sammy – if indeed that was the entity's real name, and not a masquerade – wary of Darren and Mike because he believed they were trying to get rid of him? Before the couple had called the researchers in they had solicited the help of a number of psychics and mediums, some of whom had attempted to move Sammy 'into the light' along with various and sundry other spirits they claimed had taken up residence in the household. As is usually the case, such efforts came to nothing. However, the repeated attempts to dislodge Sammy from a place he obviously saw as his home may well have contributed to his negative views about Darren and Mike. Or at least, that was one hypothesis.

The researchers had to face up to another possibility. Up to this juncture they had seen no evidence of trickery on the part of Marc, Marianne and Marianne's brother Ian. However – and they were open with the family about this from the outset – they would be failing in their duty to research things properly if they didn't take in to account at least the possibility of fraud. After all, it wouldn't be the first time someone had, for their own reasons, faked poltergeist-like activity as a method of attention-seeking, money making or purely mischief-making. If the messages *had* been faked, then the perpetrator could have made it *look* as if Sammy didn't want to talk to the researchers as a way of explaining why he wasn't so keen to use the doodle-board in their presence. Faking such messages in the presence of Mike and Darren would have been almost impossible.

The sheer number of messages was nevertheless extraordinary, and an entire chapter will be devoted to their examination later in this volume.

CHAPTER THIRTEEN

Pennies from Heaven

The researchers had assumed that June was going to stay during their entire visit, but she wasn't able to. She thanked them for the help they had extended to her daughter and Marc, and then left. After a short break the three investigators, accompanied by Marianne, Marc and Ian, ascended the stairs once again. True to form, the entity was waiting for them.

In Robert's bedroom were Marianne, Marc, Ian, Mike and the two Darrens.

Darren Olley was sitting near the window with his back to a chest of drawers. To his right sat Marc. Mike was sitting on Robert's bed, to the left of Darren Olley. As Darren Ritson reset his camera, with Marc and Marianne looking on, there was a clattering noise. Marc jumped up and spun around. There behind him, resting on the chest of drawers, was a pencil. It had seemingly dropped out of nowhere.

Darren Olley turned and stared at Mike.

'I saw that. I *saw* that … I *saw* it move.'

Darren, always careful to eliminate fraud or hoaxing, added, 'I'm pretty sure that pencil wasn't there before. Anyway, we'll be able to tell when we review the footage that Darren Olley and I took earlier. We panned across the chest of drawers several times, and if the pencil was there we'll have picked it up on camera.'

Later analysis proved that the pencil, wherever it had come from, had not been lying on the chest of drawers before the researchers entered the room. Darren Olley wondered if Marc had placed the pencil behind his ear earlier, and that it had inadvertently been dislodged and fallen onto the chest of drawers behind his head. Again, a review of the video footage proved that Marc did not have a pencil lodged behind his ear when he went into the room.

The researchers decided to vacate the room temporarily while an effort was made to record any anomalous sounds that may manifest themselves on tape. Darren set his equipment to record. Mike placed his digital recorder on top of a cardboard box by the door which led into the room. He checked that the counter was turning and that the recording light was on.

'I hope that the polt or whatever's in here doesn't pinch my recorder or break it – then I'd really be pissed.'

The two Darren's laughed as everyone present filed out of young Robert's bedroom. To keep things right, Darren filmed the exit simply to prove for the benefit of the camera that no one was left in the room before it was 'locked off' and the motion sensors activated. Mike, Darren Olley, Ian, Marianne and Marc were all standing on the upper landing waiting for Darren to leave the room. The party would then descend the stairwell together.

At this point Mike was facing the door of Robert's room. Directly to his right was the stairwell. Just before the first steps, on the left-hand wall, was a socket containing a night-light. As already detailed, this night-light had mysteriously unplugged itself from the socket during the researchers' first visit, although trickery on the part of Marc couldn't be ruled out entirely as only he had been present on the landing for those few, brief seconds. Still, the researchers felt that fraud was unlikely. This time the circumstances were entirely different, as Darren had his camera running and was actually walking towards the landing when, for a second time, the night-light flew out of the socket.

On the downside, it was disappointing that the actual dislocation of the night-light from the socket wasn't caught on camera. However, a closer analysis of what actually transpired was crucial in establishing whether everything experienced up to that point had been one, huge exercise in deception.

Suddenly, as Darren walked towards the door of Robert's room to join the others on the landing, the bathroom door flew open. Both Mike and Darren Olley can testify that no one touched the door at any point. Then there was a distinct *click* which seemed to emanate from the floor area of the landing. Almost simultaneously, those on the landing turned their heads and looked downwards. The night-light had unplugged itself from the socket once again and was now in the middle of the landing.

Marc was standing directly next to Mike and Darren Olley on the landing, and it would have been absolutely impossible for him to have bent down and removed the night-light manually without being seen. It would also have been impossible for him to have stretched out his leg and in some way kicked at the night-light until it fell from its position in the socket.

Fortunately, on analysis later, the footage on Darren's camera proved that no one had moved or in any way manoeuvred themselves towards the night-light at that point. The camera obviously didn't pick up the night-light exiting the socket as it was around the corner on the landing. However, the camera *did* pick up the entire party standing on the landing at the precise moment it ejected itself, and it is clear that no one present was responsible. The researchers believed, and still believe, that this incident alone proved that at least some of the activity in the household was genuine. Whether a lesser proportion of the events had been faked is an issue that they will return to later in this book.

After photographing the night-light as it lay on the landing floor, everyone then went downstairs. Despite his apparent reluctance, the researchers wanted to give Sammy the opportunity to write something on the doodle-board which had been placed in the cupboard.

After twenty minutes or so, the researchers decided it was time to check whether Sammy, or any other entity for that matter, had been active in the bedroom during their presence. Everyone then ascended the stairwell to check. The results were startling to say the least.

On entering the room Mike immediately checked his digital recorder. To his dismay, not only had it been turned off, but the entire recording made up to that point had been erased. This is something that just can't be done accidentally. Erasing a recording is a three-step process with a number of fail-safes built in to prevent accidental erasure. Whoever or whatever had erased the recording had done so deliberately.

Marianne, Marc, Ian, the two Darrens and Mike positioned themselves around the room. Some sat upon the floor, some upon Robert's bed, others on chairs. Darren Olley sat by the window, and placed the kit-bag containing his equipment on the floor. Shortly thereafter he moved the bag and noticed that the base was wet. He looked down at the floor and was astonished to see an ice cube glistening on the carpet, half-melted. No one could explain how it got there, but its appearance seemed to kick-start a whole series of odd events which took place in rapid succession.

Mike was sitting on the bed. On the wall opposite was a large, hammock-like net that contained literally dozens of fluffy toys; bunny rabbits, teddy bears and the like. Suddenly, Mike noticed a small, black, spherical object slowly lower itself from the point where the right-hand (facing) side of the net was secured to the wall. He couldn't make out what the object was, but it ever-so-slowly floated downwards like a feather in a gentle breeze. In order to get others to see it he shouted, 'Hey! Look! Can you see that? There ... on the wall!'

Marc, on the other side of the room, was the first to react. He looked towards the spot where Mike was pointing and exclaimed, 'Yes, I can see it!'

At this juncture the object slowly descended behind a chest of drawers. At no point did it make any noise. There was a mad scramble as the researchers pulled the drawers away from the wall. Behind them was the piece of wood that the entity had stolen from Marc earlier in the investigation.

'Look!' he shouted, *'There's* the wood I've been looking for!'

Also on the floor was the black object that Mike had observed floating to the ground from the toy hammock. Marianne picked it up. It was a small, plastic head with two cartoon-like white eyes and a large, comical nose. It had been part of a free gift that Robert had found inside a chocolate egg. Marianne placed the object on the chest of drawers and Mike took several photographs.

Mike remarked later, as he had on other occasions, 'If someone faked that I'd love to know how they did it.'

While all present were discussing this latest happening, there was a loud crashing noise from the direction of the landing. The toilet door was open. Curiously, the window in the toilet was also open. Marianne insisted it had been shut all the time, and Mike verified that when he'd used the toilet earlier the window had not been ajar.

On the floor of the toilet were two bottles of bleach. They had apparently been knocked from the window-ledge onto the floor.

Someone suggested, quite reasonably, that because the window was open a gust of wind may have blown the bottles from the window-ledge and sent them crashing to the floor. There were two problems with this theory.

Firstly, it did not explain how the window itself had come to be open when both Marianne and Mike could testify that it had been shut. Secondly, although one bottle was virtually empty and quite light, and could just possibly have been blown off the window-ledge by a strong gust of wind, the second bottle was full and very heavy indeed. Those who examined it agreed that the idea of it been blown off the window-ledge onto the floor was completely untenable. Other theories, such as the window being blown inwards and colliding with the bottles, were also discounted. The window only opens one way – outwards.

On returning to Robert's room after their brief distraction in the toilet the researchers made a rather sinister discovery. On the floor by the cupboard in Robert's room was a knife. It was small, but very sharp and had been somehow transported from a drawer in the kitchen to Robert's room.

Seemingly enjoying himself, the entity decided to carry out a trick that by now was something of an old favourite. It took the small, yellow nut from Robert's toy workbench and threw it across the room.

One other curious incident took place at this time. On the ceiling of Robert's room there are two small holes. On entering the room Mike noticed that a cardboard 'Tigger' figure that had been stuck to the wall next to the toy hammock was now on the floor. Marianne stated that the figure had been attached to the wall by double-sided sticky pads. On examination it was found that the pads were now missing. Bizarrely, the pads were found to have been placed neatly over the holes in the ceiling, as if the entity had been engaging in a bit of makeshift DIY during the investigators' absence.

Time for another break, the researchers agreed.

Downstairs, the investigators found that the polt – which was increasingly being seen by Darren and Mike as something entirely distinct from 'Sammy' in the bedroom – had been very busy indeed. It had taken an entire tray of ice cubes and distributed them liberally across the shelves in the fridge-freezer. Both film and stills were taken before everyone gathered at the kitchen table. At this point Mike started to take witness statements. He began with Ian. Shortly thereafter the two Darrens decided to go back upstairs to Robert's room to carry out one or two further tests. This left Mike, Ian, Marc and Marianne in the kitchen. The polt, it seemed, hadn't finished.

Suddenly there was a sharp *crack* on the wooden floor in the kitchen area. There, lying in isolation, was a penny. Where it had come from no one could say, but it sounded as if it had been dropped from a great height.

Two minutes later there was another loud crack, and, in the same location, Mike found a five-penny piece. It lay only inches from where the penny had come to rest. This was rapidly followed by a second penny.

Marc pointed out that there was a plate on a shelf in the kitchen which contained a large amount of loose change. The shelf was more or less directly above the position on the floor where the coins had appeared, but as no one could say with any certainty how much money had been in the plate, or what the denominations were, it was impossible to say with any certainty that that was where they'd came from.

As Marc's chair was quite close to the place where the coins had landed it was possible that, on the first occasion, the penny had slipped from his pocket and fallen through the hole in the back of the plastic chair onto the floor. It was also possible that Marc may have surreptitiously knocked the coin or thrown it. On the following two occasions, however, Mike feels that this was unlikely. He watched Marc carefully and at no point when the second two coins fell, did he move or do anything which would have indicated he was responsible. In fact, when the third coin fell his elbows were on the table and his hands were cupped underneath his chin.

'The Darrens will be annoyed they've missed this', Mike quipped.

In the centre of the table was a pink and white coloured bag belonging to Marianne. Without warning the shoulder strap began to move. The movement was gentle at first, as if someone was gently poking it with their finger. Mike asked everyone to move their arms and legs away from the table. Ian, Marc and Marianne complied. For a few seconds nothing happened, and then the bag strap started to move again. Ian then pointed to a glass of water standing on the other end of the table. The water in it seemed to be vibrating. With every passing second the vibration got stronger before abruptly coming to an end. Just then, the two Darrens came back downstairs and joined the others around the table.

At this point a general conversation ensued, and the researchers again tried to reassure the others that the polt activity was probably reaching its peak and would soon die out. Suddenly, the dining room table slid approximately five inches across the floor and collided with Darren's leg, making him wince. Marc, as a reflex, grabbed the table with both hands and moved it back. Mike and Darren Olley looked under the table immediately to see if someone could have moved it with their leg or foot, but no one was in close proximity. Besides, the table, fashioned from thick pine, is extremely heavy and moving it surreptitiously would have been difficult indeed.

CHAPTER FOURTEEN

Moving Pictures

One of the remarkable features of this case, from the investigators' point of view, was the volume of messages left on the doodle-board by 'Sammy'. Polts will often leave messages, but not normally this many. Both Darren and Mike were quite pleased about this, as such messages can often present more evidence and clues regarding the nature of the message writer than one would imagine.

The first thing that struck the investigators was that, at least superficially, the handwriting was not consistent. In short, it did not appear that the same hand had been responsible for penning all of the messages. This led Darren and Mike to reach a number of hypotheses which could explain this.

Hypothesis 1: The messages were written by one entity, but who inexplicably changed the style of its handwriting from message to message.

Hypothesis 2: The messages were written by a number of different entities, all of whom were collectively claiming to be 'Sammy'.

Hypothesis 3: Some of the messages were genuine and had been written by a single entity, while an unknown person had been responsible for faking the others.

Hypothesis 4: Some of the messages were genuine and had been written by a single entity, while more than one person had been responsible for faking the others.

Hypothesis 5: Some of the messages were genuine and had been written by a number of different entities, while an unknown person had been responsible for faking the others.

Hypothesis 6: Some of the messages were genuine and had been written by a number of different entities, while a number of unknown persons had been responsible for faking the others.

Hypothesis 7: A single individual had faked all of the messages, but had deliberately altered their handwriting from message to message.

Hypothesis 8: More than one person had faked all of the messages.

Researchers much prefer to have a nice set of simple options. Complicated scenarios are tougher to work with, harder to bring into focus. Nevertheless, Darren and Mike were happy to work with what they had, and what they had were eight possibilities, only one of which could be correct.

To narrow down the hypotheses, Darren and Mike first turned their attention to the style of handwriting on each message ostensibly left by Sammy. In all there were thirteen messages, so each message was given a number corresponding to the chronological order in which they were written.

The researchers then turned their attention to the handwriting styles evident on each message and looked for distinctive features that would help identify the writer. Please understand that the authors are not professional graphologists and, therefore, do not use professional terminology in the text that follows. The following analysis is merely some educated guesswork by well-meaning amateurs.

In the thirteen messages left by 'Sammy' the following distinct characteristics were noted in some, but not all, of the text:

TAILED 'O'

In a number of messages the letter 'O' is consistently topped off with a small but distinctive flourish.

LONG–TAILED 'K'

In a number of messages the letter 'K' possesses a distinctively long tail.

THE ROUNDED 'N'

In a number of messages the letter 'N' is distinctive because there are no sharp angles. The angles are distinctly softened and rounded.

USE OF THE CAPITAL 'E'

In a number of messages the letter 'E' is capitalised distinctively, whereas in other messages the cursive 'E' is used.

LONG–TAILED 'Y'

In a number of messages the letter 'Y' has a distinctively long tail.

THE FANCY 'O'

In one message the letter 'O' is finished with a large, distinctive, ornate flourish

To try and establish whether there was some commonality between the messages in terms of authorship, the researchers went through every message and noted which distinctive features were present in each. The following chart illustrates the results.

Pic No:	1	2	3	4	5	6	7	8	9	10	11	12	13
Feature:													
TAILED 'O'				•					•	•			
LONG-TAILED 'K'			•		•								
ROUNDED 'N									•	•	•		
CAPITALISED 'E'	•			•	•								
LONG-TAILED 'Y'		•				•							
FANCY 'O'								•					

By comparing the appearance of the distinctive features on the messages the researchers felt reasonably confident that the cross-correspondences would help them identify which messages were penned by the same hand.

Messages 5, 10 and 11, for example, all contained the highly distinctive 'O' capped by a small but consistent flourish. Messages 10 and 11 also contained the letter 'N' with its distinctive rounded angles. Although message 9 did not contain the 'tailed 'O', it did contain the rounded 'N', which led Darren and Mike to conclude that messages 5, 9, 10 and 11 were from the same source.

Pictures 2, 6 and 8 contained the same, distinctive capitalised letter 'E'. In each case the top horizontal bar of the letter is detached from the rest of the letter, while the vertical bar also becomes the lower horizontal bar in one fluid swoop. Interestingly, in message 2 it appears as if the writer has attempted to connect the top horizontal bar to the vertical bar by adding a small flourish as an afterthought.

Message 8, as well as containing the distinctive capitalised 'E', also contains the equally distinctive long-tailed 'Y'. As message 3 also contained the same long-tailed 'Y' the authors concluded that messages 2, 3, 6 and 8 were probably written by the same hand.

Message 4 contained a distinctive long-tailed 'K'. This was also found in message 6. As the writer of message 6 was also the writer of messages 2, 3 and 8, it was concluded that messages 2, 3, 4, 6, and 8 were probably written by the same hand.

There are a number of peculiarities about the messages. Some appear to be written in a childish hand while others appear to have been penned by someone much older. Even those that superficially seem dissimilar often have strong cross-correspondences that seemed to point to a common author. One possibility the researchers had to face was that one person had faked all the messages but had made an effort to disguise their handwriting. The cross-correspondences may have been 'slips' where the natural style of the writer came through despite his or her attempts to disguise their true identity. Of course, a less prosaic explanation is that all of the messages were penned by a disembodied spirit, or perhaps a poltergeist, and that the entity made similar efforts to confuse the investigators by changing its handwriting style. Disembodied spirits are, one presumes, as susceptible to the temptations of trickery as we humans.

Some messages were dissimilar in ways that strongly suggested to the authors that more than one hand was at work. For example, the letter 'O' in message 7 and the same letter in message 12 are completely different. The letter trace on message 7 begins and ends on the left, while on message 12 it begins and ends on the right.

The authors, however, decided that the help of at least one professional graphologist was needed before any definite conclusions could be reached. Being a professional paranormal investigator does not make you a handwriting expert any more than being a surgeon makes you an expert car mechanic. After some discussion they opted to employ the services of two handwriting experts. The first was Dennis Duez, one of the USA's leading handwriting analysts. Dennis, who works from his offices in Pennsylvania, has appeared on *Fox News* and other media outlets in a professional capacity, and his opinion is highly valued. His professional abilities have been described as 'jaw-dropping', which is probably as good as you'll get by way of a professional testimony.

The second expert was Dana White, who works from a private office in London.

To try and gain some clarity on the issue, the authors wanted to know whether more than one 'hand' had been involved in creating the messages. They also wanted to know whether there was any evidence that the writer or writers had attempted to change the style of their handwriting consciously in an effort to deceive the researchers. Depending on the results of both Mr Duez's and Mrs White's analyses, the researchers hoped to be able to definitely rule out – or rule in – fraud. If fraud was not an issue – and up to this point the researchers had no solid reason to think it was – then it was hoped that the graphological analysis may provide some insight into the number and nature of the entities that were leaving such extraordinary messages on Robert's doodle-board. To Mike and Darren's knowledge, graphological analysis of poltergeist messages had never been conducted before, although it later came to their attention that Harry Price had carried out a similar experiment.

Mike first contacted Dennis Duez on Monday 7 August. He found him charming, affable and helpful. Mike had been worried that the expert would, after hearing the story, have merely thought to himself, 'Wacko!' and replaced the receiver in its cradle. Mike need not have worried. Mr Duez listened patiently and then told him exactly how the researchers needed to proceed.

Firstly, Mike sent Dennis an e-mail with the thirteen 'message' pictures attached. The pictures had all been taken by Marianne using the camera facility on her mobile phone. No fault of hers – she'd done her best – but the quality was not particularly good. Fortunately, Mike is an expert at photo restoration and enhancement which he carries out as part of his business. He downloaded the images onto his computer and then, using the best software available, enhanced them as much as was humanly and technologically possible. The results weren't brilliant, but they would at least allow Dennis Duez to make an initial judgement.

Next, Mike sent Dennis samples of Marianne's handwriting for comparison. Samples of Marc's and Ian's handwriting were sent the following day.

Two days later, copies of the doodle-board messages were sent to Dana White. Then, all the researchers could do was wait.

CHAPTER FIFTEEN

The Fib Factor

From the very outset, Darren and Mike were convinced that Marianne was genuine. From the second visit onwards they were also pretty convinced that at least some of the phenomena taking place in the house were truly paranormal. And yet, to be thoroughly professional, the researchers simply had to make every effort to eliminate the possibility of trickery. They had their professional reputations to maintain, and, in addition, helping the family deal with what can only be described as a nightmare situation would only be made more difficult if one or more of the victims were exaggerating the phenomena or even engaging in wholesale fraud.

From the outset this was made abundantly clear to all parties concerned, and no one seemed to have a problem with it. At the first meeting Mike made the position clear:

'Look, its not that we don't trust you, or even that we don't *want* to trust you, but you have to see things from our perspective. There certainly seems to be something genuinely strange taking place in your home, but there are legions of cynics and sceptics out there who will be only too happy to shoot us down in flames if we don't make every effort to rule out deception.'

Both Marianne and Marc said they fully understood the position and certainly didn't take offence at it.

There are a number of sceptics who simply can't accept that paranormal phenomena are a reality. They will come up with the most bizarre explanations for poltergeist and related activity, and often their hypotheses are harder to believe than the notion that there are things in this world that we simply don't understand.

In most cases the sceptics will go down one of three well-worn routes when trying to explain away paranormal phenomena.

Firstly, they will attempt to find 'rational' or 'scientific' explanations for things that seem to be unexplainable. That unnerving 'bump in the night' is probably just your central heating system cooling down. The apparition of your deceased grandmother was really just a trick of the light, and so on. In most cases, it has to be said, they're probably right. The vast majority of allegedly paranormal phenomena *can* be explained away rationally.

But not all. There is a hard residue of cases that simply defy logical explanation.

Ah', say the sceptics, 'but that's only because we don't have sufficient data. If we had the time and resources to study this or that case fully, a rational explanation would surely be found.'

Well, the authors disagree. Experience has taught them that truly extraordinary things do happen to ordinary people, and in such cases both science and logic are often found wanting.

A second line of attack is to claim that witnesses to paranormal phenomena are either mentally ill or simply deluded. Again, there is a degree of truth in this. Mike often receives mail from readers who claim to hear disembodied voices, for example. In many cases unusual circumstances, such as prolonged sleep deprivation, can precipitate such symptoms. Psychoses can do the same. Fortunately, there are treatments available which, in many cases, greatly reduce the symptoms or even stop them altogether. In the long term, cognitive therapy can prevent those same symptoms reoccurring. However, the authors are aware of numerous cases where disembodied voices have been heard by multiple witnesses. In situations such as this the sceptics will often claim that 'mass hallucination' is responsible, even though the evidence for the existence of such a phenomenon is very tenuous indeed.

In true cases of mass hallucination two factors have to be at work simultaneously; these are *suggestion* and *pareidolia*.

'Suggestion' is the process in which one individual consciously or unconsciously guides the thoughts of another.

Imagine a scenario in which a person takes a drink from a glass and then passes the same glass to a friend. The friend then takes a drink, assuming that the glass contains water. If the first person then clutches his or her throat and falls to the ground pretending to have been poisoned, then the power of suggestion may actually make the second person believe that they are experiencing the same symptoms. They too may fall to the ground, experiencing what, to them, are the very real symptoms of poisoning. It's possible, then, that if a person says, 'Look! There's a ghost!' the power of suggestion may be strong enough to make bystanders think that they can see a ghost too, even if there is no apparition there.

'Pareidolia' is the process by which vague auditory, olfactory or visual stimuli are misinterpreted as something more specific. All humans have the ability to do this. Simply stare at some passing clouds for a few moments and you'll see human-like faces if you wish to. Gaze into the flames of a fire and you will, if you try hard enough, see racing cars, a gaggle of geese and a two-headed elephant. You aren't going crazy; you're just allowing your mind to visualise a framework while your imagination fills in the gaps.

Here is an example of how suggestion and pareidolia work together:

Imagine that you are sitting in a church. In front of you, behind the altar or pulpit, is a beautiful stained-glass window. As the rays of the sun stream into the church through the window your eyes are bewildered by a cascade of light and colour. Suddenly, your eyes perceive a vaguely – human shape made up of sunbeams, colours and possibly the outline of solid objects in the background. The spiritual environment you find yourself in, coupled with the fact that you are meditating on religious matters, may suggest to you that you are undergoing a vision or spiritual experience. Pareidolia may then transform the vaguely human shape into nothing less than a glorious vision of the Virgin Mary.

If you then nudge the person next to you and tell them excitedly what you can 'see', the process may then start to work within them too. Before you know it, the entire congregation may be 'seeing' the Blessed Virgin Mother.

Now it must be pointed out that such instances of 'mass hallucination' are extremely rare. For this reason alone we need to be careful when trotting out this explanation as the answer to all multiple-witness paranormal events. Another reason for caution is that in some case the witnesses all seem to have the same experience simultaneously. Yet another is that there may well be hard, corroborating evidence to support the idea that the phenomenon had an objective reality and was not simply imagined.

Mike knows of one case in which two witnesses – both paranormal investigators – saw the apparition of a lady in a white dress float across the landing of an abandoned mansion house. A third investigator who was nearby, but who saw nothing, testified that both the experients 'nearly jumped out of their skin with fright' at exactly the same second when the ghost allegedly appeared.

The third investigator immediately asked the experients to refrain from any further conversation and draw a sketch of what they'd seen. To his surprise, both drawings were almost identical. The devil was also in the detail, as they say, for both witnesses placed a headband around the head of the ghost and what looked like a large coin or medallion in the centre of the forehead. They also claimed that the ghostly woman's eyes seemed to be staring intently at the ceiling.

It later came to light that other visitors to the building had seen exactly the same apparition. In cases such as this it just seems impossible to imagine that 'mass hallucination' is a viable explanation.

There is no doubt that some mental illnesses can make people think that they're seeing things that have no objective reality, but, as with 'scientific' explanations, it simply isn't possible to apply this conclusion to all instances of paranormal phenomena.

A third tactic used by sceptics is to accuse witnesses of out right fraud. Mike has personally investigated a number of ghost and UFO sightings where the alleged experients were later found to have lied. Sometimes, fraudsters engage in this type of activity to draw attention to themselves. Oftentimes it will be for some imagined pecuniary gain, the participants in the hoax believing that newspapers will pay them huge sums of money for their story. Occasionally, the hoax will be attempted purely for 'fun'.

The problem with some sceptics is that they are quite happy to accuse experients of lying even when the evidence simply doesn't support that conclusion.

In June 2002, Mike gave a lecture to a group of retired business-men entitled, 'Investigating the Unknown'. In the audience was a psychologist who asked Mike whether he personally had ever witnessed anything he couldn't explain with his own eyes. Mike answered in the affirmative, and related an incident in which he had seen, along with another witness, a cut-glass ashtray spontane-ously rise from a coffee table and gently lower itself to the floor.

At this point, the psychologist became extremely angry and shouted, 'That can't be the truth!'

Mike politely asked the questioner if he was accusing him of lying.

'No', he replied, 'I'm just saying that what you've said can't be true, and you know it.' 'In other words, I'm lying.'

For some reason the man didn't want to use the word, 'lying', but felt comfortable making the allegation that Mike was knowingly saying things that weren't true. This sort of sophistry would make an interesting psychological case study in itself, the authors think.

The man continued:

'What you've just said is scientifically impossible!'

'Well', said Mike, 'I'm sorry about that. But it doesn't alter the fact that we saw what we saw. If science can't explain what we saw, then *the scientists* have the problem. If the only way that you can prevent yourself panicking is to accuse me of deception, and demean my character, then go right ahead.'

The authors have seen such belligerence many times before. Sceptics who pride themselves on taking a 'scientific approach' to the paranormal often have no moral scruples when it comes to proving their case. Witnesses have been accused of every vice under the sun by sceptics in an effort to undermine their tes-timony. Some sceptics are so anally retentive that destroying a person's reputation or ruining their character is seen as a small price to pay when the credibility of orthodox scientific doctrine is at stake.

Not all hoaxers are malicious in their intent, however, and the authors actually have a great deal of sympathy with some individuals who have felt compelled to engage in trickery. Just why this is so is an issue that we need to address.

It is difficult to overestimate the terror felt by experients who are the victims of poltergeist activity. The thought that a malevolent, invisible entity is stalking you in your own home, and that even your closest family members might think that you are either mentally, ill, stupid or engaging in trickery, can have a catastrophic effect on a person's happiness and peace of mind. Time after time, the authors have interviewed witnesses whose sincerity was beyond doubt, only to find later that they had engaged in a degree of deceit when testifying to the details of what they were going through.

Some years ago, Mike knew an elderly woman who was enduring a number of distressing physical symptoms. She was subjected to a battery of diagnostic tests, all of which drew a blank. One day, the woman apparently collapsed at home and was rushed to her local hospital in an ambulance. Further tests were carried out, and it was discovered that she had a previously undiagnosed condition that was directly responsible for her symptoms. She was given the correct treatment and eventually recovered.

Later, the woman's daughter confided in Mike that her mother had actually faked the collapse at her home, knowing that she would thereafter be hospitalised. She gambled that, by pretending to be worse than she actually was, the doctors would take her more seriously and carry out further tests to ascertain exactly what was wrong. The woman was really ill; her deceit was not carried out gladly, but simply as a ruse that would get people to listen to her. In this case the gamble worked.

Victims of the poltergeist phenomenon often find themselves in a very similar position. They know that what they are going through is real, but they have a well-grounded fear that no one will take them seriously. They worry that investigators may, after finding no objective evidence, abandon any interest in the case and leave them alone and helpless. To circumvent this possibility, poltergeist victims will often exaggerate the severity of the attendant phenomena in an effort to convince investigators that what they are going through is very, very real and not simply a figment of their imagination. Their deceit is not malicious; it is simply a cry for help.

In the case of the family in question, there were three experients who could theoretically have been guilty of exaggeration, fraud and deceit. These were Marianne, Marc and Marianne's brother Ian. The authors felt that Marianne was an unlikely candidate. Ostensibly, she had had as much opportunity to fake the polt phenomena as her partner and her brother. However, both Darren and Mike felt that her demeanour just didn't lend itself to this conclusion. When she appeared frightened, her fear was palpably genuine. When she related her experiences, she did so with candour, often correcting herself over minor details that were of little consequence. Never for a moment had she done or said anything to arouse suspicion. All the evidence indicated that she was being totally candid with the investigators. If Marianne was faking it, then she was the best faker they'd ever come across.

Now for Marc.

Marianne and Marc seemed to have a solid, stable relationship. Marc appeared kind, courteous and responsible. He also seemed to be a loving, caring stepfather to little Robert. The authors had seen little to dent this conclusion, but this in itself doesn't rule out the possibility that he may, for good motives or bad, have engaged in some form of deceit.

After the third visit to the household, Darren and Mike talked at length about the possibility that Marc may have been trying to deceive Marianne and/or the researchers.

By nature, Marc is quiet. He is both sociable and hospitable, but not given to engaging in lengthy conversation. Marc doesn't wear his heart on his sleeve, and his thoughts are largely inscrutable. For some time the authors were undecided as to whether he was the sort of person who would, potentially, engage in trickery. Unlike Marianne, he was just too hard to read.

On reviewing the huge catalogue of incidents that had taken place within the home, it became obvious that Marc could easily have faked some of them. The question was, had he? Had Marc ever done or said anything to make the authors suspicious? It was true that Marc's deadpan demeanour made it more difficult to judge whether he was trustworthy or not, but this wasn't Marc's fault. Both Mike and Darren decided that another review of the accumulated data was the only way forward.

From the outset, it seemed apparent that even if Marc had engaged in some form of deceit he simply couldn't have been responsible for all the phenomena presenting themselves in the household. Marianne's mother, June, had witnessed things when Marc wasn't even at home. So had Marianne and, apparently, her brother Ian. Further, the authors themselves, along with their colleague Darren Olley, had observed a number of phenomena which Marc simply couldn't have faked without the use of some extremely sophisticated and witheringly expensive equipment.

Marc *could* have faked the incident with the pencil, for instance, which occurred on the third visit to the house. On the other hand, he could *not* have faked the incident with the night-light which took place at the same time. He *could* have faked at least one of the incidents where the coins dropped to the floor in the kitchen, but he could *not* have faked the slow, floating descent of the object from the toy hammock to the floor.

Having eliminated the possibility that the entire phenomenon had been masterminded by Marc with Machiavellian cunning, the authors then had to ask themselves whether he could, at least potentially, have been responsible for some of it. If Marc had been engaged in trickery, there were a number of possible motives that could have precipitated such action.

Was Marc trying to create a story he could sell to the papers? The authors doubted it. He appeared a little too streetwise, a little too savvy for that. The authors had never met Marc's friends, but they couldn't imagine them being the sort that would have sympathised with him if he'd taken such a course of action. They would, Mike thought, have ribbed him mercilessly. Marc just didn't strike the authors as someone who would revel in media attention. Mike has worked in the media for years, and he viewed Marc as the sort that would squirm at the thought of being paraded in public as a poltergeist victim. In fact, the desire for anonymity was something that both Marc and Marianne had expressed from the earliest days of the investigation. This would change later, but not for financial reasons. Eventually, both Marianne and Marc concluded that openly identifying themselves when the case was made public would probably bring a short but intense flurry of media attention, but that this was infinitely preferable to years of speculation on the part of other investigators who had a burning desire to track them down. Later still, Marianne once again decided that anonymity was to be preferred, but for other reasons. The family had already been identified in a two-part feature published in a national magazine and on a number of web sites, but after Marianne's second change of heart the authors agreed to revert to her original desire for anonymity. It was, of course, impossible to metaphorically rewind the tape and undo the previous exposure of the family's true identity in the media. However, out of respect for their wishes we have once again preserved that anonymity, at least in the pages of this book.

Could Marc have been exaggerating the polt phenomena in a sincere effort to ensure that the investigators maintained their interest in the case? This too struck the authors as unlikely. On two occasions Marc had seemed genuinely afraid when the polt made its presence felt, but the rest of the time, at least when Mike and Darren were present, he seemed to be handling the situation very well. He was getting on with his life – 'functioning', if you like – and did not at any time display the symptoms of extreme stress that are normally associated with polt activity.

There was of course a third possibility, and that was that Marc may have been faking some of the phenomena purely out of mischievousness.

It was true that there was something 'laddish' about Marc, and the authors don't mean that unkindly. Despite his quiet demeanour, he had a good sense of humour and the authors imagined that, if he was in a playful mood, he could just have faked an incident or two 'for a laugh'. In fact, within days of their discussion on the subject the possibility arose that Marc may have done exactly that.

On Thursday 3 August, Marianne went out into the back garden. She happened to glance up at Robert's bedroom window and, to her astonishment, saw a teddy-bear hanging from the ledge. The previous few days had been very quiet, and Marianne was angry that, just as the polt seemed to have disappeared, it had apparently come back with a vengeance. Perhaps it had never really gone away. Distinctly unhappy, she went back inside and stormed up the stairs. Quite simply, she'd had enough.

Marc followed her into Robert's room.

'Look', she shouted to the invisible entity, 'You have to stop this! You're frightening me and you're frightening Robert. This has to stop and it has to stop now!'

At this juncture, Marc openly confessed to Marianne that he had been responsible for hanging the teddy-bear out of the window.

Marc's explanation was that he had glanced down from Robert's bedroom window and happened to see the youngster playing in the garden. On instinct, he'd picked up a teddy-bear and hung it out of the window for Robert to see. He had then seemingly got distracted and shut the window, forgetting that the teddy-bear was still hanging outside.

The story sounded unlikely to the two researchers, but they decided to reserve judgement.

Whatever the truth, it is unlikely that Marc, whatever his motives, could have grasped the far-reaching consequences of his actions.

From the investigators' point of view, Marc's admission was of great impact. If Marc could 'accidentally' upset his partner, who could say that he hadn't also *deliberately* attempted to trick Darren and Mike 'for a laugh'? No matter what the outcome of the investigation, cynics could – and undoubtedly would – now point to Marc and accuse him of being responsible for every seemingly paranormal incident in the household. His motives for engaging in such a course of action – whether calculated fraud, playful mischievousness or, as he claims, mere forgetfulness – were of little consequence. The authors were now forced to rethink everything that had occurred since the beginning of the investigation. There was a very large question mark hanging over Marc, now.

At the outset, Marianne had admitted that the polt phenomena had started around the same time Marc moved in with her. This seemed suspicious, but it was not conclusive. It was just possible that Marc was the 'focus' in this case, and had unwittingly precipitated the polt activity by his presence. In other words, he may have been responsible for the infestation, but not *knowingly* responsible.

Unless Marc readily admitted that he'd been responsible for hoaxing alleged paranormal incidents, the question would remain unresolved. The authors, although acknowledging that *some* of the incidents could have been faked by Marc, had never 'caught him red-handed', so to speak. If he *had* been responsible for some of the more extraordinary phenomena then he had taken a great risk, for some of them had been carried out in the presence of two – and on one occasion three – seasoned investigators. He could so easily have been caught, and to this day Mike thinks it unlikely that he would have taken the chance.

Another point that needs to be addressed was whether Marc had deliberately carried out the teddy-bear incident to frighten Marianne. If so, wasn't such a 'joke' both unnecessary and cruel?

Mike thought that the prank, if such it was, had to be seen in a larger context. Marc had never struck Mike as a vindictive or cruel person. If the incident with the teddy-bear was a hoax it was undoubtedly thoughtless and ill-timed; but it is unlikely that he meant to hurt or upset his partner. Perhaps he was simply trying to 'lighten the mood'. After all, the diminution in polt activity had made the couple relax to a degree. Maybe Marc thought that it was now 'safe' to play such a prank, and perhaps he grossly miscalculated the effect that it would have had on Marianne. These were, at least, the speculations that both Darren and Mike were batting back and forth between them.

There seemed to be some circumstantial evidence that Marc may indeed have engaged in an innocent prank – at least from his perspective.

Darren recalls an incident that took place during the investigators' second visit to Lock Street:

We had just left Robert's bedroom. Mike and Marianne were in front of me, heading down the stairs. Marc and Ian were behind me, and they were laughing ... messing around, if you like.

Suddenly, one of them shouted, 'Hey, was that you? Did you do that?'

The other one – I'm not sure who – said, 'No ... it wasn't me!'

Eventually, one of them admitted playing a prank of some sort on the other. My impression was that one of them had touched the other, thrown something ... I don't know what, exactly; but it was obvious to me that one of them had done something to mimic poltergeist activity in an effort to frighten the other. When the joke was admitted, they both burst out laughing.

At first, this incident seems to be damning, and simply reinforces the notion that someone – on this occasion either Marc or Ian – was engaging in some form of trickery. On closer examination, however, their behaviour may turn out to be a powerful witness for the defence.

The first thing that we can say is that neither Ian nor Marc thought that such behaviour was inappropriate. The fact that they were prepared to engage in such banter openly, and in front of one of the authors, demonstrates that there was a degree of innocence attached to it.

Even more telling is the fact that the person on the receiving end of the prank at first took it seriously, seemingly considering the possibility that whatever had happened had been a genuine manifestation of polt activity. This indicates that, to Ian and Marc, at least *some* of the activity in the house was genuine. If it had all been faked from 'the get-go', the recipient of the joke would not have asked whether or not the perpetrator was responsible.

Marc, the investigators opined, should not have left the teddy bear hanging out of Robert's window, plain and simple. However they conceded that Marianne's partner couldn't rewind the metaphorical tape and undo what he'd done. Interestingly, though, the consequences did not stop there.

Later in the day, Marianne decided to leave the house and go to her local supermarket which was only 100yds away. Marc was relaxing in the bath.

On her return she opened the front door with her key and stepped inside the passageway. Almost immediately, she heard Marc shouting down the stairs.

'Marianne! Get up here, quickly!'

Marianne ran up the stairs to see what was wrong, and found Marc in a state of high excitement.

According to Marc, he'd been lying in the bath when he'd heard a door slam. He also stuttered something about a light going out. Marianne quickly checked in all the rooms, but everything seemed in order.

Shortly after, Marianne went into her bedroom and her eye caught sight of something peeking out from under the quilt. It was Robert's doodle-board, and Sammy had seemingly left a message on it.

HI MAM, it said.

Underneath was what appeared to be a drawing of a young boy wearing something akin to a tracksuit. There also appeared to be a motif or logo of some kind on the boy's right breast, or maybe it was a pocket. It was difficult to tell.

Marianne immediately photographed the message and sent it to Mike's own mobile phone as a multimedia message.

Mike rang Marianne and thanked her for the picture. He asked her to relate the circumstances in which she found the doodle-board, and she did – after telling him about the teddy bear incident earlier in the day. This disturbed Mike. Marc had now admitted to doing something a little foolhardy, and this would inevitably have a great impact on how future researchers would view the latest doodle-board message.

The implication, for sceptics, would be obvious; Marianne had left the house for a few minutes, during which time Marc must have hastily scribbled a message on the doodle-board and left it under the bed quilt before jumping back in the bath. This would also now cast doubt on the veracity of the previous messages. No matter how earnestly Marianne insisted that Marc had not hoaxed them, no sceptic worth his salt would be inclined to believe him. By apparently messing around with the teddy bear, Marc had, perhaps unwittingly, cast doubt on the veracity of much that had happened before that point and possibly everything that happened afterwards.

Marianne was, in her own mind, certain that Marc had not faked the new message on the doodle-board. Her belief was that Marc's 'prank' – if such it was – had actually encouraged Sammy to leave a new message. Mike asked her what had led her to this conclusion, and he couldn't deny that what she had to say certainly made sense.

Because the polt activity – and the possibly related activity in Robert's bedroom – had diminished over the previous few days, Marianne had not tried to communicate with Sammy. Deep down, she still wanted 'the whole thing to just go away', which was perfectly understandable. However, when Marc, whether accidentally or deliberately, left the teddy bear hanging from the bedroom window it led her to think that the entity was still active, and motivated her to go into Robert's bedroom and talk to 'Sammy' again. This act, she believed, had prompted Sammy to open up the lines of dialogue with Marianne once more and write her another message. It was certainly possible, but it was also still possible that Marc had written the message as a prank.

From an investigative point of view, it seemed unlikely that Marc could have fully grasped the ramifications of his actions. Whether or not he had faked other instances of polt activity, the authors could not say at this point. In the instance where he had apparently left the teddy bear hanging out of the window he had readily admitted it. He didn't have to do this, as no one had caught him in the act. Had Marc not admitted to Marianne what he'd done, it is highly likely that everyone concerned, including the authors, would have tentatively accepted the event as a genuine manifestation of poltergeist infestation. So, just why did Marc admit to his role in the incident? To the authors, the only answer to this question that made sense was that he felt guilty about upsetting Marianne again just after she seemed to be calming down. But if Marc felt guilty because of his actions, is it likely that he would then have carried out a polt-related practical joke just hours later? Probably not.

The authors were reluctantly prepared to give Marc the benefit of the doubt and accept that his prank with the teddy bear, whether deliberate or accidental, was probably a one-off incident carried out without any dark agenda. Later, an entirely different conclusion would manifest itself; that Marc hadn't hung the teddy bear out of the window at all.

Towards the end of the investigation, when the polt activity seemed to be dying down and something akin to normality was returning to the household, Marc made a startling confession to Marianne. Yes, he had admitted hanging the teddy bear out of the window, but his story – which the researchers had always viewed as odd to say the very least – had been fabricated. According to Marc he hadn't even touched the teddy bear, let alone displayed it from the upper floor of their house for the neighbours to see. Whoever had done it, it hadn't been anyone living in the house. Marc had concluded, almost certainly correctly, we think, that it must have been the poltergeist. Marianne explained to both Darren and Mike what had happened next:

> Marc said he could see how upset I was at the teddy bear incident – particularly as things seemed to have been dying down. I was *really* upset, you know ... He didn't want me getting worried or stressed again, because he remembered what you both had said – that it would only make things worse. Because of that he pretended that *he* had 'accidentally' left the bear hanging out of the window so I wouldn't think the polt was back and get even more freaked out.

With hindsight this explanation makes perfect sense, and the authors wondered why they hadn't considered the possibility earlier. Marc clearly loves Marianne, and it is easy to imagine him wanting to take the rap for the polt's wrongdoing if he thought it would make her feel better.

In the final analysis Marc's credibility as an experient was important, but it wasn't crucial. The authors broadly believed that

Marc could not have been responsible for every incident which took place in the household. At worst, he could only be guilty of exaggerating an already pre-existing phenomenon, and not creating it from scratch.

Finally, we need to put Marianne's brother Ian under the spotlight. Was there any likelihood that he could have engaged in any trickery? Again, the balance of probabilities was against such an idea, although it couldn't be ruled out.

Theoretically, Ian could have been responsible for faking some of the phenomena, but not all. There were simply too many occasions when he had been absent during bouts of polt activity. Further, why fake polt phenomena in the house of your sister, knowing that it wouldn't be long before someone noticed that 'things happened' only when you were around and at no other time?

Ian's experiences with the polt seemed to have genuinely unnerved him. As he related them to the authors during their first visit, he looked uncomfortable, uneasy even. Mike and Darren got the feeling that recounting his experiences was coming perilously close to reliving them.

June, Marianne and Ian himself had all testified that when the polt first began to manifest itself, Ian had been sceptical. It was only when he experienced the symptoms of the polt infestation first-hand that his scepticism waned rapidly.

Ian seemed to have a good relationship with Marc and obviously knows him far better than the authors do. If Ian suspected that Marc had carried out the odd prank in an effort to tease the authors then, out of loyalty, he may have just smiled and turned a blind eye. However, it is hard to imagine that he would have participated in anything that would cause such severe distress to his sister. On that basis, the authors currently have no evidence that Ian has taken part in any orchestrated effort to deceive.

On Tuesday 8 August, Mike and Darren discussed the whole issue of fraud and the likelihood or otherwise that they'd been hoodwinked.

'With hindsight', said Mike, 'the chances of investigating a case of this magnitude and getting everyone to behave perfectly are remote indeed. As far as the last message is concerned, we'll have to wait and see what Dennis Duez comes up with in his analysis. Its possible Marc faked it, but we just don't know. Maybe things happened just like he said.'

'Anyway', answered Darren, 'there's not a single person involved who could have faked everything, and we've seen things with our own eyes that just *couldn't* have been faked'.

Mike agreed.

The jury was still out as far as the pictures of the written messages on the doodle-board were concerned. The researchers hoped that Dennis Duez and Dana White would be able to shed some light on their authenticity.

Apart from the issue of the messages, both Darren and Mike now felt that they had enough evidence to construct a working hypothesis concerning what exactly had transpired in the household. The final bits of the jigsaw were, they believed, falling nicely into place.

CHAPTER SIXTEEN

The Polt Personality

One week after sending Dana White the pictures of the doodle-board messages, the authors received her report. This turned out to be a photo-by-photo analysis, and was both illuminating and disturbing.

First, however, Dana provided the investigators with her general impressions.

Her overall feeling was that the messages – or at least, most of them – had been written 'in a modern hand' and by an adult. Significantly, however, she also felt that a) at least one of the messages may actually have been written by a child, and b) the writer had on occasion attempted to disguise his or her handwriting so that it would appear to be childlike. The writer, she felt, was male and two of his main character traits were stubbornness and obstinacy. He was also a man who did not know the meaning of the word compromise.

'This chap writes in a direct manner and doesn't like to beat about the bush', she explained.

On the positive side, the writer shows a tendency towards industry and enterprise.

'He knows what he wants and how to get it, and he'd certainly know how to make the most of an opportunity.'

On the negative side, said Dana, the writer showed clear signs of being distressed. In fact, she said, he was in desperate need of help. Exactly what kind of help, however, she was unable to say.

One of the intriguing things pointed out by Dana was that an unusual number of letters were actually shaped like numerals. The letter 'S' would sometimes appear more like a '5' or even a '7', and the letter 'G' would be stylised so that it looked more like an '8'.

This was a clear indication that the man was money-orientated.

The writer also had a tendency to switch from cursives to capitals.

'This means that often he isn't understood, and is trying to get his point across forcefully', she added. 'In fact, he wants to be the centre of attention'.

In Picture one, Dana White was also struck by the writer's use of the abbreviations 'CU'. She pointed out that this was very similar to the abbreviations used by young people when they send text messages, and may give further clues to the identity of the writer.

In Picture two, where the writer had simply written the word 'DIE', she pointed out that the central horizontal bar has a curious inflection that actually makes the bar look like a sword. This 'dagger inflection' was extremely disturbing to Dana White.

'The centre bar on the 'E' represents the heart, and tells you something about what this person is feeling inside. They are disturbed, anxious and full of tension. I see a lot of anxiety there. To be honest it's very creepy.'

The third message analysed by Dana White contained the words, 'I am sorry', or at least the researchers thought that it did. Dana wasn't so sure.

'What you see as the letter 'I' is actually a 'J', and I'm certain that the word 'am' is not that at all. To be honest I think that it's a surname following on from the initial letter of the first name. In short, the man's first-name initial is J, and the word that follows it is a scrawled surname that is difficult to read. It may be something like 'Barry'. The message, then, may read something like, 'J. Barry. Sorry.''

Further analysis of the remaining characteristics largely confirmed what Dana White had picked up earlier. The author of the messages was stubborn, determined and had a desire to be noticed. Disturbingly, she also felt that he was 'out of control' to some degree and had difficulty writing.

'On some messages his handwriting is all over the place, and the letters aren't matched up. This man is filled with nervous tension, neurotic even. There are also indications that he had to write these messages quickly, as if he didn't have much time.'

She also picked up other positive characteristics, however, that seemed to be completely contradictory.

'In some respects this man is heart-orientated, emotional. However, he can also be incredibly cold-blooded. The bottom line is that this writer has an extremely disturbed mind.'

The researchers, of course, had still to receive a report from Dennis Duez in Pennsylvania. However, Dana White's analysis had given them something to work with in the meantime. It had also put Darren and Mike on the horns of a most terrible dilemma.

The writers had noticed that there were distinct similarities between the handwriting on the doodle-boards and the handwriting of Marc Karlsonn. One obvious and exceedingly grim question presented itself to Mike and Darren; could Marc be a disturbed – possibly even psychopathic – individual masquerading as a quiet, unassuming young man in whose mouth butter seemingly would not melt? If so, then what on earth would the researchers tell Marianne – 'Excuse me love, but you're living with a total nutter – you'd better pack your bags and get out'?

The investigators had no reason to doubt the accuracy of Dana White's analysis. What they needed, however, was a workable scenario into which her analysis would fit comfortably.

The first problem was the clearly definable personality of the doodle-board writer. He was controlling, domineering, aggressive and money-orientated. Marc was none of these things, and Marianne's testimony had been consistent throughout: he was a caring, unassuming partner who had shown nothing but kindness and love to both her and her young son. The writer displayed handwriting characteristics that were uncannily similar to Marc's, but he possessed a personality that was radically different. What could be the explanation for such a conundrum?

Mike came up with what he believed then – and believes now – to be the answer.

Most experts in the field of poltergeist research believe that the poltergeist itself is nothing more and nothing less than some form of externalised energy; negative energy, created by great stress, that reaches a point where it can no longer be contained within its human host. When that polt-energy bubbles over and externalises itself from the host, it can act and behave very much like a sentient human being. Because this polt had its origins within Marc – the authors were by now becoming increasingly convinced that he was the primary focus – then it was easily to understand why it may have retained some of his handwriting and other characteristics. By way of an analogy, a man can spend several hours in a pub without smoking or drinking, but when he leaves his clothes will still smell of stale tobacco and beer.

The poltergeist, then, may be something that retains some of the characteristics of its human host even after it externalises itself. However, if Dana White's analysis of the doodle-board messages was correct, then the handwriting was not just characteristic of the polt, it was also characteristic of Marc. Remember, the handwriting of both Marc and the polt were very similar.

There are two possible explanations for this, neither of which involve labelling poor Marc as crazy.

Firstly, Marc is apparently dyslexic and this means that the attribution of character traits within his handwriting may not be based on a platform which possesses the same degree of scientific solidity. Secondly, no one knows how long the polt-energy had been building up in Marc. For all we know, it may have been there latently since his early childhood. If the polt-energy had manifested itself on a low level for all that time, then there was a possibility that Marc may actually have been subconsciously allowing some of the polt's characteristics to influence *his* handwriting, instead of the other way around. Whatever the truth of the matter, there was no doubt in the minds of the researchers that the character traits displayed on the doodle-board messages were *not* those of Marc. However, they would later prove to be extremely consistent with the personality of the polt.

There is a final postscript to Dana White's analysis of the doodle-board messages that is truly extraordinary.

On the day she began her examination of the images, she
printed them off and took them into her garden where she could
look at them in peaceful surroundings. Suddenly she became
aware of a presence nearby. She 'felt' – but did not actually see –
a man gazing at her. He was tall, with straight black hair and a
long black coat. To all intents and purposes, he was the same man
that Robert had seen on numerous occasions in his bedroom.
Why this entity – whoever or whatever he was – had chosen to
make his presence felt to Dana White in this way we may never
know. However, her testimony simply added much credibility to
the notion that whatever was happening at Lock Street was real,
and that the entities involved could seemingly touch the lives of
those who lived far away from that quiet, unassuming little row
of houses.

Dennis Duez's report, when it came, was well worth the wait.
It was concise but comprehensive, and shook the authors to the
soles of their boots.

Firstly, the researchers wish to say that the conclusions Mr Duez
came to through his careful analysis are not disputed. The authors
accept them fully, and will always be grateful to him for his services. However, the observations made stunned them completely
and led them to look at central aspects of the case in an entirely
different light. For legal reasons, the authors do not intend to
publish his full findings in this book, but they will make some
comment on them.

The point of the exercise had been to establish whether the
principal experients could have faked some or all of the messages left upon the doodle-board. The authors – not experts in the
field of graphological analysis – had been struck by the similarities
between Marc's handwriting and that of the polt. Even Marianne
had commented on this, and Marc himself told the authors that
this fact disturbed him. From the outset, Marc never denied that
these similarities existed; but he did vigorously deny writing the
messages. Careful analysis of the evidence accumulated over the
course of the investigation had convinced the authors that Marc

simply could not have written the messages, despite the similarity in the handwriting. To the authors' satisfaction, nothing in Mr Duez's report hinted at the principal experients – including Marc – as potential culprits.

Dennis Duez is an expert handwriting analyst however, and he is of the opinion that none of the messages on the doodle-boards were genuine.

'All in all, it appears that evidence of a poltergeist incident has been severely compromised by the planting of false evidence from the very beginning, and continuing "seeding".'

Dennis's handwriting analysis report conclusively identified 'one human as the person who had authored five of the thirteen alleged poltergeist writings'.

According to Dennis, the strongest support for the 'seeding of evidence' theory, is that 'the first piece of writing attributed to the onset of this particular phase of the poltergeist actions on Robert's doodle-board was that it was conclusively identified as one of those five composed by a human hand and not a poltergeist'.

When one looks at his reasoning, it is obvious what drew him to this conclusion and any handwriting expert *not* experienced in the field of paranormal research may well have arrived at the same idea. The valuable insight provided by Dennis's report and its conclusions has convinced the authors that the exercise was extremely worthwhile. The researchers would encourage all investigators who have allegedly polt-written messages to have them analysed in a similar manner. Without his insight, the investigators may well have found themselves wandering down any number of blind alleys.

After reviewing the reports of the graphologists, the authors came to the conclusion that Marc had not faked the doodle-board messages. Their belief that he was the polt-focus in this particular infestation was, however, strengthened enormously.

CHAPTER SEVENTEEN

Cut-Throat Cuddlies

There was one aspect of the entire investigation that had hung over Darren and Mike like a dark, brooding cloud. So much of the evidence seemed to point irresistibly to the phenomena in the household being truly paranormal, and yet neither researcher was able to successfully rid themselves of the notion that Marc may – no matter how unlikely it seemed – have successfully tricked them. Due in part to the reports submitted by the handwriting analysts, the authors now knew that he had not faked the doodle-board messages, but what about the other phenomena? Despite all their previous certainty, was it just possible that he had, by employing incredible ingenuity and sleight of hand, falsified at least some of the seemingly paranormal events that had so bemused the witnesses? Again, the question presented itself; if Marc had not falsified every event, could he at least have been responsible for a substantial number of them? In spite of a paucity of evidence, both Darren and Mike had a growing suspicion that he may not have been as innocent as he made out. True, Marc hadn't actually done or said anything obvious to justify such a conclusion, but the idea continued to manifest itself, illogically but persistently, whenever the researchers reviewed their case notes. The unease the investigators felt wasn't helped by the incident in which Marc had apparently left a cuddly toy hanging from Robert's bedroom window. Perhaps it was that, more than anything else, that made Darren and Mike begin to doubt his innocence. Unfortunately, at this juncture Marc had not yet divulged the truth to Marianne about this incident; namely, that the polt had been responsible for it after all.

With every passing day, Marc's role as the 'unknown quantity' in the investigation proved to be a growing source of frustration to the investigators. There was something so obvious about Marianne's innocence that the investigators just knew she wasn't trying to fool them. But Marc . . .

The possibility of Marc engaging in a sustained campaign of trickery was the main topic of conversation when Darren and Mike met for breakfast in the Market Cafe on Friday 25 August.

'I really don't know what to make of it', said Mike. 'We haven't caught him out trying to deceive us, so why don't we trust him in the same way we trust Marianne? It's a question for which I really don't have an answer. For some reason I just can't get the thought out of my head that he might be pulling the wool over our eyes. I genuinely can't see how he could have caused *everything* to happen through deceit, but I still can't help but wonder if he isn't 'hamming it up', as they say . . . you know; making a genuine phenomenon look worse by exaggerating it. I can't say he is, but neither can I bring myself to say that he isn't.'

Mike then told Darren that he had asked Marianne if the researchers could bring someone new into the investigation; a long-time colleague and friend, Jill Butler. Jill was psychic, mediumistic and quite knowledgeable about the sort of activity that was presenting itself at Lock Street. Both researchers felt that a fresh pair of eyes might give some added insight into the case. Just as importantly, Jill wasn't the sort of person who 'saw spirits around every corner' whenever she had an audience. She was level-headed and not given to melodrama.

At 10.30am, Darren and Mike finished eating and left the cafe. Jill showed up minutes later.

'Hi!' she said cheerily. 'My car's over in the car park. Are you ready?'

The trio made their way through the bustling market, looking forward to another tussle with the unknown. As they drove towards the Peterworth household, the investigators apprised her of the case in some detail.

Marianne looked stressed. She smiled, was gracious as usual and offered everyone coffee, but the strain was showing on her face. She'd had a tiff with Marc several nights previously, and, true to form, the polt had resurfaced. Robert's 'Tigger' toy had been found sitting in the toddler's blue, plastic seat, which was in turn sitting atop the matching plastic table.

But there was worse. Later that evening, Marianne decided to take a bath. She ran the hot water, submerged herself and tried to relax. It was difficult, but she was making heroic efforts not to let the polt upset her. She closed her eyes as the tension in her muscles began to ebb away. For a few minutes, all was well, and then, without so much as a second's warning, the bathroom door flew open with such fury that it was a miracle it didn't disengage itself from the hinges. Marianne, terrified, sat bolt upright.

From her vantage point in the bath, Marianne could see her own bedroom door, which was closed. Reflected on its white, gloss-painted surface she could see the delicate glow of the table lamp in Robert's room opposite. Something was moving in her son's room, as the light from the lamp was being interrupted continually. The changing shadows danced upon her own bedroom door in a way that left her feeling distinctly uneasy. She could also hear footsteps on the creaking floorboards. Then, after the footfalls stopped, she heard the cupboard door in Robert's room open, followed by a 'rummaging noise'. Hoping against hope, she wanted the person in the room to be Marc. She shouted out, but there was no answer. She shouted again, but louder this time.

As the personage in Robert's room continued to move around, causing the shadows on her own bedroom door to dance all the faster, she heard the kitchen door downstairs open. Moments later, Marc appeared on the lower landing and walked up the stairs.

'Did you shout, Marianne?'

Marianne checked the reflections on the door again. Whoever or whatever she'd heard in Robert's room was still there, and it obviously wasn't her partner. The shadows were still dancing, the footfalls still audible. Then, just as Marc reached the upper landing, everything fell silent. The moving shadows had been replaced once again by the gentle, steady glow of the table lamp.

'Marc! There's someone in Robert's room!'

Marianne had already exited the bath and joined Marc on the landing. Gingerly they entered her son's bedroom, but there was nothing out of place. All that could be heard was the deep, rhythmic breathing of a sleeping child. Marianne admitted later that at this juncture she just wanted to cry.

Jill talked to both Marc and Marianne in some depth. She openly admitted that she could sense a number of negative emotions in the living room, including unhappiness, fear and rage. Something had happened at this location, she said, and it hadn't been pleasant. She also felt a connection with someone who had killed themselves under very tragic circumstances.

At this point, Mike tentatively suggested that Jill might want to take a peek in Robert's room. After all, this was where the bulk of the activity was now centred as the polt, although not gone altogether, temporarily seemed to be taking a back seat. Jill agreed.

Marianne left the room first, followed by Darren, Jill, Mike and Marc in that order. In single file they ascended the stairs. Mike knew something was wrong the moment he saw Marianne turn off the landing recess which led to Robert's room.

'Oh my God . . . oh, no . . . it's started again.'

'Oh, *shit'*, said Darren.

Mike entered the room and instantly saw the cause of their discomfort.

The entity had been at work. In the centre of the room stood the small, blue table in its usual position. Next to it was the matching blue chair. The chair was vacant, but not the table, though. On it sat one of Robert's cuddly toys, Mr Bunny Rabbit. Mr Bunny Rabbit had, tucked under his right 'paw', a large, vicious-looking carving knife that the polt had seemingly pinched from the kitchen. The other end was laid across the neck of another fluffy toy, a duck, which was also on the table, lying prostrate. Mike commented on the scene later:

To be honest, it was obscene – sickening. It wasn't just the image of one fluffy toy trying to decapitate another – it was more than that.

The two playthings had been posed with great care. The rabbit had its head raised slightly and its shoulders arched back, giving it a distinctly haughty appearance. The duck's feet were in the air, its arms by its side. Its eyes stared vacantly at the ceiling. It was bizarre, but you could almost sense the helplessness emanating from it.

'It reminded me of the previous incident, in which the larger bunny-rabbit was sitting in the bucket chair on the landing with the box-cutter blade in its hand. There was something evil about the way it sat in that chair, arms outstretched ... as if it had just slit its wrists.

Marianne then noticed something else. On a shelf there stood a framed Christening Prayer, a heartfelt plea to God that the child to whom it was given – in this case Robert – should be kept safe. The entity had turned the prayer around so that it faced the wall. Hanging from the shelf, slightly to the right, was a toy policeman. Several cuddly toys hung from the shelf, actually; but the policeman was different. The cord from which he dangled had been wrapped tightly around his neck. Marianne began to shake. If the entity was trying to frighten her, it had succeeded.

There was a surprising element to this unpleasant little vignette. Neither Jill Butler nor Mike could detect any malign spiritual presence it the room whatsoever. Despite the obscene nature of the cameo in front of them, it was as if all the evil within it was *locked* within it and could not invade the rest of the space around it.

Despite the immensely powerful impact of the image, it wasn't long before another thought came to mind.

'This is too much,' Mike whispered. 'This can't be right. It was petering out, but now ... this looks ...'

'Staged?' added Darren, under his breath.

'Possibly ...'

Numb, everyone but Darren and Mike went back downstairs. The two investigators were unable to believe that the polt – or whatever was responsible – could have been kind enough to put on such a spectacular show.

Mike looked at Darren.

'Marc?'

'Could be. We're going to have to sort this out. We're just going to have to tell them about our suspicions.'

'You're right. I think this *was* staged.'

Darren suddenly looked at Mike knowingly.

'Mike . . . something's just tapped me on the back of the neck.'

It seemed that the entity might have been annoyed that the authors doubted its ability, and had tapped Darren's neck as a reprimand.

Mike and Darren returned to the living room while Marc was talking to Jill in the kitchen.

'Don't get upset, Marianne', said Darren, 'but we need to ask you this. I think you know what we're thinking. Where was Marc when this happened ... was he the last one upstairs?'

'Yes he was . . . but I honestly don't think he did this. I *know* he didn't.'

'But we need to be sure, Marianne . . . and the truth is we can't be.' added Mike.

Although the investigators didn't know it just then, challenging Marc's veracity may have been one of the wisest decisions made during the entire investigation. Mike and Darren were coming very close to laying at Marc's feet the blame for faking the incident upstairs. It was just like too many Hollywood movies to be true, they felt. However, it seems that the polt may have been listening in to the conversation and, to put it bluntly, was getting pretty pissed off at the fact that someone else was being given the credit for its handiwork. This would soon prove to be Marc's 'get out of jail free' card in a way the researchers could never have expected.

If Marc wasn't faking some of the phenomena, then things had become truly worrying. Whereas the incidents in Robert's room had, until that juncture, been 'mischievous' in nature, they were now taking on the same, sinister quality that characterised the phenomena that had occurred elsewhere in the house. This meant that the polt may now have begun to invade Robert's bedroom and 'muscle in' on the small piece of territory hitherto used by 'Sammy' alone.

Mike's suspicions were seemingly confirmed when he asked Marianne whether Sammy was 'visiting' Robert as frequently as he normally did.

'Its funny you should mention that', she replied. 'Robert still talks about Sammy, but not as much. He doesn't seem to come around as frequently as he used to.'

To Mike, this meant that the polt may now have been effectively on the verge of evicting Sammy from the house. This may also have explained why some of the doodle-board messages seemed to be written by an adult *pretending* to be a child. The polt, Mike thought, may now be masquerading as Sammy in an effort to fool both the householders and the investigators regarding his true nature.

CHAPTER EIGHTEEN

Voices from Beyond

Jill, Mike and Darren continued to speak with Marc and Marianne, trying to extract anything that could shed further light on what was becoming an increasingly complex mystery. At some point, Marc ventured into the kitchen. Instinctively, Darren followed him. Marc poured himself a glass of water and stood chatting to Darren. Darren was, at this stage, standing directly in the doorway between the kitchen and the living-room. Seven feet away, in the living room itself, sat Mike. Mike could see Darren clearly. He could also see Marc clearly, who was standing just inside the kitchen and slightly to Darren's right. Both Darren and Marc were approximately 12ft away from the patio doors that led out into the garden. The patio doors were very slightly ajar.

Suddenly, there was a loud clatter which came from the direction of the garden. Marc looked at Darren, who in turn looked at Mike. Before any of the other adults present could speak, Darren exclaimed, 'I saw them ... I *saw* them drop!' Young Robert, who was playing in the garden, shouted, 'What was *that?*'

All five adults ran into the back garden. On the ground were two large, blue building blocks which had been stored in a box in Robert's room.

Robert giggled excitedly.

'Look!' he laughed. 'They came from up high . . . from where the roof is!'

Mike and Jill gently took Robert to one side and questioned him. Had the blocks fallen from the roof?

'No', said Robert, they had came from 'up by the roof. Where exactly had they come from? 'From out of the window', he retorted. Which window?

'From my window . . . the window in my room.' Marianne spoke up.

'Mike . . . you *saw* those blocks upstairs. You *know* they were in Robert's room!'

'I know they were', said Mike. 'I did see them.'

Mike, then, had seen the blocks in Robert's room. Darren had seen the blocks fall from the direction of Robert's bedroom window onto the path. More tellingly, however, everyone had seen Darren 'lock off or insulate Robert's room only five minutes previously. No one, therefore, could have entered the room and thrown the blocks downstairs without their actions being a) detected, and b) recorded on the video camera which had been left running in Robert's room before the room was sealed off. In addition, the camera was facing the door, so if anyone had entered Robert's room they would have been filmed doing so.

As everyone re-entered the house, Darren decided to go and check on his camera which was upstairs in Robert's room. He walked towards the door that led from the kitchen into the hall, and Marianne followed. As Marianne entered the doorway from the hallway she found something behind it. She picked the object up. It was a large, plastic paint-ball pistol. Somehow, it had been spirited away from Marc's wardrobe and ended up in the kitchen.

The pistol was quite large – too large for Marc to have concealed about his person. Besides, when the building blocks fell into the garden – after apparently ejecting themselves through the closed window of Robert's room – everyone left the house together as a group, and re-entered as a group. Mike was watching Marc constantly, and never for so much as a second did he venture near the hallway or the kitchen.

Darren retrieved his camera from the bedroom and immediately began to look at the footage. Because the camera had been facing the door of Robert's room, one cannot see the window. However, at the precise moment that the blocks dropped from the window to the pavement outside, a terrific thud can be heard on the footage. Darren later remarked, correctly, that the noise sounded like someone violently thumping the pane of glass with their fist.

The reason the investigators knew that the bang coincided with the fall of the blocks from the window was because at the moment the blocks fell Darren noted the precise time. This corresponded exactly with the digital clock time on the video camera footage at the moment when the bang can be heard.

As Darren analysed the footage, Marc walked into the living room and sat down on the sofa. The others were in the kitchen, except for Mike, who was standing in the doorway between the kitchen and the hall. He looked at Marc, who was cradling his head in his hands, and wondered. He decided to talk to him in private.

Mike had taken no more than two steps towards the living room doorway when Marc turned and looked at him. Suddenly Mike heard a faint but distinct *whump* behind him. At that same moment Marc exclaimed, 'Mike . . . what was that? Something just flew down the stairs behind you.'

Mike turned and found yet another displaced fluffy toy – a black and white beagle – lying on the floor behind him. It could only have come from the direction of the stairwell, which was the only place out of Mike's line of vision. He raced upstairs, but there was no one there.

Darren and Jill went upstairs to check the camera. They took Robert with them, in the hope that he would communicate with Sammy. They asked Mike if he wanted to come too, but he declined.

'I'll stay here with Marianne and Marc. Then, if anything happens, I'll be a witness to it and they can't be accused of cheating.'

During the course of the morning, Marianne had received a series of calls on her landline phone. Whenever she picked up the receiver, the line would go dead. She presumed that they were from automated direct selling centres, and didn't seem to think they were anything sinister.

Just before Jill and Darren took Robert to his room, the phone rang again. Marianne dialled the caller-retrieve function and stared at Marc.

'Marc . . . the call was from *your* phone!'

Mike asked Marc where his mobile phone was. He said, 'It's in the kitchen', and went to retrieve it. He returned momentarily and declared, 'My phone . . . it's gone. It's just disappeared.'

Already suspicious, Mike and Darren could both see a workable scenario here. Marc may have been making the calls to the landline surreptitiously from his mobile phone, and then disconnecting the call as soon as Marianne answered. He could now be claiming that his phone had 'disappeared' simply to prevent the investigators from examining the phone's call log.

Marianne said, 'Here, Marc; use my mobile phone to ring yours. When we hear the ring-tone we'll know where it is.'

Without hesitation, Marc agreed. He deftly pressed a number of buttons on Marianne's phone until the word 'Marc' was displayed, and then activated the 'call' function. Within seconds, the words 'Phone Busy' displayed on the screen.

'Look', he said. 'It's engaged.'

Wherever Marc's phone was, it was in use. Just as Mike was beginning to wonder whether Marc had deliberately rung a number to keep the line open before hiding his phone, the landline rang. Marianne picked up the phone and listened. Everyone present waited in anticipation, watching carefully as a look of astonishment crept over her face.

'It's an automated message. Listen, I'll play it again.'

It's not commonly known, but if you use a mobile phone to send a text message to a landline the message will automatically be translated into a voice message. Instead of reading the message on a screen, you will hear it repeated verbally by a human — but distinctly robotic — voice.

Everyone gathered around the phone and strained to hear. Suddenly the automated voice spurted forth the message once again: *Hi, Hi, Hi, Hi, Hi* . . . . indefinitely.

Marianne saved the message and then disconnected the call. Later, the investigators established that the call had been made at precisely 11.33am. It was received at 11.35am, two minutes later.

Baffled, Jill, Darren and young Robert ascended the stairs. Mike, Marianne and Marc sat around the kitchen table.

It was Marc who spotted his mobile phone first, sitting in the centre of the table.

'My God ... I can't believe it.'

Mike wasn't sure whether he believed it or not, but he knew that Marc hadn't gone anywhere near the kitchen table.

Mike removed his own mobile phone from his pocket and placed it next to Marc's. Without being asked, Marianne did the same. She also placed the cordless landline handset, which was still in her hand, on the table.

All the phones are now in sight, so hopefully we can exclude trickery', said Mike.

Marc, Marianne and Mike talked for a while, and then, at 11.55am, the landline phone on the middle of the table rang. It was another automated voice message. It had been sent exactly two minutes previously, at 11.53am. This time, it said, *Hello, Hello* . . .

Another call came in at 12 noon. This time it simply said, *Sorry* . . .

Some of the calls had been sent from Marc's phone, which we'd checked to make sure contained the correct SIM card. However, at no time had Marc touched his mobile which was sitting directly in front of Mike on the table. Several similar calls then came in from the landline.

The question was, could Marc have sent the messages from his phone without touching it? This was an issue the researchers would have to address later.

Eventually, Darren, Jill and Robert came downstairs. Mike told them about the phone messages. Darren and Mike both agreed that the messages were very similar in tone to the message left upon the doodle-board, and it seemed to be a reasonable assumption that they both came from the same source.

Before the investigators left, the entity threw a battery-operated toy car down the stairs and generally carried on in its now predictable manner. Mike decided to talk to Robert before calling it a day. After all, Sammy was his friend.

CHAPTER NINETEEN

Conversations with Robert – and Sammy

Robert is a delightful child. He smiles constantly and is extremely polite. He warms easily to strangers and finds no difficulty in making conversation. For a three-year-old he is very articulate.

When Mike spoke to him, he was sitting comfortably on one of the two leather sofas in the living room. Sitting next to him was Marc. What follows is a transcript of the conversation. Robert's responses to Mike's questions are italicised.

Tell me about Sammy.
He's my friend.
How old is he?
Three.
Do you like him?
Sometimes.
What do you mean, 'sometimes'?
Sometimes he's naughty.
Really? What does he do?
He throws things.
What sort of things?
Toys ... lots of things.
What do you do when he throws things?
I tell him to stop.
Does he?

Mmmm?
Does he stop?
Sometimes.
Does he ever get angry?
Sometimes he pushes me. He pushed me over.
When, today?
[Robert nods his head].
What does Sammy look like?
He has blue skin.
Really?
Yes. His skin has bubbles on it.
What sort of bubbles?
Where he got burnt.
In a fire?
Mmmm… yes; in the fire.

Mike wanted to know more about the enigmatic Sammy. As Robert was the only one who seemed to be able to see him and converse with him directly, then any further details would have to be gleaned from him.

Where does Sammy live?
In a house.
Where is the house?
By the Monster House.
Where's the Monster House?
Over there … [pointing to the living room window].
Does a monster live there?
I don't know. That's what Sammy calls it.
Does Sammy speak to you?
Yes!
What does he say?
I don't know.
What do you say to him?
I tell him not to be naughty.
What does he say back?
I don't know.

As the conversation progressed, several things became obvious to Mike. Firstly, Sammy could not or would not divulge to Robert exactly where he lived. In his research into QCCs, Mike had found that this was a curious common denominator that cut across all cultural and geographical boundaries. Quasi-corporeal Companions *never* divulged exactly where they came from, but would only give essentially useless clues, such as, 'Over there', 'From far away' or 'In a house'.

Another interesting feature of the discussion was Robert's inability to articulate anything that Sammy had said to him. He could tell you with ease what Sammy did, but never what Sammy *said*. Again, this is a common feature with several types of QCC, although Mike has no idea why.

Mike asked Robert if Sammy came around every day to see him.
Not now.

This also reinforced Mike's suspicions that the polt may have been metaphorically if not literally pushing Sammy out of the house. If this was the case, why was the polt only doing this now? It could only be because his power was growing.

Robert became distracted and was seemingly tired of answering questions. He told Marc that he wanted a book that had apparently ended up under the sofa. Marc obliged, and got down on his hands and knees. He steadied himself with his right hand upon the floor and then slid his left hand under the sofa in an effort to locate Robert's book. Darren came into the room at this point. Suddenly, the now familiar yellow plastic nut, which had been upstairs in Robert's room, fell from the ceiling and hit Marc on the right shoulder. Both Darren and Mike saw this happen.

As the investigators prepared to go, the entity presented itself one last time by once again utilising the yellow plastic nut. It came bouncing down the stairs before coming to rest two steps from the bottom.

As Jill, Darren and Mike journeyed back to the town centre, they mused over the rather spectacular display that the entity had provided in just a few, short hours.

'You know', said Darren, 'It's peculiar . ..'

'I know exactly what you're thinking', added Mike.

CHAPTER TWENTY

The Rage of the Wraith

Darren and Mike had reached an impasse regarding Marc. Despite their best efforts, they hadn't been able to rule out the possibility of trickery on his part, but neither had they been able to positively rule it in.

After leaving Lock Street, Darren decided to accompany Mike back to his office to assess the situation. Halfway through their journey, Mike's mobile rang. He pressed the 'unlock' keys and was surprised to see that a multimedia message was waiting for him in his inbox.

'I've got a feeling that this might be from Marianne', he muttered, and he was right. He took one look at the picture and then showed it to Darren.

'Jesus!' said Darren.

Mike immediately returned the call.

'Marianne? It's Mike. What the hell happened?'

'Mike, you won't believe it. Have you seen the picture? How could it *do* that?'

To understand the true significance of what had happened, it will be necessary to rewind the tape, metaphorically speaking, and return to the point where the investigators left Marianne and Marc's home.

Jill had offered to drop both Mike and Darren back in the town centre. She had parked her car at the rear of Lock Street, and it was a simple matter to drive back onto the adjacent main road. Unfortunately, she wasn't too familiar with the estate where the family lived, and she took a wrong turning. Darren and Mike pointed this out almost immediately, at which point Jill reversed the car and headed back in the opposite direction. This led them to go past the back of the house they had just left.

As the car cruised past the back garden of Marianne and Marc's home, Mike happened to glance at it. Through the gaps in the fencing, he clearly saw Robert standing next to the patio doors at the rear of the dining area. He was, Mike noted, actually outside the house and standing on the garden path. One of the patio doors was open, and Robert was holding it, simultaneously looking inside the house. It was as if he was waiting for someone. Mike said later that it looked as if he was politely holding the door open for someone else just before they too exited the house and joined him.

He was right. Although neither Marianne nor Marc had mentioned this to the investigators, they had decided earlier in the day to take Robert to a local nursery for a 'taster session' before he began full-time attendance later in the year. As soon as Mike, Darren and Jill had left, they immediately put their coats on in preparation for the short walk to the nursery itself. Robert, eager to go, had gone outside and held the patio door open for the couple who joined him moments later. This is important, for it proved to the investigators' satisfaction that the three occupants of the home had vacated the premises less than two minutes after they had. During that incredibly short interval, Marianne testified later, neither she, Marc nor Robert had ventured upstairs.

As soon as you left we immediately put our jackets on and left the house. Marc wasn't out of my sight for a second, and nor was Robert.'

Jill dropped the two investigators off, and merely minutes later Mike received the multimedia message from Marianne's phone.

What had happened was this: after taking Robert to the nursery, Marianne and Marc immediately returned home. The couple entered by the rear door and, straightaway, Marianne noticed that the yellow nut was once again lying on the stairs. Both Marianne and Marc gingerly walked up the stairwell together, not knowing quite what to expect:

> When we got to the top of the stairs Marc looked nervous. In fact, he looked scared. I asked him what was wrong. He said, 'I don't know, Marianne ... I just get a bad feeling. Something's not right.
>
> We decided to look in Robert's room. When we opened the door, we saw that the room had been completely trashed. Robert's bed was in the middle of the floor, the bedclothes were strewn all over the place, the table and chairs had all been knocked over ... I just couldn't believe it. Marc just freaked.'

The multimedia message that Marianne had sent Mike contained a picture of the devastation. There was absolutely no way that anyone could have trashed Robert's room so extensively without making some noise, and, furthermore, it could not have been done within less than two minutes while under the watchful gaze of one's partner.

Both Marianne and Marc were badly shaken by this latest outrage. What had begun as a relatively mild poltergeist infestation was now taking on the proportions of a horror novel. Marianne and Marc, unfortunately, seemed to be the two principal characters.

A remarkable image of a bottle balancing on edge of its own accord. This still picture is from videotaped footage recorded by Mike Hallowell.

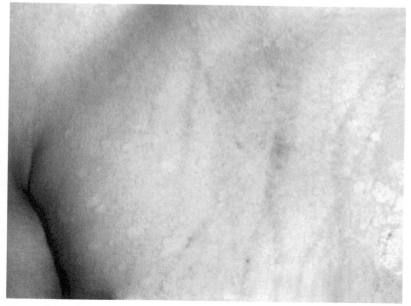

Cuts and scratches on the front of Marc's torso – image taken from video footage.

A disturbing theatrical 'arrangement' found in Robert's room by the authors – the first of a string of astonishing phenomena that lasted throughout the rest of the day.

Darren W. Ritson examines the warped – and now restored – table.

A toy rabbit in a chair that was found at the top of the stairwell with a box cutter blade in its left hand.

Intimidating messages left for the authors by the poltergeist: 'JUST GO NOW' and 'STOP IT NOW'.

Classic poltergeist manifestations – three candleholders stacked neatly on the landing window-ledge.

The large carving knife thrown at Marianne by the poltergeist seconds after it clattered to the floor.

The Statuette of 'the African Lady' which sat on the shelf in the hallway was found to have been relocated to the staircase by the poltergeist.

Darren and Michael with Guy Lyon Playfair at a meeting of the Incorporated Society for Psychical Research, where they were invited to lecture on the case.

This chair and bin had been mysteriously placed *behind* the closed bedroom door while the room was empty. Upon our entry into Robert's room, the opening door moved the chair and bin to the location that you see in the image.

The book thrown to the floor in Mike Hallowell's study by the poltergeist.

This toy building block was found on the toilet floor, upside down, and filled with water – yet another of the poltergeists antics that bewildered all present.

The ornamental candle holders on a window ledge at the top of the staircase; the second picture shows that one of the objects has clearly been moved.

Displaced objects: The top two images show the plastic nut in its resting position after it had been violently catapulted by the poltergeist at South Shields. The bottom two images show ice cubes that appeared spontaneously that had of course previously been in the freezer – one is found in the refrigerator and the other in an upstairs bedroom.

CHAPTER TWENTY-ONE

Marc in the Clear

As described earlier, on their journey back to the town centre both Darren and Mike had arrived at a similar conclusion almost simultaneously. Darren articulated his thoughts first.

'You know', said Darren, 'It's peculiar. All during the investigation, we've had doubts about Marc. Today, for the first time, we expressed those doubts to Marianne – in the house – and what happens? Almost immediately a string of incidents occur for which there is no way he could be responsible. I think the polt was trying to tell us something.'

'So do I', Mike responded. 'You know what I think? I think we pissed it off royally, that's what I think. We were on the verge of giving the credit for its antics to Marc, and it didn't like that one little bit. It was as if it then had to do something – anything – to prove that Marc wasn't responsible. It didn't want him to get the credit for its own creativity.'

When the two investigators arrived at Mike's office, Mike's wife Jackie fixed them something to eat and made coffee. Then they sat down and began to sift through the events of the day. Darren, with typical thoroughness, insisted that they should start by writing down a chronological list of everything that had occurred.

During this, the fourth visit to Lock Street, there had been ten separate incidents which were, at least superficially, paranormal in nature. Of these ten incidents, there were five in which Marc simply couldn't have played a part. (It was also looking extremely unlikely that he could have hoaxed the bizarre activity involving the telephones, although there was a slight doubt about this that the investigators needed to clear up later. It was possible that Marc could have programmed his phone to send the messages at a pre-arranged time, or even sent them from a computer. Further investigation ruled this out, however.)

For example, when the two large building blocks had cascaded into the garden – having egressed from the bedroom window, according to young Robert – Marc was standing inside the dining room immediately next to Darren. He was also in plain view of Mike. For Marc to have hoaxed this incident it would first have been necessary for him to throw the blocks across the dining room without either Mike or Darren noticing. This notion is in itself absurd. Secondly, the blocks would have had to pass through an extremely narrow gap between the patio doors, which were only slightly ajar.

Had Marc even slightly miscalculated, the blocks would simply have bounced off the doors back inside the dining room and his trickery would have been undone. Marc simply couldn't have faked the incident with the blocks.

He also couldn't have faked the incident in which the toy beagle flew down the stairwell and landed just behind Mike in the hall. At that time, Marc was in the living room at the other end of the house. Even so, the door that joins the hall to the living room was wide open and Mike could see Marc clearly as he sat upon the sofa.

After pawing over the accumulated data for some time – and at long last giving Marc the all-clear – the investigators decided to fix another hot drink.

Now it just so happened that in Mike's office, upon a bookshelf, was a hardback copy of George B. Hodgson's *The Borough of South Shields*. This volume – the definitive work on the Borough of South Tyneside's capital town – weighs almost four pounds. To put it mildly, it's hardly a lightweight pamphlet that can be carried away on a gentle midsummer breeze. As the investigators walked away from Mike's office there was an almighty bang from behind them. They both flinched and ducked simultaneously. When they turned round, *The Borough of South Shields* was lying in the middle of the office floor.

'Do you think we've brought back something with us?' asked Darren.

'I hope not', said Mike. 'Jackie will hit the roof.

CHAPTER TWENTY-TWO

Confrontation

Marianne rang Mike later in the day. She'd calmed down a little, but was naturally still very upset about what the entity had done to Robert's room. She asked Mike if he would maybe 'smudge' the place again, as it really had helped the first time. Mike said he'd go the following day. Jill Butler had agreed to come too, but then she had to cancel as a business meeting had cropped up that she couldn't avoid.

Mike arrived just after 3pm, and Marianne opened the door.

'Hi, Mike; thanks for coming. Marc's not in from work yet, I'm afraid. Would you like a coffee?'

'Sounds like a good idea to me.'

Before carrying out the smudging ritual, Mike took the opportunity to talk with Marianne some more about the problem in general. He explained that because he believed that the poltergeist was essentially energy, and not a sentient being, it couldn't be 'banished' in the same way that one could ritually banish an evil spirit. The smudging would work, but if the circumstances in or around the house changed then it may be cancelled out.

'It's a bit like turning off the TV. While it's off you get silence, but if you switch it on again you'll surely get a picture. If circumstances alter, it could return. Mind you, I don't expect it to last for much longer. As I've told you before, it's already well past its sell-by date.'

Marianne looked puzzled.

'So Mike, why does it seem to be getting worse?'

'Look', said Mike, 'I'm not going to kid you. This poltergeist is unusual. It's not following the typical pattern. Usually that may indicate that trickery is involved, but we've now pretty much ruled that out. So, what we have here is, quite simply, an unusual polt that hasn't read the rulebook.

'Normally, a polt would have burnt itself out by now, but this one is being particularly stubborn. Polts are like wasps, you know.'

'*Wasps?*'

'Yes. Wasps thrive on carbohydrates, which are secreted by larvae in the nest. However, in late August the queen stops producing larvae, so the workers have to go outside the nest to find the carbohydrate they need. That's when you see them climbing into discarded soft drink cans and candy wrappers; they're desperate to feed. The older they get the more they need, so feeding becomes an even bigger problem. Then they'll devour rotten fruit, and this makes them bad-tempered and likely to sting people. Eventually it becomes physically impossible for them to take in the amount of carbohydrate they need to survive, and they die.

'I think polts are the same. Like the wasp, they have a life cycle. They thrive on negative energy and fear. As they get older, they need more and more, so they have to ramp up the fear factor in the place they normally inhabit. As they get towards the end of their life cycle, I think they become desperate. The negative energy generated subconsciously by the focus is not inexhaustible, and the polt senses this. The only way to survive is to generate more fear. That's why, as they get near the end of their life cycle, they become wilder and more belligerent. They're like the angry wasp that just can't feed enough to satiate its hunger.'

'So why is this one lasting longer than normal?'

'That's the puzzle. Other than the stress caused by this current situation, both Marc and you seem to be pretty happy together. The polt seemed to be dying, but then, suddenly, it bounced back stronger than ever. I know I suggested yesterday that it may have been the little tiff you had with Marc that awakened it a little, but after what it did in the bedroom, I'm not sure. Its feeding somewhere else – somewhere close to here – and the food supply must be enormous. Whatever it's doing, it's feeding to a degree which seems to enable it to sustain itself almost indefinitely.' Marianne looked Mike in the eye.

'Truthfully, Mike, do you think the smudging will work?'

'It will make life difficult for the polt, but it may not stop it altogether. There is a chance it might make it worse in the short-term, but that's not a bad thing.'

'How can making it worse not be bad?'

'Because the more energy it burns up, the faster it will die. It's getting desperate, so it's redoubling its efforts to generate more fear. To the polt, fear equals food. That's why it trashed Robert's room; it's going to new lengths, now.'

'I'm not bothered, Mike, as long as it goes. I've put up with it for this long, if it got worse in the short-term I'd cope, as long as I knew it was going to go sooner.'

'There are no guarantees, but we can only do our best. Whatever happens, neither Darren nor I will walk away until it's sorted.'

'I know, Mike, and I appreciate that. But I don't understand; if the poltergeist can feed well nearby, why is it becoming desperate?'

'Because poltergeists are person-centred, not place-centred, remember? If you, Marc and Robert moved house, what would it do then?'

'Who do you think the focus is, then, Mike?'

At one point we thought it could be Robert, but now I'm not sure. To be honest, Darren and I are really starting to think it could be Marc'

Mike smudged the entire house and silently uttered Indian prayers. The pleasant aroma of sage and sweetgrass drifted into every room. The polt did not react in any way, but Mike knew it was watching, biding its time.

As Mike left, he gave some final advice to Marianne.

'I may just have stopped it dead in its tracks, but I don't think so. It's possible that it may be very, very angry now; angry at you and Marc for bringing Darren and I in to help, angry at us for agreeing. Ring me if you need me – any time, day or night, I don't care.'

'I promise', said Marianne.

It was a promise she'd be forced to keep within the space of a day.

In some respects, the entity had hidden its true nature well. Oh, it had done the things that most polts do; thrown stuff around, trashed the odd room or two, thrown coins on the floor ... even engaged in obscene theatrics with Robert's cuddly toys. But it had done nothing that would metaphorically hit the headlines, at least in paranormal circles.

That would soon change, though. Unbeknownst to Mike and Darren, the polt wasn't just angry; it was furious. It was probably around this time that it decided blood would have to be spilt.

CHAPTER TWENTY-THREE

Evil is as Evil Does

Mike and his wife went shopping at their local ASDA store on the Saturday afternoon, stocking up on a few items. After a hot bath, they snacked on stuffed vine leaves, falafel and a bottle of red wine. Mike had recorded an episode of *Law & Order; Criminal Intent,* which starred one of his favourite actors, Vincent D'Onofrio. He and Jackie settled into the sofa and relaxed, the entire scene was one of domestic bliss.

By 11.30pm, Jackie was tired and went to bed. Mike said he'd follow her up shortly after he had seen the headlines on *Sky News.* He turned the volume up. Both the lounge door and the kitchen door across the hall were closed, too. Three barriers, all in all, which prevented him from hearing his mobile phone beeping on the kitchen workbench at precisely 11.36pm. He had an incoming message, but was unaware of it:

Sorry to text u so late if u r up can u call me its urgent

Mike, unaware of the message, continued to review the headlines.

At precisely 11.40pm, Mike's mobile rang, and this time he heard it. It was Marianne, and she sounded hysterical.

'Mike . . . can you help? It's attacked Marc'

Mike rang a taxi and arrived at Lock Street just after midnight. As he approached the house, he noticed how distinguishable it was from those adjacent to it. The hour was late and most dwellings were in darkness. Conversely, Marianne's home was lit up like a Christmas tree; every light and lamp seemed to be switched on.

Mike rang the bell and Marianne answered. Marc was standing just behind her, and ostensibly looked okay. He wasn't, though, as Mike would soon discover.

The couple and Mike walked into the kitchen, and the first thing the investigator noticed was the dining table. It was littered with the symbols of stress relief; two mugs of half-drunk tea, a cigarette packet, disposable lighters and a half-full ashtray. The tea mugs stood in pools of liquid. It appeared as if the table had been jarred, causing the contents of the mugs to overspill onto the surface.

Marianne grabbed a cloth and wiped up the mess.

'Sorry about that', she whispered. '*It* did that before; *it* moved the table.'

Mike told her not to worry about it.

'Okay', said Mike, 'Tell me all about it. But first, where's Robert?'

'He's okay', said Marc. 'He's asleep next door in the living room. We keep checking on him.'

It was Marianne, as usual, who related the story.

At around 10.10pm, the couple were watching TV in the living room when they both heard a rhythmic banging noise which seemed to be coming from upstairs. They both ascended the stairwell. First, they checked on Robert, who was fast asleep. However, when they checked the master bedroom they found Robert's blue, plastic bucket-seat on top of their bed.

At 11pm, the couple had gone to bed. Again, Marc and Marianne checked on little Robert to make sure he was sleeping soundly. Since 'things started' – the euphemism Marianne often used for the onset of the polt infestation – it had been even more important for her to make regular checks on the child to ensure that he was okay. Up to that juncture, the polt hadn't attacked her son, but she had no confidence in the notion that such a thing was impossible. At any rate, Robert seemed fine.

As they entered the master bedroom, everything seemed okay there, too. They got undressed, climbed into bed and Marc turned out the bedside lamp. After allowing a suitable hiatus for the couple to relax, the polt decided to have some fun.

Marc fell asleep first. Marianne, who was merely dozing, suddenly felt something hit her in the face. It was a stuffed dog – one of the cuddly toys belonging to Robert with which the entity had such a fascination. Seconds later another stuffed toy hit her, at which point she shouted for Marc. Startled, Marianne's partner sat bolt upright in bed, rubbing his eyes.

'What's wrong?'

'It's *throwing* things at me!'

Marc turned the lamp on and then gazed at the toys on the bed.

'Marianne . . . there's something wrong.' 'What do you mean?' 'Look . . . look at the quilt'.

Marc pointed to the bottom of the bed. Slowly but surely the quilt cover was moving, as if being gently caressed by an unseen hand. Then the 'unseen hand' took hold of the quilt and started tugging at it. Marianne and Marc grabbed hold of the quilt at the other end of the bed and pulled in the opposite direction. The couple and the entity then proceeded to engage in a short but intense tug of war before the quilt suddenly dropped to the bed. Sanity seemed to have been restored, but only momentarily.

'Marianne . . . there's something else wrong. My body feels like its burning.'

Marianne told Marc to remove his T-shirt, which he did. Slowly she cast her eyes over his torso, and was curious to notice a few random scratches. They were small, almost insignificant, but she did wonder where they had come from.

'Can you see anything?' asked Marc.

'Just a few little scratches . . . nothing else; although one of them is starting to look a little inflamed. It's red around the edges now, although it wasn't a few seconds ago.'

Then Marianne noticed several more scratches that she hadn't noticed at first. Marc noticed more appearing on the other side of his body.

'Marianne ... I'm burning. Look at these marks ... what's happening to me?'

'I don't know', she replied, 'but this is crazy. I'm going to ring Mike.'

Mike listened to the tale intently as it unfolded.

'Marc, can I have a look at the scratches?'

'Sure', he replied, as he removed the T-shirt. Meanwhile, Marianne fixed Mike some coffee.

Mike was horrified. He counted at least thirteen separate scratches on Marc's torso. Some were large, others small and faint. Some were vertical, others horizontal, but all seemed to be scattered randomly. With the exception of a number of vaguely parallel scratches on his left side, just over the ribcage, there was nothing to suggest that these marks had been made by an animal. Besides, Marianne had actually seen them appear.

'Polt scratches can sometimes disappear quite quickly, so I need to get these documented.'

Mike removed his camera from its pouch and started snapping. After he'd finished, Marc replaced his shirt and sat back down at the table. As he did so, the polt moved the dining chair sharply from left to right and he almost fell on the floor. Marianne, sitting on the chair next to him, jumped. She was now extremely nervous, and Mike wondered how much more of this she could handle.

'There's something else we forgot to mention', said Marianne. 'When you said earlier that you would order a taxi straight away to bring you here, Marc said that we should give you the money to cover the fare. As he said that, a crumpled-up £10 note flew across from the kitchen and landed next to me. It was almost as if it was saying, 'Here's his taxi money!' It was weird.'

'Well, we know one thing; the polt is listening to you when you talk to each other.'

Later, this fact would prove to be of great significance as the investigation progressed.

'Okay', Mike said, 'why don't we all go upstairs and you can demonstrate to me exactly what happened in the bedroom'.

Marianne admitted she was nervous, frightened to ascend the stairwell. Mike offered to go up first, alone, and have a quick look around while the couple waited downstairs.

Understandably, they were only too glad to let him act as a scout on that particular expedition.

As he walked up the stairs Mike inhaled deeply, casting his eyes in all directions, looking for something – anything – that may indicate that the polt had been recently active in that location. There was nothing; no toys or items of clothing strewn over the stairs, no rocking horses hanging from the loft hatch. Neither did he sense the cloying, heavy atmosphere that often accompanies polt activity. The stairwell looked and felt completely normal, in fact. After Mike gave the couple the all-clear, Marc and Marianne ascended the stairs and joined him on the landing.

Mike checked the toilet first, but there was nothing out of place in there. The bathroom was fine, too.

Slowly, carefully, Mike activated his digital sound recorder and opened the door to Robert's room. He was barely able to believe the evidence of his own eyes. He took a deep breath and realised that he was going to have to tell the couple, now standing just behind him, about something they were patently unaware of.

'Erm . . . was the bed in the middle of the floor?'

'No' said Marianne, her voice trembling.

'Well ... it is now.'

Marianne followed Mike into the room, and became visibly distressed.

'Woah! Oh, God . . .! Everything's moved . . . *everything!* The lamp is on the *floor. ..!'*

Mike immediately started taking pictures.

The three witnesses, stunned, started to acclimatise themselves to the scene of utter devastation which surrounded them. Robert's room looked like a bombsite. Toys and items of furniture were strewn everywhere.

Suddenly, the door to the toy cupboard swung open violently, but without making even the faintest noise. Marianne was the first to react.

'The cupboard door opened! *God. ..!'*

Mike, Marianne and Marc then walked into the master bedroom. At first, everything seemed to be normal, but then the

Japanese-style light-shade hanging from the rose in the middle of the ceiling started to sway back and forth.

Marianne then mentioned that it had done something similar earlier, just after the light cord in the bathroom had started to sway and a towel jumped off the towel rail, landing unceremoniously in the middle of the floor.

'I can't believe the state of the bairn's room . . . it's absolutely *trashed* . . . '

At precisely 12.54am, the trio retreated to the landing, and Mike shut the door to the master bedroom firmly behind him. Almost immediately Marianne shouted 'Woah!' as the door flew open again. Mike saw it open out of the corner of his eye, and then all three watched as the door to Marianne's wardrobe was wrenched open too. Mike took more photographs and then shut the wardrobe door.

Back in Robert's room, the polt had again been active. As detailed earlier in this volume, the poltergeist (and/or sometimes 'Sammy') had displayed an inordinate fascination for a blue, plastic table and matching chair that Robert used. The table was now in the centre of the room, behind the bed. From his vantage point, Mike noticed that it looked distinctly odd. He walked towards it, carefully dodging the detritus that littered the floor.

Mike's first impression was that the table looked as if it had been melted. It had a subtle but unusual 'sheen', as if it had been highly polished. To Mike the table actually looked hot, like melted wax. More than that, it had lost its shape and now reminded him of something one may see in a Salvador Dali painting. Its centre was sunken, as if, in a semi-molten state, and it looked as if it had begun to collapse in on itself. One of the legs had warped outwards so that its foot was now approximately two inches from the floor. The other legs seemed to have buckled inwards, making its appearance even more bizarre.

Mike carefully extended a forefinger and touched the table. It was cold to the touch. Marianne just exploded.

'Eh? It's been totally mangled! God ... do you know what it is? This is the *second* table it's broken! How can it *do* that?'

Mike now placed the flat of his hand upon the table-top and gently rocked it back and forth. Due to the twisted legs, it now wobbled crazily. There were no visible stress fractures in the plastic, and it still glowed slightly. Had Mike not known better, he could well have assumed that it had been freshly moulded that way.

Even stranger, Mike noted that Robert's china mug was still perched on top of the table where the youngster had left it. Whatever force had distorted the table, it had apparently done so in such a way that the objects on the table's surface had remained undisturbed.

As Mike took another photograph, something else moved just within his peripheral vision. It was on the landing just outside of Robert's room. Marianne saw it too, and screeched.

The entity strode slowly but purposefully from the bathroom and walked across the landing into the master bedroom. As it passed the door to Robert's room, it paused momentarily and stared icily at Mike. It was large – maybe two metres in height – and midnight black. It was a three-dimensional silhouette that radiated sheer evil. It had no eyes, and yet it appeared to be staring. Its face, devoid of all features, was nevertheless menacing. Mike stared back, and then calmly spoke into his digital recorder.

'For the benefit of the tape, something – or someone – has just walked from the bathroom into Marianne and Marc's room . . . '

'Woah . . .!' said Marianne again, 'Did *you* see someone there . . .?'

'Yes I did . . . just like a black shape . . . but it's gone now.'

Now Marianne was *really* frightened, and the situation wasn't helped when some toy bells belonging to Robert left their normal home in his toy hammock and, jingling merrily, presented themselves at Marianne's feet. The room then went icy-cold.

There was, Marianne then noticed, a large, irregular stain on the carpet near the bed.

'Look, it's poured a cup of juice on the floor and then put the cup back on the table. There's a big wet patch on the floor!'

Mike didn't want to alarm Marianne and Marc, so, when the couple were looking the other way, he deftly bent down and rubbed the fingers of his left hand over the damp patch. He then raised his fingers to his nose and inhaled. The pungent odour of stale urine filled his nostrils. The polt had pissed on the floor. He decided not to enlighten the couple about this novel twist, as right now they had enough on their plate to worry about.

Mike had had just about enough of the entity and its antics. On the audio tape, he can be heard challenging the polt openly.

'Okay ... whoever you are ... you're obviously not a very happy chappie, and we know why. So ... alright, you've had a go at Marc, why don't you have a go at *me,* now?'

Marianne, hardly able to believe that Mike seemed to be openly challenging the polt to a duel, exclaimed, 'God ...!'

Mike continued.

'So why aren't you doing anything *now,* then?'

As if in response, the polt threw a five-pence coin on the floor at Mike's feet. Mike picked it up and placed it on top of a chest of drawers. Marc then flinched. A faint rumbling–cum–pounding sound was emanating from the master bedroom.

'What was that? Did you hear that?'

Marianne said she was scared to look. Mike said that he'd investigate.

As the investigator entered the master bedroom, Marianne followed. On the audio recording, in a trembling voice, she can be heard saying, 'What is it Mike?'

Mike noticed that the sash from Marianne's dressing gown, which had been lying on the floor beside a chest of drawers, was now draped across the floor. Mike started to describe the experience verbally for the benefit of the sound recorder when, suddenly, he saw something shoot through the doorway from the direction of the landing and hit Marc in the centre of his back. It clattered loudly to the floor. Mike looked down at the object. It was a battery-operated toy car belonging to Robert. Marianne – to use her own highly-appropriate terminology - 'freaked' again.

'Jesus! *Shit!'*

Mike looked at Marc and smiled. 'Where do you think that came from?' 'I'm fucked if *I* know!'

Mike took yet another photograph and then challenged the polt a second time.

'Whoever you are, why not just have a go at me? *I'm* here now. Throw something at *me!* Scratch *me!* Do something to *me,* now! So why aren't you having a go at *me?* Why aren't you doing anything to *me,* now? Is it because you know I'm on your case?'

The polt's reaction was to violently wrench open the door to Marianne's wardrobe. Mike closed it again – this was becoming something of a habit – just as Marc also noticed that it had opened one of the drawers in the chest next to Marc's side of the bed. Mike checked on his camera's screen the photographs he'd taken moments earlier, when they were last in the room, and the drawer was clearly shut. Marianne looked at the image and gasped.

The polt, obviously still wanting to play, then started to pull at the quilt upon the bed. It was as if an unseen hand was lifting the cover up to a height of six to eight inches and then putting it back down.

'Whoah!' shouted Marianne, 'The quilt is moving! Did you see it go up like that?'

Marianne then screeched again as the polt pulled open the wardrobe door before turning its attention once again to the quilt.

As Mike started to film the open wardrobe door, a faint, rhythmic beeping noise could be heard. It sounded like someone pressing the keys on a mobile phone pad, but as there were no mobile phones in the room apart from Mike's, the source remains a mystery.

Mike decided to take a second photograph of the bed in Robert's room. Should it be moved again by the polt, they would have both a 'before' picture and an 'after' picture to compare it with.

Nothing was out of place on the stairwell as they descended. Although they didn't know it at the time, this was the last occasion they would be able to say that for the rest of the evening.

After reaching the hallway, Mike opened the kitchen door and entered. He turned right to walk to the dining area, and was amazed to see one of the dining chairs now blocking his way. During their absence, it had been moved away from the table and placed in the centre of the floor.

Marianne asked if anyone else wanted tea or coffee. Marc said yes, but Mike declined. Marianne walked away from the table towards the kitchen sink to fill the kettle. As she approached the taps, she glanced to her left and suddenly shouted with surprise.

'Look at *this*!'

Mike and Marc went over to where Marianne was standing. Adjacent to the door which leads from the kitchen to the hall there is a full-length cupboard. The cupboard door had been opened to its full extent so that it now almost totally obscured the door leading into the hall.

'I was the last one in, and I *know* that the door was shut.' said Mike. 'If that door had been open, we couldn't have opened the hall door without hitting it.'

Mike shut the cupboard door, paying careful attention to the locking mechanism as he did so. As the door closed, the ball mechanism made a distinctive 'click'. The hinges also creaked unceremoniously. Mike opened and closed the door several times, adjusting both the speed and the amount of pressure upon the handle each time. It was impossible to open or close the door without making a considerable amount of noise.

Mike, Marianne and Marc walked back to the dining area. Mike sat down, followed by Marianne. Marc attempted to sit down, but the chair suddenly shot backwards. Marc just managed to grab it with his left hand and steady himself, his backside coming perilously close to hitting the floor. He looked at Mike quizzically.

'That's the second time it's done that to me. What's it got against me?'

Mike purposely avoided answering the question for one, simple reason. He didn't want to worry Marc any more than was necessary. The truth was that the polt had attacked him viciously earlier in the evening, and now it seemed to be trying to humiliate him whenever he was sitting at the table. On previous occasions, everyone sitting around the table would be annoyed by the chair-moving stunt, but now it only seemed interested in victimising Marc. Mike knew for certain now that Marc *was* the focus.

Marianne, however, voiced forth a suggestion. The normally inscrutable Marc had lost his temper earlier in the evening and called the polt names, using several colourful adjectives and expletives.

'Mike, do you think he could have upset it by shouting at it like that?'

'It's certainly possible . . . but who can say?' Mike studied Marc. He appeared ill. His hands were trembling and his face looked pallid and sickly. Are you okay?'

'Yes, well . . . no, not really. This whole thing has got me stressed out. Look at how my hands are shaking; they're like this all the time, now.'

For a while, the trio discussed the events of the previous hours. Mike tried to calm the couple down, but it was a difficult task. Who could blame them for being so frightened?

Mike didn't want them to discuss things too much; he was worried that the fear would become too entrenched.

'Okay, let's take another look upstairs. Anyway, I have an idea – something I want to try out.'

Mike went first, retracing their steps through the kitchen towards the door that led to the hall. The cupboard door, which Mike had left shut, was now open again. Without saying anything, Mike simply closed it. He opened the hall door and almost stood upon a baseball cap belonging to Marc. Inches away lay a coat belonging to Robert. Neither article had been there when they entered earlier, and they weren't there when they gathered to observe the mysteriously-opening cupboard door. The reason the researchers can say that confidently is that the hall door is almost entirely composed of glass panels. The cap, at least, would have been easily seen, as would part of the toddler's coat.

One again, Mike and the distinctly nervous couple ascended the stairwell. Their fear was palpable, and Marc's breathing was becoming laboured.

'Shall we look in Robert's room again?' asked Marianne.

'Not yet', replied Mike. 'There's something else I want to do first.'

In the master bedroom, Mike could see nothing amiss.

'What I'd like to do', he explained, 'is to try and provoke the polt into pulling at the bedclothes again. If you'd both like to get into bed, just as you normally would, I'll sit back here and see what happens.'

Marc disappeared momentarily and reappeared with Robert's diminutive but comfortable red chair for Mike to sit on. Mike walked over to the bedroom door and glanced into Robert's room. Marc had only been in there for seconds, but Mike needed to be sure that he hadn't surreptitiously done anything untoward at the same time. This was to protect Marc's reputation as well as his own. The room was exactly as they'd left it except for the fact that it no longer contained the red chair.

Mike re-entered the master bedroom and took his seat. Marc and Marianne were now in bed. Ironically the couple looked cosy, relaxed even. Nothing, of course, could have been further from the truth.

Mike aimed his camera at the couple and said, 'Okay, smile! Let's have one for the album!'

Marc managed to raise a faint smile, but just as the shutter clicked, Marianne jumped up and said, 'It's moving the quilt!'

Mike looked at the foot of the bed, and could see a faint movement. However, it was so faint it was impossible to say whether he was witnessing anything conclusive. Nevertheless, on the chance that the movements may become more pronounced, he decided to shoot some film footage. Just as he was about to press the 'record' button, the polt dropped the quilt back into place.

'I feel really nervous', whispered Marianne. 'If anything else happens I don't know if I could cope.'

'It's doing my head in', added Marc.

Mike did record a short piece of footage, but nothing happened. He turned off his camera. Just then, almost as if the polt had waited for him to stop filming, the wardrobe door that had opened earlier opened once again. Mike watched as, in complete silence, it moved outwards. An item of clothing stored on the base shelf inside – from the other side of the room Mike couldn't make out what it was – fell forwards and hung crazily from the aperture between the door and the wardrobe itself.

Marc was the first to get out of bed. He walked towards the bedroom wall that faced the foot of the bed and leaned against it. He stared up to the ceiling and said, 'This is making me feel sick'.

Marc seemed not to have noticed the fact that the wardrobe door was now ajar, and due to the couple's comments about their increasing nervousness, Mike decided not to mention anything about the incident. However, he took a picture of the open door. On the photo, a dejected Marc can be seen staring into space.

Eventually Marc got back into bed, and almost instantaneously complained that his body felt hot. Mike asked him to sit up and take off his T-shirt. At first, he didn't actually remove his shirt, but simply lifted it up to chest level and displayed his back. The cuts made earlier in the evening had all but disappeared, but in less than a minute a number of angry weals and scratches started to appear again before Mike and Marianne's eyes. Mike switched his camera to the movie function once again and began to film.

'You could actually watch the scratches forming', Mike said later. 'First an elongated red patch, then sharply defined scratches within it. Shortly afterwards, cuts started to appear on the right-hand facing side of his back; they immediately bled. Then his skin started to change colour. It went dark, almost as if it was sunburnt. At one point, there was more red, angry, discoloured, cut and scratched flesh than ordinary. I'd seen film and stills of poltergeist scratches appearing before, but nothing like this. You'd have thought he'd been given the cat o' nine tails. It was horrendous.'

Before Mike's very eyes, Marc's torso went from being virtually unmarked to looking as if it had been attacked with a cleaver. This sick bastard of a polt was simultaneously plumbing new depths and reaching new heights as it went about its twisted work.

Just after removing his shirt fully, Marc complained that his head was stinging. He turned to the camera and, sure enough, there was a large, discoloured patch on his forehead. Mike wondered whether Marc had been resting his head on the wall above the bed when he'd been filming his back, but both he and Marianne insisted that he hadn't.

Mike switched off his camera when the appearance of the weals on Marc's back and forehead seemed to have petered out. Almost instantaneously, however, Marc complained that his chest was hurting. Mike switched on his camera again, and started filming.

This time the weals weren't as deep, angry or bloody as the ones on his back, but they were certainly there.

Once again, Marianne asked whether Marc's earlier attempt to scold the poltergeist could have precipitated his ugly persecution. Again, Mike could only say, 'It's possible'. The truth was, he didn't really know.

Marc was becoming increasingly uncomfortable. His entire upper torso was now 'on fire'. Marianne, who was looking increasingly exhausted, suggested that he go to the bathroom and splash himself with cold water. He did. Marianne threw back the covers and lay there in her pyjamas, staring wistfully into space. It was obvious what she was thinking; *why the hell is this happening to us?*

Mike panned the camera round towards the door and followed Marc towards the bathroom. He had doused himself liberally in cold water and his wounds, despite their terrible appearance earlier, had now faded remarkably quickly. The scratches and cuts were still there, but the redness had disappeared.

Exactly forty-two seconds after Mike left the bedroom, followed by Marianne, they entered Robert's bedroom to see what, if anything, had happened since they were last in there. Marianne was the first to spot something truly extraordinary.

'The table's fixed!'

The plastic table, which only a short while before had been twisted out of all proportion and rendered useless, was now in perfect condition. Marianne could do nothing but gasp in astonishment.

'Well', said Mike, 'at least you've got your table back'.

Mike focused the camera on the table. The tabletop was now perfectly flat, the legs were perfectly straight and no one would ever have guessed that it had been through such a bizarre transformation. It was as if it had never been damaged.

Mike took a snap of the miraculously restored table and then turned his camera off. Within seconds, Marc pointed out something that Mike had missed.

'Hey look! The bed is back where it's supposed to be!'

Mike looked at the bed and, sure enough, it had been moved back to its normal position against the wall.

Mike turned his camera back on and filmed the bed in its normal resting place. It was not until later, when reviewing the footage in his office, that he noticed something extremely odd.

When Mike, Marianne and Marc had entered Robert's room, the door had been firmly shut. Mike remembers distinctly grasping the handle firmly and pushing forward to open the door. The three witnesses entered the room and walked into the centre of the floor. Marianne commented, 'The chair has moved', and it had. It was now lying adjacent to Robert's bed, on its side. However, when Mike filmed the bed in its normal position against the wall, the chair can be seen lying up against the door in a position that it was *not* in when they first entered the room. After analysing the footage, Mike could only come to one conclusion. When they had entered the room, the chair was lying on its side near the bed. For a brief few seconds the chair was out of the sight of the witnesses as they examined the table. During those few seconds, the chair had moved, silently, and came to rest up against the bedroom door in a position it was not in when they first entered the room. This translocation had occurred literally behind the witnesses' back, only inches away from them. When Mike realised this he admitted, later, that his stomach tightened and he felt something akin to real fear. The polt was now *really* playing games with them, *really* enjoying itself.

'Look', said Mike, why don't we tidy up the room while we're in here and try to restore an air of normality?'

The three set to work, and, within a few minutes, little Robert's room was in pristine condition, except for the piss stain on the floor.

After the tidy-up, Mike, Marianne and Marc descended the stairwell, making sure that all the rooms upstairs were tidy, in order and presentable. Mike followed the other two down the stairs so that, later, no accusations could be made that either Marianne or Marc had dropped anything on the way down. This was fortuitous, because when they got to the bottom of the stairwell Marianne looked behind her and exclaimed, 'Oh my God, what's that?'

On the middle landing, in plain sight, was a miniature tool box from one of Robert's toys. Mike would testify later that there was absolutely no way on God's earth that either of the householders could have dropped it there surreptitiously.

'If anyone suggests to me that either Marianne or Marc did that, then they're talking bollocks. They couldn't have; plain and simple.'

Mike took a picture of the toy before Marc removed it.

Mike opened the door that led from the hallway into the kitchen and proceeded towards the dining area. In the centre of the walkway was another of Marc's baseball caps. Mike knew that it hadn't been there when they left, as he was the last one to vacate the kitchen before they had gone upstairs.

The three witnesses, now feeling slightly battle-fatigued, sat around the kitchen table. Once again, the polt tried to pull the chair away from Marc as he sat down.

Marianne lit up a cigarette, drawing upon it as if her life depended on a nicotine fix. Who could blame her?

Mike commented later, 'Despite everything that had happened, she still had the presence of mind to keep a meticulous log of events and to photograph everything with the camera facility on her mobile phone. Marianne was a gem.'

At one point, Mike asked Marianne to check the door that leads from the kitchen to the hallway, as he was busy analysing the pictures and film taken earlier in the evening. The door had repeatedly been found open even though Mike had made sure it was shut minutes previously. Marianne rose from the table, and as she did so, her chair jerked backwards and collided with the wall. Both her hands were on the table, and Mike could not see how she could have moved the chair with such force simply by using her legs. She looked shocked, but didn't say anything. She walked into the kitchen and said that the door leading into the hallway was still shut, but pointed out that an eye-level cupboard door was now wide open. The door was not open when the trio passed into the kitchen, and they would have had to close the door to walk past the cupboard into the kitchen area. Mike took a picture of the open door and then closed it firmly.

Mike had noticed during the course of the evening that Marc was repeatedly belching, and, every time he did so, his facial expression indicated that he looked distinctly uncomfortable. Now he was looking very pale indeed, and was cradling his head in his hands. Mike asked him if he was okay.

'I have a gluten allergy, which upsets me sometimes, but it's just the stress of this whole situation that's getting to me now. Before you came I was so stressed I started to vomit. I think I'm going to be sick again, but I don't feel like going upstairs in case anything happens.'

He then managed to raise a faint smile.

'Look' said Mike, 'if you need to go to the toilet then go, and we'll come up the stairs with you. You'll be okay, honest.'

Mike, Marc and Marianne then walked through the kitchen area, only to find the large cupboard door and the door leading into the hallway open again.

'See?' said Mike, 'You have a polite poltergeist; it opens doors for you'.

The first thing Mike noticed was that the poltergeist had deposited a five-pence piece on the third stair. 'It's generous, too.'

At the top of the stairwell, everything looked okay. The doors to all the bedrooms were shut, although Mike realised that this was no guarantee that the rooms behind them had remained untouched.

Marc opened the toilet door and stared inside, transfixed. 'Look', he whispered.

The lid of the toilet seat was down, and, standing upon it was a large, ceramic ornamental pig. Marc, looking extremely dejected, made a move to pick up the pig so that he could evacuate his stomach. Mike asked him to wait for a few seconds, if possible, till he took a picture. Marc then went about his business. When he exited the toilet, he looked paler still, but a little brighter.

A quick check of the two bedrooms revealed nothing. This was unusual, but a welcome relief.

Marianne and Marc descended the stairwell yet again, followed by Mike. Marianne noticed that the polt had left yet another five-pence piece, while Marc pointed out that, further down the stairwell, it had gifted the couple a plastic clothes peg. It wasn't exactly a box of continental chocolates, but no one was in the mood to complain. Mike took the customary photographs and then walked through the hall doorway into the kitchen. The full-length cupboard door was open again, requiring another photograph. Marc simply pushed the door shut without comment; it had all been said before.

More tea and cigarettes followed. Then more chat. The polt threw a five pence piece from the kitchen, and it clattered to the floor next to the snoozing Bounder. The dog jumped up with a start. Marianne walked over to Bounder's blanket and retrieved the coin.

'You know', said Mike, 'if it keeps giving you money at this rate you could consider taking early retirement.'

The comment, meant to lighten the mood, elicited two faint smiles.

After a short break, the trio decided to venture upstairs again. Nothing was out of place. No trashed rooms, no pigs in the toilet. On the way down, they found another of Marc's baseball caps on the lower landing. Mike took another picture, and, although fascinated by the evening's events, was finding the process of capturing every incident on camera rather monotonous. Still, a paranormal researcher has to do what a paranormal researcher has to do.

Marc picked up the cap and placed it on the upright of the handrail on the middle landing. Three weary souls then walked down to the hallway, only to find the same cap lying on the floor.

'It's playing mind games with us now' said Mike. 'It's taunting us.'

At this juncture Mike felt uneasy. The polt was behaving in a somewhat juvenile manner, but he kept recalling the attack on Marc. He wondered if the events of that evening, bad as they were, were simply a relative period of calm before the arrival of a maelstrom of immense proportions. He couldn't have been more right.

When they next ventured up the stairs – shutting numerous cupboard doors on the way, of course – they found a small, plastic cartoon-type character lying next to the toilet door. Yet again, the rooms seemed to have been left undisturbed. On seeing this, Marianne and Marc visibly relaxed. However, as they returned downstairs with Mike, Marc stumbled over something several stairs down from the upper landing. It was a child's book.

On entering the kitchen, Marianne pushed shut the full-length cupboard door.

Are either of you at work tomorrow?' Mike asked, as he looked at the clock on the wall. It was almost 3am.

'We both are', said Marianne. 'We start at 7.45am.'

'Then I think you need some sleep. The way I see it, you have a number of options. You can go to your mother's for what little remains of the night. Another option is to simply go to bed as normal and keep your fingers crossed that nothing happens. A third possibility is that you can sleep in the living room upon the sofas. The other question is what shall I do? I can go home now if you like, but if you want I can 'hold the fort' so to speak while you get some shut-eye. I don't mind staying here till morning if you like.'

Both Marianne and Marc were emphatic that they wanted Mike to stay.

'But what will you do?' asked Marianne.

'I'll just sit here at the kitchen table, watching and waiting. If anything happens, then I'll deal with it. Mind you, I'm not expecting *too* much to happen; the polt has probably exhausted itself. I think that's why it's degenerated to simply opening doors and leaving small tokens of its presence on the stairs. I'll only wake you if it's absolutely necessary.'

Just before Marc and Marianne joined Robert in the living room, Mike noticed that the kitchen area seemed to be filled with a faint but distinct haze. It was barely visible, but definitely there.

'Can you see that?'

'Yes', said Marianne, 'I can. Could it just be the smoke from the cigarettes?'

'Possibly', said Mike, although he was secretly harbouring a darker interpretation that he didn't want to share with the couple at that juncture. The polt within the household was very strong, extremely aggressive and had lasted far longer than most others. It had proved itself to be both cunning and creative, displaying most of the typical symptoms of polt infestation. But not all. One of the most serious symptoms is commonly called *fire-starting* by researchers. In such cases, the polt will initiate small, spontaneous fires with no obvious cause. For example, victims may find circular burn marks on bedclothes and carpets. Fortunately, such polt-fires tend to extinguish themselves just as mysteriously as they start. Mike sincerely hoped that the polt was not about to escalate the infestation to another level.

Suddenly, Mike felt a sensation of pressure on the back of his neck. It was coming from the strap of his camera pouch. He looked down at the camera, which was hanging at waist level, and realised that someone or something was pulling the pouch downwards quite forcefully.

'Something is pulling at my camera'.

The camera now felt like a lead weight around his neck, and he was having difficulty in keeping his head up. Marianne looked alarmed.

'Mike ... maybe you should take it off. My God ... I hope it doesn't try to strangle you.'

Mike felt as if he was caught between a rock and a hard place. On one hand, he had no desire to be throttled by the polt. On the other, he was intrigued and wanted the experience to continue for investigative purposes. In the event, the choice was taken away from him. Just as suddenly as it had started, the pulling sensation stopped. At that juncture both Marc and Marianne joined Robert in the living room in an attempt to get some much-needed sleep.

The polt had gone relatively quiet, but it hadn't quite retired for the evening.

CHAPTER TWENTY-FOUR

In the Still of the Night

Mike wasn't sure what to do. He wanted to sleep, but couldn't as he didn't want to miss anything. He had a book in his bag – ironically, a battered paperback copy of *Stranger than Science* by Frank Edwards – but was too tired to read. He decided to keep a log of the evening's events in his notebook. He glanced at the clock again, and saw that it was just after 3am.

Like many parents, Marianne had purchased a baby monitor for Robert, or, at least, a baby monitor to be used on Robert's behalf. For the uninitiated, these devices consist of a two-way speaker-microphone that can be plugged in to any conventional electricity supply. One unit is installed in the bedroom of the child, the other normally in the living area downstairs. If the child coughs, cries or in some way gets distressed the parents are immediately aware of it and can then attend to baby. When the monitor detects a noise, an array of green lights flash to alert the parents. This is particularly helpful if the parents are hearing-impaired.

Marianne brought the unit from the living room – a 'WalkAbout Classic' manufactured by Tomy – and plugged it in to a socket before placing the unit itself on the dining table. The other, matching unit was still in Robert's bedroom. If the polt made a noise up there, then Mike would hopefully hear it.

Darren had noted during an earlier visit that Marc rarely showed any emotion on his face, even when confronted by seemingly paranormal phenomena of reasonable magnitude. When the investigators found the bunny rabbit trying to cut the duck's throat, for example, he didn't look shocked at all, unlike Marianne, who looked as if the sky had fallen in. It was this seeming lack of emotional response that had made the investigators suspicious of Marc, and Mike was intrigued by it. Even though earlier in the evening his torso had been covered in welts, he seemed unusually calm. Mike decided that he would have to put Marc to the test one more time to see how he reacted when confronted by something which, from his perspective, would seem to be truly paranormal. If his face maintained its usual dead-pan expression then Mike would, he decided, accept the fact that Marc simply wasn't the type of person who displayed his emotions readily. The investigators had now ruled out Marc as a wholesale fraudster, but the issue of his rather muted emotional responses was puzzling and needed to be sorted out.

Mike felt guilty about what he intended to do, but believed he had no option. The next morning Mike would test Marc. He then set about engineering an event which looked like something truly paranormal, but was faked. When Marc woke up, he planned to draw Marc's attention to it. Mike has stated categorically that he will not divulge the exact nature of this experiment, as he doesn't wish to provide pranksters with an instruction manual that could help them fool investigators in the future. Also, if further doubts ever arose about Marc's credibility, then the test could be employed for a second time. This would have been difficult to do if others had prior knowledge of it.

Mike has not even divulged exactly what he did to Darren or other investigators, as he feels that to do so would inevitably detract from all the other genuine phenomena that took place.

'What happened is between Marc and I, and, to be honest, I don't know if Marc himself even realises the exact moment when I tried to catch him out. In any event, no one else needs to know.'

The results of Mike's little test will be examined presently. Just after Marianne and Marc left Mike alone in the dining area, Bounder suddenly jumped up from his bed and stared into the corner of the room beside the patio doors. The couple also have a cat named Midnight. Midnight has his own basket which, bizarrely, sits on top of the refrigerator/freezer in the dining area. Why Midnight preferred such an elevated living space Mike didn't know, but he seemed perfectly happy there. At the exact moment that Bounder reacted to something seemingly invisible however, so did Midnight. The cat stood up in his basket, arched its back and stared at the exact same location. He meowed, spat and then apparently went back to sleep. Bounder stared at the corner for a few seconds more and then also returned to the Land of Nod.

At 3.12am precisely, Mike heard a faint thump emanating from the baby monitor. He decided to investigate. Once again, Marc's baseball cap was on the floor in the hallway. Yet another five pence piece had appeared on the stairs. Mike quietly ascended the stairwell and noted that the door to the cupboard on the upper landing was wide open. It had definitely been closed when he had last descended the stairs with Marc and Marianne. A quick check of the rooms indicated nothing out of order.

Back downstairs, Mike settled into the dining chair and made a few brief notes. At 3.33am exactly, Bounder began to whimper in his sleep. He sat up, looked around the dining room as if expecting to see something and then settled back down.

By this time, Mike was extremely tired and deluded himself into thinking that if he merely rested his head on his arms upon the dining table he could rest without falling asleep. First, though, he opened his bag, removed a half-drunk bottle of mineral water and took a swig before replacing the top and placing the bottle on the table.

Mike has no doubt that, under normal circumstances, he probably would have fallen asleep as he rested his head. However, the polt seemed to want company and Mike was the only person available.

Mike's eyes had been closed for no more than a minute when he suddenly felt 'rather strange' as he described it later.

It was as if the entire room was filled with static electricity. My skin started to tingle and the hairs on my arms stood on end. The same thing then happened to the hairs on the back of my neck.

I opened my eyes and looked around, and at first everything seemed normal. Then my attention was drawn to the bottle of mineral water on the table, and I couldn't believe what I was seeing. Instead of standing flat on its base, the bottle was tipped sharply on an angle. I could see no way that its position could be explained by the conventional laws of physics. In scientific terms, the position the bottle had adopted seemed to be impossible.

Mike hurriedly removed his camera, switched it to the 'movie' setting and began to film. Hardly able to believe his luck, he reset the camera and filmed again. And again. He gently squeezed the bottle. Then he poked it with his finger. It wobbled distinctly and then returned to its normal – or rather, distinctly abnormal -position. He shook the table hard. Again, the bottle wobbled, but it didn't fall over. Fascinated now, Mike prodded the base of the bottle hard with the forefinger of his right hand. The bottle fell over with a crashing noise that seemed totally disproportionate to its size, weight and proximity to the table itself.

Mike picked up the bottle and looked at it. He examined the base carefully and found that a small area on the edge of the base had been slightly flattened. He attempted to balance the bottle on this small area, but found it impossible. He made a mental note to try again the following morning. Slowly, the statically-charged air returned to normal.

At 4.12am, the dining-room table moved approximately four inches without any help from Mike, Bounder or Midnight. Six minutes later the atmosphere again became charged with static, and Mike wondered if the polt was going to engage in some more fun with the water bottle. It didn't.

For over an hour, the house was in complete silence. The polt lay dormant but then, at 5.31am, it moved a dining-room chair. Four minutes later it moved the chair back again, which was extremely thoughtful of it and saved Mike the bother.

At 6.25am, the family arose. Mike drew Marc's attention to his faked 'paranormal event'. His face displayed no visible reaction, but his *words* proved to Mike that he was genuinely puzzled by the incident. Mike became convinced at this point that Marc's sometimes muted reactions were not, in and of themselves, a sign of deceit or evasiveness on his part.

Mike then showed Marianne the footage of the bottle balancing on its edge upon the dining table. He also showed Marianne the actual bottle and pointed out the slightly flattened point on the edge where, just possibly, the bottle could be balanced in a bizarre manner without the aid of paranormal powers or by engaging the services of the resident poltergeist.

'Have you tried to balance it, Mike?'

'I did, but it didn't work. Mind you, I was tired and not focusing as well as I normally do.'

In Marianne's presence, Mike again tried to balance the bottle on the edge of the base, but to no avail. On two occasions, it seemed to balance for a split second, but then toppled over. Mike then tried drinking a mouthful of water from the bottle to see if that would make a difference. He didn't do this on the basis of science; it was merely something between a wild guess and a hunch. Intriguingly, Mike *did* then manage to get the bottle to balance on its edge after a few goes. The question is, what had been responsible for the bottle balancing in such a strange manner during the night? Mike isn't sure.

'From a viewpoint of hard evidence, there's not much to work with. There was only one witness present; myself. Further, there are numerous ways I could have faked the incident. In addition to this, the fact that the damaged base made it just possible to balance the bottle on its edge under some circumstances means that a rational explanation was available, even if highly unlikely.

Did I knock the bottle with my arm when I was dosing, and coincidentally hit it with just the right amount of force, and at the right trajectory, to tip it onto the damaged, slightly flattened area on the edge of the base? It seems unlikely, but I can't rule it out.

The reason I feel that something paranormal was involved was that when I tried to destabilise the bottle by shaking the table, or poking it with my finger, it still stayed in its weird, lop-sided position. But then again, when I pushed it harder it *did* fall over, so who knows.

Every time I review the footage it sends a chill down my spine, but I wouldn't like anyone to come to any definitive conclusions about the cause.

Mike caught a taxi home. He really needed to sleep, but the adrenalin was still pumping. He downloaded all the pictures and footage into his PC and then began to categorise them. How cynics would or could attempt to explain away the growing body of evidence would prove interesting.

CHAPTER TWENTY-FIVE

Come Out, Come Out, Wherever You Are

Sunday 27 August started relatively quietly. The polt remained dormant during the day, which at least afforded Marc and Marianne the opportunity to rest.

At 5pm, Marianne went upstairs and happened to enter Robert's room. She noticed that several drawers in one of the storage chests had been pulled open, and the blue bucket seat – with which the polt had an obvious fascination – was standing on top of the table. The metal trash can had also been moved from its usual position by the bedroom door.

At precisely 5.15pm, Marianne also found a felt-tip pen floating in the bath. Exactly fifteen minutes later another four felt-tip pens were found attached to the side of Robert's bedroom door with adhesive tape.

This was all typical behaviour for the polt, and by now the family were becoming accustomed to it. They didn't like it, obviously, but it was no longer frightening them to the degree that it once had. Perhaps that is why the polt was now ramping up the fear factor by engaging in new types of activity that were calculated to terrorise the couple. The attack on Marc the previous evening was perhaps the best example.

But now the polt was about to try something new.

The investigators were aware that, on rare occasions, polts had been known to physically translocate people as well as physical objects. The entity that had victimised the family in question had already proved that it could do both. It had, on numerous occasions, thrown objects through Robert's bedroom window even when the window was shut and the blinds were down. Those objects would cascade to the garden below – sometimes breaking, sometimes not – while leaving the window itself intact.

On one occasion, the polt had moved Robert. It had taken him from his bed, carefully wrapped him in a blanket and placed him on the floor. It had then secured him to the floor by placing the blue, plastic table over the top of the sleeping youngster.

Moving the youngster a few feet from his bed to the floor is one thing. Making him disappear altogether is, of course, quite another.

Earlier in the evening, Marianne and Marc had put Robert to bed. They then went downstairs and watched TV in an effort to relax. At 9.30pm, they both went upstairs. Marianne went into the bathroom while Marc went to check on Robert. He opened the bedroom door and instantly let out a yell. Marianne, who came running from the bathroom to see what was wrong, found Marc wide-eyed and horror-stricken.

'It's Robert; he's *gone.*'

Frantically the couple searched the house, ransacking cupboards and looking under beds. There was no sign of the child.

One can only try to imagine the fear that coursed through the couple at this point. If the polt was indeed exploring new ways of instilling fear into this family, it had hit upon a very effective tactic indeed.

In some respects, this was a new low in the activity of this particular entity. It had never frightened Robert himself, and had always ensured that it was Marc, Marianne or Ian who discovered the evidence of its more sinister workings. Now, without frightening Robert directly, it was nevertheless using him to wreak havoc in the psyches of both Marianne and Marc.

Once again, the couple frantically tore through their home in an effort to find the boy. Eventually they came to one of the wardrobes in the master bedroom, the closet in which Marc keeps his clothes. They'd already looked in here, but desperation insisted that they try again. They opened the door and, to their profound relief, found Robert. He was tightly cocooned in a blanket; so tightly he would have been unable to extract himself of his own volition. He was sound asleep.

As soon as Robert had been carried downstairs and secured in the living room, Marianne rang Mike. Her voice was trembling and she could barely formulate her words. He tried to reassure her that everything would be okay, but it was a mammoth task. Why *should* she believe that everything was going to be okay after all Marc and she had been through?

Mike told her to keep making notes and take photographs, and she dutifully agreed.

Mercifully, the polt allowed the family to spend the rest of the evening together without incident. Wisely, they allowed Robert to sleep in their bed with them. In all probability, this would not have prevented the polt from doing the same thing again had it wanted to, but both Marc and Marianne felt better for it.

CHAPTER TWENTY-SIX

Die, Bitch

There are different ways to threaten people. Threats may be indirect and subtle, or direct and brutal. Those who try to instil fear in others usually don't mind what tactic they use, as long as it works. Its *horses for courses,* as they say.

With hindsight, it is clear that the polt that terrorised the house in Lock Street was happy to use every weapon in its armoury. It had tried the relatively gentle approach – moving objects around, throwing the odd coin, here and there – and for a while, this had worked. Marianne and Marc, never having experienced anything like this before, naturally found it very difficult to cope with.

But then things changed. As the researchers explained to the couple more about the nature of poltergeists their fear lessened somewhat. The polt didn't like this, for the lessening of the fear also meant the lessening of its food source. So, as you may imagine, it had to adapt its *modus operandi* to these new circumstances.

It began by leaving messages on Robert's doodle-board. Nothing sinister – apart from the one time when it left the message 'DIE' – but it was a change, and it unnerved the couple somewhat. When they got used to the doodle-board messages, it started to mess around with the phones. This unnerved them too, particularly Marianne. But then the researchers explained that they shouldn't worry; it was just all part of the polt's game plan to get them scared. Once again, the fear subsided somewhat. And, once again, the polt became hungry.

So the polt rounded on Marc, transforming his upper torso from something lithe and pink into something scarred and red. He looked like he'd been savaged by a mad dog.

And then it had hidden young Robert from the watchful gaze of his doting mother.

By this juncture both Darren and Mike were convinced that the entire phenomenon was – at long last, and despite their previous bouts of premature optimism – reaching its peak. They just couldn't see how anything remotely like a typical poltergeist could sustain itself indefinitely while using up such vast amounts of dark energy. Mike felt that the polt was becoming increasingly desperate. Its renewed vigour meant only one thing to him; its days were numbered, and it was now pulling out all the stops in a frenzied effort to stay alive. Mike has never thought of poltergeists as sane, but this one was becoming truly demented.

At 5pm, on Monday 28 August, the polt threw the little yellow nut from Robert's junior workbench down the stairs. It just missed Marc. The couple finished eating, and then decided to check upstairs. They inspected their own bedroom first. Everything seemed fine, but suddenly they heard what sounded like an ominous scraping noise coming from Robert's room.

'It sounded like something large and heavy was being forcibly scraped across the wall,' said Marc. 'It really made us jump. After a while we plucked up the courage to take a look.'

The polt had certainly been active in Robert's room. It had placed the red wooden chair on top of the blue plastic table, and then placed the blue, plastic chair on top of the red one. Marc and Marianne quickly dismantled this spontaneous bit of furniture sculpture before retiring to their own room once again. However, another scraping noise, although not as loud or as sustained as the first, made them go once again into Robert's bedroom. This time it wasn't so bad; the polt had simply moved the table.

It turned out that this bit of furniture rearranging was merely the preamble to something far, far worse. The polt was about to get really, *really* nasty.

By 5.15pm, the couple had returned downstairs. Robert was playing happily in the garden on his buggy. At 5.20pm, Marianne's mobile phone rang. She looked at the number on the illuminated screen, and was astonished to see that it was the number of their home's internal landline. Someone was ringing Marianne's mobile phone *from within the house*. She knew that it couldn't have been Marc, for he was standing right next to her. Apprehensively she accepted the call, but the phone went dead. Over the next ten minutes, this same process was repeated over and over again. Each time Marianne accepted the call, the polt immediately terminated it.

At 5.35pm, Marianne's mobile phone rang again. This time, however, the call was coming from Marc's mobile phone. When she drew this to Marc's attention, he immediately pulled his phone from his pocket and showed it to Marianne. It was not in use, it was not dialling out and the key-lock was in place. And yet the number displaying itself on the screen of Marianne's mobile phone *was* indeed Marc's.

Marc put his phone down on the dining table just as Marianne drew his attention to noises coming from upstairs. Something was being dragged across the floor. They went upstairs and checked Robert's room, and to their dismay found that the polt had been busier than ever. The bed had been moved into the centre of the floor, the red chair was back on top of the blue table and the heavy storage boxes had been moved from their normal position.

They returned to the kitchen. Marc went to use his mobile phone, but it was no longer on the table where he'd left it. Just then, the landline telephone rang, and Marc's mobile number appeared on the screen. Acting on a hunch, Marc wondered if the polt had taken the phone upstairs. Marianne listened carefully, and could actually hear Marc's footsteps as he ascended the stairs. She then heard the bedroom door open, and at that very second, the line went dead. Marc picked up his phone, which was lying in full view on their bed. It was no longer in use.

At 5.45pm, Marc and Marianne were standing in the hallway when the polt threw a toy down the stairwell. It was another of Robert's 'cartoon character' toys; a plastic man with stylised, elongated arms, legs and neck. Sinisterly, the neck had been twisted 360 degrees and the head bent backwards. Marianne photographed the toy with her phone and sent Mike a copy to his mobile. When he received it, he studied the image for a few minutes and then decided to give her a ring. Just then, his own phone rang. Marianne had decided to ring him. 'Hi, Mike; did you get the picture?'

Mike said that he had, and asked Marianne to give him a resume of the day's events. Mike could tell by her voice that she was distinctly upset, and said that he would come straight over.

After Mike and Marianne had finished speaking, she went to the hall and found on the stairs a small figurine of an African lady which normally stands on a shelf in the hallway. She then went back into the kitchen and waited for Mike to arrive. Marc sat with her.

At 6.05pm, her mobile phone beeped, indicating that she had a text message waiting to be received. The text had ostensibly been sent from Marc's phone, which was sitting – switched off – on the table between them. Marc's mobile phone showed no signs of life, and the screen was not illuminated. With great apprehension, Marianne opened the message. The words on the screen simply said, *Get you bich*.

Marc, desperate to stop whatever was transpiring, opened up the battery case on his phone and took the battery out. He then placed the battery, battery cover and phone back down on the table.

Two minutes after the first text message, another one arrived. This one was far more sinister and, incredibly, it was being sent from Marc's mobile phone even though he'd removed the battery. Marianne opened the message, which said, *You're dead*.

It was at this point that Mike arrived at the rear of the house. Marc walked down the garden path and opened the gate. As they both walked up to the house Marianne came running out. Her arms and hands were shaking uncontrollably, and her appearance can only be described as pitiful. Even during Mike's time in the Police Service he could not remember seeing a victim in such a state of abject terror.

'Mike! Please help! It says it's going to kill me!'

Inside the house, Mike endeavoured to calm the terrified Marianne down. This wasn't helped by the fact that a battery-operated 'Cookie Monster' toy spontaneously burst into life, even though the switch that operated it was set to the 'off position. In addition, the toy figurine that had been unceremoniously mangled at the neck now appeared on the kitchen bench, miraculously restored. The polt then began to throw knives around the kitchen, some of them narrowly missing Marianne. Shaking, she took photographs of them *in situ* where they landed, as did Mike with his digital camera.

At 6.16pm, in Mike's presence, another text message arrived on Marianne's mobile phone; *It you bitch*. Not very articulate, but extremely frightening nonetheless. Mike picked up Marc's phone and examined it. There was no residual power in the phone, and, just to make doubly sure, he deftly slid the SIM card half-way out of its holder so that it was no longer connected. He then placed the phone back on the table. If there was a remote chance that Marc had pre-programmed his phone to send these messages – even though Mike thought it highly unlikely – then it wouldn't be able to do so now.

Mike asked Marc if he could see the scratches and cuts that the polt had inflicted upon him the previous evening. Marc removed his T-shirt, and Mike was astonished to see that that there was virtually no sign of the wounds. There were three, faint scratches on the right-hand side of his torso, over the ribcage, but the rest of his body was now perfectly healed. Later, two highly-qualified and experienced nurses would say that it was physically impossible for wounds such as those Mike filmed appearing to disappear like that in less than forty-eight hours. Mike filmed Marc's miraculously healed body.

At 6.20pm, the polt picked up the remote control for the TV, which had been sitting on the kitchen bench, and threw it to the floor. All the while Mike was urging the couple to stay calm.

'Remember, its trying to frighten you. Don't let it win. Don't give in to it. *Don't give it what it wants.*'

Mike said he'd like to take a look upstairs if the couple didn't mind, and they said that they had absolutely no objections. To make sure he was ready, should anything happen, he removed his camera from the pouch and set it to the 'movie' function. He then ascended the stairs. As he did so, the polt removed a cooking pan from the kitchen table. Marianne's eyes were only averted for a second. One moment the pan was there, the next it was gone, as they say.

When Mike got to the top of the stairwell, he checked the toilet and bathroom. Everything seemed okay. Next he decided to check Robert's room, but stopped just as he was about to open the door. From inside he could hear the sound of a child giggling hysterically. Later Mike would say that it sounded like a toddler having his ribs tickled. He tried to open the door, but it wouldn't budge. He tried again, but still no joy. Still, from inside, came the eerie sound of a laughing child. This was not normal laughter, no matter how joyous it may have sounded superficially. There was a malign, sickening quality to it that Mike found particularly disturbing. He felt the muscles in his stomach go as tight as a drum. By hurling his entire bodyweight against the door while simultaneously holding the handle he eventually gained ingress. At the very moment the door opened, the laughter stopped. The room was still, now, and immaculately tidy save for one cuddly toy lying by the bed. Marianne later told Mike that the toy had not been lying on the floor before, but had been sitting securely in the toy hammock on the wall opposite.

At that moment, Marianne went to the foot of the stairs. She had heard the loud, weird giggling from Robert's room even as she sat in the kitchen. She'd also heard the thumping noise of Mike's frame colliding with the door as he attempted to open it. Worried that Mike was in trouble, she shouted up the stairs and asked him if he was okay. He answered in the affirmative just as loud bangs and thumps started to emanate from the master bedroom.

'It's in *your* room, now!' he shouted. 'I'm going in!'

Once again, despite his best efforts, the door into the master bedroom refused to budge. Something was pushing forcefully against it from the other side. It would give an inch or two momentarily, and then spring back again.

Meanwhile, unknown to Mike, Robert had suddenly started to laugh hysterically in the living room for no apparent reason.

This time Mike decided to try a new tactic. He switched on his camera again in the hope that if he did manage to open the door he may be lucky enough to catch something – anything – on film. As he shoulder-charged the door – this time successfully – he pressed the 'record' button. On the footage, one can clearly see the polt's handiwork. The double bed had been dragged into the centre of the floor. A roll of carpet that had been stored neatly against a wall now straddled a chest of drawers like a bizarre bridge. Numerous objects and artefacts littered the floor.

Suddenly there was another loud bang from Robert's room just as Marianne arrived at the top of the stairs. Strangely, although Marc, Marianne and Mike all heard the noise, it cannot be heard on the film footage.

Mike had already re-entered Robert's room with his camera. Marianne followed him in, only to be told by Mike that the polt had actually set-to in *her* room, not her son's. They both re-entered the master bedroom. Marianne, clearly distressed, simply shouted, 'Oh my word . . . oh, my God . . .!'

Downstairs, the pan had been restored to the kitchen table, which was one small mercy. But then at 6.30pm, another text message was received. Again, it was Marc's number on the display screen. Before Marianne had time to open it, the kitchen table screeched back and forth across the floor wildly. Ignoring this latest intrusion as best she could, she opened the message; *The bitch will die today.*

Almost immediately, another one arrived; *going to die today going to get you.*

At 6.40, the polt seemed to have tired sending text messages and swapped to sending automated voice messages instead. The first one said, in a chilling, robotic voice; *the bitch will die today bitch gonna get you o.k. mam.*

With a shaking hand, Marianne handed the phone to Mike so he could replay the message and hear it too. The message was evil, sinister and intimidating. However, what struck Mike most forcefully were the words *o.k. mam.* These words were exactly the same ones that 'Sammy' had used in one of his doodle-board messages. This seemed to reinforce a chilling possibility first postulated by Darren; that there really was no Sammy; 'Sammy' may have simply been the polt in disguise all along. The authors will look at this possibility in greater depth later.

At 7pm, the polt threw a carving knife from the kitchen, which landed perilously close to Marianne.

'See?' said Mike. 'See what I mean?' Fear! Everything it does is geared to frighten you. Don't be frightened!'

At this juncture, the polt backed off and gave the couple a much-needed break. Just then, Marianne's brother Ian arrived. Mike tried to apprise him of the situation, but he seemed stunned.

'Why is it doing this? What's the point?'

'The point is, Ian, that it's trying to survive. It needs to feed, and the only way it can feed is to scare your sister and Marc out of their wits.'

Suddenly, Marianne frowned and looked puzzled. Mike asked her what was wrong.

'It's strange; I've just thought of something that doesn't make sense. I've just remembered that my landline telephone is set to 'incoming calls only'. It's been like that since 23 August, because I forgot to pay the bill. How can it be ringing my mobile from the landline when the landline can only receive calls and not make them?'

Mike picked up the landline receiver and tried to dial his home number. He was unable to as, just like Marianne had stated, it was only able to receive calls, not make them. This didn't seem to stop the *polt* making calls from the landline, of course.

Mike asked Marianne if she'd managed to take any notes. She had, God bless her. While enduring this maelstrom of evil, she had, at every brief interval, sat down and recorded the experience.

'Look, Mike; I've written down two pages of notes just tonight ...'

Mike clearly saw the two pages, covered in Marianne's hand-writing, as she turned them over.

'I'll write some more, later', she whispered, clutching the note-pad nervously in her hands. Mike wondered if writing down her experiences like this was in some way therapeutic for her. He hoped so, as she certainly deserved something.

Suddenly the refrigerator jumped, as if someone had stumbled against it. Marc, standing nearby, flinched.

'Did you see that?'

'Yes, it moved.'

'No . . . not just that; something fell down the back ... I saw something go down the back of the fridge.' Mike hadn't seen anything.

Marianne decided that she, Robert and Marc should stop at her mother's for the night. Mike thought that, under the circumstances, it would probably be a good idea.

'Let me give you the notes I've written before you go.'

Marianne opened her notepad and found her hand-written notes; or at least, she found one page of them. The second page had disappeared completely.

The refrigerator shuddered weirdly again and both Marc and Ian decided to pull it away from the wall. As they did so, Mike peered behind it and saw what he thought was a penny. It turned out to be a small dog biscuit which Bounder had probably knocked there when he'd been feeding, as both his feeding bowl and his water dish sit next to the refrigerator.

From her vantage point at the other side of the table, Marianne could see a little further underneath, and she suddenly stooped down and thrust her hand behind the refrigerator.

'Wait a minute ... I can see something.'

She pulled out a crumpled piece of paper – the second page of her hand-written notes that had disappeared minutes earlier.

'My God ... I don't believe it. It's my notes! But Mike, you *saw* both pages just a minute ago. The notebook has never left my hands!'

And it hadn't, as Mike would later testify.

Mike asked the couple if they wanted a lift in the car to Marianne's mother's, but they politely declined. She only lived a short distance away;

'Look, please ring me later when you get to June's and let me know that you're all okay.'

Marianne said she would.

When the opportunity arose, Mike deftly pushed the SIM card back into place on Marc's mobile phone as it lay upon the table, and then he left. Any residual doubts he'd had that Marc had been responsible for sending such wicked text and voice messages to his partner had now evaporated completely

Later that evening, Marianne rang Mike from her mum's house. She still sounded distressed. Perhaps trying to play the polt at its own game, Marc had rung their landline phone from his now reassembled mobile. No one should have answered, of course, because their house was empty. Regardless, someone – or something – picked up the receiver at the other end and immediately replaced it, thereby ending the call. It could only have been the polt.

Mike tried to reassure Marianne that she'd be okay, but during the conversation she received a string of text messages from the entity. They were nasty and intimidating. They told Marianne that 'tonight is the night you will die' and that it would come for her 'when you're asleep'.

'Mike, please tell me that it hasn't come with me to my mum's. I couldn't stand it.'

Literally one second later the polt sent her another text message. It had obviously been listening: *Please donwt gow now. I will just com with you bich.*

'Mike, I'm frightened to go to sleep!'

Another text message: *I cann get you when you awake and I'll come for you when you're asleep bich.*

'My God, you're right! Its listening to everything we're saying!'

Mike again reassured Marianne that the polt was just trying to intimidate her.

'When you wake up tomorrow morning, and you're still alive, you'll realise that all these threats have just been empty words.'

And they were. She rang Mike the next day, from work, and told him that everything was okay

'See? I told you', he said.

Later, the couple bravely returned to their home with little Robert. Everything was pretty much in order, although a few bits and pieces had been moved around in Robert's room. While at June's house Marc's travel pass had gone missing. Marianne found it in the centre of the floor in Robert's bedroom.

Everyone, including Mike and Darren, were now hoping that the worst was over.

It was not to be.

CHAPTER TWENTY-SEVEN

More Phone Fun

Mike has a good friend called Daniel Jackson. Just as the investigation into the Lock Street poltergeist was beginning, Danny's son, Damien, was killed on active service in Afghanistan. His death hit the news headlines throughout the UK and abroad.

Mike's worry was that Danny would be besieged by the media; the last thing he needed after the death of his son. To try and take the burden off him to a degree, Mike suggested that his own media business should field all the press enquiries. Danny readily agreed.

On Saturday 26 August, Tyne Tees Television presenter Kim Inglis contacted Mike and told him that a well-wisher had forwarded a bereavement card for Danny to the TV company. Mike asked Kim to send the card to his office. He then telephoned Danny and told him that he was welcome to call in any time and pick the card up.

On Wednesday 31 August, Mike and Jackie went to bed just before midnight. At 1.55am the following morning, barely two hours later, Mike suddenly woke up. He decided to get up and drink a glass of milk before trying once again to get some rest.

At the beginning of the investigation, Mike had told both Marianne and Marc that if they were ever frightened – day or night – they should ring him. Since then, Mike had gotten into the habit of taking his mobile phone to bed with him in case they should call during the night. As he got out of bed to go downstairs, he instinctively picked up his mobile phone from the bedside table and took it with him just in case it should ring while he was in the kitchen.

Mike crept downstairs quietly in an effort not to wake his wife. She had an early start at work the next day, and needed her sleep. He placed the phone on the kitchen workbench and poured a glass of milk. He drank it and then went back to bed, forgetting to take his phone with him.

At exactly 2.02am, just as Mike got back into bed, Jackie awoke with a start.

'Mike … is that your mobile phone ringing?'

Mike listened carefully. It *was* his mobile phone, and he silently cursed himself for not bringing it back upstairs with him. As quickly as he could he descended the stairs, only for the call to disconnect seconds before he could accept it. He looked at the screen, and saw the usual message, '1 missed call'. Working on the assumption that Marianne and Marc were in trouble, he hastily unlocked his phone and looked at the number. The call had not been made by Marianne or Marc, but by his friend Danny.

Mike was mystified. Why would Danny be ringing him at this hour? He seemed to be coping with Damien's death rather well, but was it possible that he'd became depressed and needed to talk? Without further delay, he returned the call. Within seconds, Danny answered. He had just pulled into a lay-by to answer his phone.

'Hello?'

'Hi Danny, its Mike. Are you okay?' 'I'm fine; how are you?'

'I'm okay, I just wondered why you were calling so late.'

'Calling who? I don't know what you mean.'

'Danny, you just rang me seconds ago.'

'Mike, my phone has been sitting on the dashboard of my car, and the keypad is locked. I haven't phoned anyone.'

'Well, the call definitely came from your number. I have it attached to your name, and 'Danny' showed up on the screen.'

'I don't know what to say. Honestly, Mike, I haven't used my phone. The strange thing is your number *is* the last one dialled on my outgoing calls log.'

Both Danny and Mike were puzzled. Before they ended the conversation, Mike asked Danny when he was coming to pick up the bereavement card. Danny said he'd pop round after lunch later that day. Mike went back to bed, still scratching his head about the mystery phone call.

Early the next morning, after a restless night and very little sleep, Mike had a job to do. Mike is patron of a paranormal investigation group called The North East Ghost Research Team, of which Darren is the founder and principal investigator. Mike and Darren had agreed that the time may have come to bring in the team to help carry out a thorough investigation into the whole phenomenon. An arrangement was made with Marc and Marianne to bring the team in to carry out an all-night 'vigil' the following evening. Mike asked Darren what the general attitude of the team members was towards what had been going on.

'Mike, they're all really keen to take part, but I think one or two believe it's all too good to be true.'

From the standpoint of Marianne and Marc, of course, the situation wasn't 'good' at all. They were in the middle of a veritable nightmare. However, for researchers in the field opportunities like this are few and far between and it is easy to become a little cynical. Mike explains:

'I've investigated hundreds of cases allegedly involving poltergeists. Many can simply be put down to the misinterpretation of perfectly natural phenomena. Others may be genuinely paranormal, but the frequency with which incidents occur can be patchy and sporadic. You can visit the same house ten, maybe fifteen times and never see a thing, only for it to throw a saucepan at the householder less than a minute after you've departed. This is very frustrating for researchers, who can investigate a case for months and yet never see anything happen with their own eyes.'

Mike and Darren both felt it was important to impress upon the team members the unusual nature of the case. The activity was intense, frequent and sustained. The polt had also proved itself to be very, very violent. On the Thursday morning, Mike composed a thirty minute movie presentation for the team to see. It contained film, stills and audio recordings made by Darren and Mike. This would be shown to the team before the vigil in an effort to reinforce how serious the situation was.

By lunchtime, Mike had finished the presentation and decided to burn it on to a DVD so that the team could view it on their TVs. Unfortunately, Mike put the blank DVD in the 'DVD reader' instead of the 'DVD writer' and sent his computer haywire. Mike could not get the drive to eject the blank disk. Fortunately, Danny – who is something of an expert with computers – knocked at Mike's door just at that moment.

Danny fixed the problem pretty quickly and restored Mike's computer to working order. He then offered to burn the disk for Mike in case something else went wrong. Mike took no time in taking up Danny's kind offer.

Danny brought up the movie presentation on the screen, and stared at the title: The Lock Street Poltergeist; a Pictorial Guide for Investigators'.

Danny stared at the screen for a moment and then said, 'What's this, Mike?'

Mike briefly related the story to Danny from start to finish. Danny then shook his head and said, 'I'm intrigued. But you know, there's something weird I have to tell you.

'Remember during the night, when my mobile phone rang yours without me touching it?'

Mike acknowledged in the affirmative.

'Well, the thing is I was actually driving past Lock Street at that very moment.'

This bizarre coincidence led Mike to imagine all sorts of strange possibilities, including the notion that the polt, which had become very adept at using phones to spread its own particular brand of terror, had somehow 'picked up' on Danny's mobile phone when he was driving past the location it inhabited.

Jackie made coffee for Mike and Danny, and the two friends then sat in the garden. Danny wanted to know more.

There are a few things that the reader should know about Danny. He is highly intelligent, extremely articulate and very well read. He is also an astute judge of human character. He has lived on a Native American reservation for a while, and knows quite a bit about their cultural and spiritual practices. Indeed, he was married to an Indian woman for a number of years. This has created a unique bond between Danny and Mike, for obvious reasons.

As Mike told Danny more about the case, Jackie joined them in the garden. The three chatted, and then Mike heard his mobile phone ring inside the house.

'Damn! Sorry about this . . . I'll be back in a minute.'

Mike ran inside to take the call.

He pressed the button to receive the call and then stared in astonishment as the word 'Danny' appeared on the screen. He held the phone to his ear, but there was only silence. He slowly walked out into the garden and showed his friend the screen bearing his name.

'Danny . . . you're calling me!'

Danny immediately pulled out his mobile phone from his pocket and showed it to Mike.

'No I'm not; look, the keypad is locked and the phone isn't being used. It's actually switched off.'

Mike held the phone to his ear again, but the call had been disconnected. Just then, he received a text message from his phone provider saying that there was a voice message waiting for him on his message retrieval system. Mike dialled 901 and waited.

The 'message' left for him was actually several minutes of the conversation they'd just had as they sat in the garden.

'I just can't explain that; its not possible.' said Danny.

'I think I can', said Mike. 'I think the polt is listening in again, the same way that it did on Monday evening when I spoke to Marianne. My God . . . what a *bastard*!'

By now, Danny was more intrigued than ever, and wanted to know if there was any chance that he could accompany the team on the investigation the following evening. Mike said he would be delighted to have Danny along, but would need to make a courtesy call to Darren first. Darren later told Mike that Danny would be welcome, and that his expertise in a number of areas would be valued.

CHAPTER TWENTY-EIGHT

The Briefing

At 7pm on Friday 1 September, the team met at Mike's house for the briefing. Some of the investigators were familiar to him, while others he was meeting for the first time.

Mike gave a short presentation in which he related the history of the case. He then played his short 'poltumentary' on the TV At first, the investigators were simply presented with a seemingly endless succession of stills, each one showing an artefact that had been dislodged from its normal resting place by the polt. These included ice cubes on the floor, pennies on the stairwell, and so on. For most seasoned investigators this is pretty low-level stuff, and many could rightly claim to have 'seen it all before'. However, as the sinister text and voice messages that had been sent to Marianne appeared, one by one, on the TV, some began to look a little uncomfortable. This was *not* your average polt.

Next, the investigators were shown the footage of cuts, weals and wounds slowly but steadily appearing over Marc's torso. This also had an effect, and one or two present puffed their cheeks and exhaled quite sharply.

Finally, over fifteen minutes of audio recordings, on which the polt can be heard throwing things around and the terror in Marianne's voice is horribly palpable, were played out. Afterwards there was a stunned silence, and awkward glances were exchanged in profusion.

'We just want you to know what you're getting yourself into; just *what* you're taking on.' said Mike. 'This is no walk in the park, believe us. This is the *real deal* poltergeist, not some frustrated spirit that simply likes to tug at your bedclothes every now and then. It is nasty, sadistic, violent and cunning.'

Mike and Darren gave everyone present the opportunity to back out without any loss of face, but no one took it. Everyone was then asked to sign a waiver promising that they would not hold anyone responsible should they be physically or psychologically damaged by the polt.

An opportunity to ask questions was given, but few were forthcoming. Darren told the team that no guarantees could be given that anything would happen during the course of the vigil. In fact, the polt was now operating at such a frenzied pace both Darren and Mike were worried that it would burn itself out prematurely.

All we can tell you', said Darren, 'is that if it keeps up the same level of activity this evening that it has demonstrated at other times, you could well be in for a bumpy ride.'

The team then trooped into Mike's back garden, where last cigarettes were smoked pensively. Just as they were getting ready to depart for Lock Street, Mike received a text message from Marianne: *Be prepared, for a busy night. It's being very active. Come as soon as you can. I'm scared.*

Mike read out the message to the assembled team. The effect on them was both immediate and obvious. Intuitively, everyone seemed to realise at that point that this was, as Mike had said, the *real deal*.

Dusk was just setting in as three vehicles filled with investigators and equipment headed down the road to face God-knows-what at 42 Lock Street.

The polt, meanwhile, was warming up in anticipation.

CHAPTER TWENTY-NINE

Into the Darkness

When the team arrived at the rear of the house and parked their cars, Marianne and Marc could be seen standing on the garden path. Both looked nervous. Marc walked to the gate and opened it, while Bounder jumped around excitedly. After everyone had been introduced formally, Marianne lost no time in relating the catalogue of events she'd composed since Mike's last visit. The polt had been busy indeed. Later, Mike would refer to the events that transpired in the early hours of the following morning as 'Grim Saturday'.

Shortly after Mike had left on the previous Monday – the day when the polt had seriously frightened Marianne by sending her death threats – her brother Ian had accompanied the couple upstairs as they collected a few things together for their overnight stay at June's. It was 7pm. As the three stood in the centre of Robert's room, a carving knife whistled past them and clattered to the floor. It had gone missing from the kitchen earlier. As they came back downstairs – somewhat hurriedly, as you can imagine – the polt threw its favourite yellow nut at them. They ignored it, leaving it lying in the passage where it landed. The polt then picked it up again and threw it into the living room.

At 7.10pm, the couple needed to go back upstairs to retrieve something they'd forgotten. At the top of the stairwell, they found the African Lady' statuette which normally sat on a shelf in the hallway. They returned it to its normal place without comment.

Five minutes later, Marc went to sit down at the dining room table. The polt, of course, couldn't resist the temptation to pull the chair away from him as he sat down. Doing everything he could to maintain his dignity, and not let Marianne see that he was frightened, he picked himself up and sat down once again, this time holding on to the edge of the seat as he did so.

After another five minutes, as they walked down the garden path towards June's, the small, yellow plastic nut, so beloved by the polt, flew down the path after them.

After they returned home the next day, Marc received a phone call. A low-pitched, gravely voice simply said, 'I'm going', then hung up. He told Marianne about the call. Just then, her own phone beeped. She had an incoming text message. It said, *I'm back*.

For the rest of the day the polt was relatively quiet. It threw some more building blocks into the garden from Robert's room, but that was all.

The following day, Thursday 31 August, Marianne heard talking coming from inside the cupboard in Robert's room. She opened it and found one of her son's battery-operated motor cars fully lit-up. Reaching new heights of ingenuity, the polt started to speak to her through it. She just turned the toy off and shut the door.

Fifteen minutes later, at 7.15pm, Marianne and Marc were in the hall when something small and black wafted down slowly between them from the ceiling. It was a perfectly-cut square of polythene that looked as if it had been excised from a plastic bin-liner.

At 8.20pm, while they were being visited by a friend, the couple felt it was safe enough to let Robert play in his room. Almost immediately, he came back down the stairs and said that, 'something was banging on his bedroom window'. The couple decided to investigate. As they entered the hallway, they found one of their son's toy cars lying at the foot of the stairs. Robert said he had not put it there. They went upstairs, with Robert in tow, leaving their friend in the living room. Everything seemed in order. At 8.2 5pm, they brought Robert back downstairs. Marianne took

Robert into the kitchen to fix him something to eat. Marc joined their friend in the living room. As he sat down on the sofa, both heard a deep, male voice whispering over the baby monitor. They couldn't make out exactly what it was saying, but the tone of the voice frightened them. As the other monitor was in Robert's room, they decided to go back upstairs again to investigate. When they opened the door, they found that Robert's room had been trashed once again. The bed was in the middle of the floor, the blue chair had been placed on top of the matching table and other items and toys had been strewn around. Once again, they returned to the relative safety of the ground floor.

At 8.40pm, the couple and their friend heard strange banging noises emanating from the monitor. Marianne was too frightened to look, so Marc returned to the bedroom alone. Weird noises were coming from within Robert's toy cupboard. Marc took a deep breath and opened it. Robert's karaoke machine had been switched on, and was making a succession of bizarre sounds. Further, a large puddle of water was on the cupboard floor and was beginning to seep under the door. Marc's eyes set upon a toy fire engine belonging to the child. He extended his hand and touched it. It was dripping with water. Unnerved, Marc decided to go back downstairs and let Marianne know what had happened. As he left Robert's room, the cupboard door on the upper landing swung open violently, blocking his path to the stairwell. He pushed it shut and ran downstairs. At the bottom of the stairwell, he found that Robert's buggy had been moved.

Marc entered the living room and had just started to relate to Marianne and their friend what had happened, when they heard a noise in the hall. They all went to investigate. Robert's miniature 'quad bike', which was in a recess under the stairs, now had its headlights on at full beam.

Nothing further happened until after their friend had departed. Then, at 11.35pm, a small toy which Robert had been given free at a burger bar burst into life, playing the theme tune that accompanies TV adverts for the company.

Exhausted, the couple went to bed and, unsuccessfully, tried to sleep.

Earlier in the investigation, the couple told Mike and Darren that a lottery scratch card they'd purchased had gone missing. Three weeks later it had reappeared on the upper landing of the stairwell. Unnerved, Marc threw the card in the waste bin outside. To the couple's knowledge, the card was now buried under tons of waste in a municipal landfill.

At 6.20am on the day of the vigil, Marc had got up for work. He opened his wardrobe door and was astonished to see the same scratch card lying on top of a pile of clothes. Somehow, it had re-entered the house. He showed the card to Marianne, and asked her what they should do. Marianne suggested to Marc that he should tear it up. He did, but not before he made a note of the serial number. Should the card appear again, or at least one like it, they could positively identify which. Then, in front of Marianne, he ripped the card into little pieces and dumped them in the trash can in Robert's room.

Shortly after getting dressed, Marc went downstairs to fix breakfast. There, on the kitchen work-bench was the self-same scratch card. It was perfectly intact. Marc then decided that he would take the scratch card to work with him and dump it in a public litter bin in Newcastle. He did, but it reappeared in the kitchen again shortly before the investigation team arrived.

At 5.15pm, the couple heard a bang emanating from upstairs. They looked in Robert's room and found that the blue table and chair had been knocked over. Fifteen minutes later – Mike had noticed that the polt often acted in fifteen-minute cycles – the polt pulled Robert's bed into the middle of the floor and moved his storage units away from their normal position under the window.

Not long after, the couple, sitting in the kitchen, heard a loud rapping at the front door. They both went to see who it was, but there was no one there. Disturbingly, however, the door was unlocked and ajar. Mike had noticed that Marianne was fastidious about checking that her front door was locked, often giving the handle a cursory tug as she passed it on her way up or down the stairs. He had no reason to disbelieve her, then, when she told the investigators that it had definitely been locked just minutes earlier.

At 5.50pm, Marianne found the front door unlocked once again, and this time it was wide open. She shut the door and locked it, only to find it wide open again five minutes later.

At 7.15pm, the African Lady ornament had moved its position. It was still on the hall shelf, but facing in a different direction. As she went to place it back in its normal position, the headlamp on Robert's quad bike came on again. She turned it off and then went back to see to the ornament. It had moved yet again in the few seconds it had taken her to turn off the quad bike lights.

Marianne and Marc subscribe to satellite TV. At 7.40pm a message flashed on their screen reminding them that a programme was about to start. Neither Marianne nor Marc had programmed their 'digibox' to do this. The programme was titled *House of Horrors.*

At this juncture Marianne burst into tears and sent the aforementioned text message to Mike asking for the team to come quickly.

Just after sending the text, another reminder flashed on the screen, telling the couple that *Most Haunted* was about to start. The couple hadn't asked to be reminded about that, either. Other 'reminders' flashed on the screen for programmes and films that the couple hadn't programmed in – all of them were around the theme of hauntings or ghosts. Later, Mike was unable to find listings for many of the programmes as they hadn't even been scheduled to be broadcast.

The team members were taken aback that the poltergeist seemed to be in full flight, and had actually been pulling its wicked stunts literally minutes before they'd arrived. The question was, would it continue to show its hand now the team was there?

Marianne put the kettle on. Darren and Mike really felt for her. Despite her youth, she had been incredibly brave and was now determined not to let the polt drive her from her own home. Meanwhile, the team deposited their cameras and other surveillance equipment in the living room. This room was not exactly polt-free, but it was usually subject to far less activity than the rest of the house.

It was important that Marianne and Marc had time to bond with the team members before the investigation started, so for the first half hour everyone sat around the kitchen table drinking coffee and, as best they could, engaging in light-hearted banter. It worked well. For the record, the team consisted of Mike, Darren, Darren Olley, Mark Winter, Suzanne McKay, Julie Olley, Claire Smith, Glenn Hall and Mike's friend Daniel Jackson.

Eventually the team asked permission to set up their equipment in various locations around the house. In particular, they wanted to focus on Robert's room, where the bulk of the activity seemed to be taking place.

Darren gave the team what may best be described as a technical briefing. Organising vigils is his speciality. He dictated who would accompany who, instructed everyone present that no one – absolutely no one – was to go anywhere in the house unaccompanied. Even if anyone visited the toilet, then someone would go with them. The 'smallest room' would also be inspected both before and after they had relieved themselves.

To be honest, I feel that we need to carry out this investigation a little differently', he said.

Instead of having teams stationed permanently in each room, for the first part of the night at least I think we should all stay together in the kitchen. Periodically we'll then check the other rooms together.

Everyone agreed that this sounded like a good idea. The polt seemed to do its best work unobserved, except when it was cutting up Marc, that is.

Darren placed a log sheet on the kitchen table.

'Every incident must be logged here immediately after it happens. You don't have to go into great detail, as full reports will be written up later, but you must log the exact time and the essential details.'

Everyone in the house then made for the stairwell for a brief guided tour. Thankfully, the polt had decided not to disappoint them. On the middle landing, halfway up the stairwell, sat the

African Lady ornament which was normally situated on the shelf above the radiator in the hall.

Darren checked the time on his watch – it was 8.45pm – and made a log entry before the tour continued. By the time all the protocols had been correctly observed it was 8.53pm.

Darren went to the front of the group gathered in the hallway and proceeded up the stairs, followed by Mike and the others. All the doors were closed. He gently pushed open the door leading into Robert's room only to find it was blocked. Through a gap of approximately one inch, Mike and Darren could see that the trash can from Robert's room was hard up against the door on the inside. Both investigators judged that it would have been nigh impossible to pull the trash can towards the inside of the door from the outside before shutting it. Mike took a photograph, other cameras started clicking and, when the task of evidence-gathering had been dutifully completed, Darren pushed the door open further. When the gap was large enough, he reached in and grabbed hold of the trash can to prevent it falling over. He managed to move it to one side before opening the door fully.

As the team entered one by one, they noted that Robert's bed had been moved away from the wall. Robert has several pairs of slippers and training shoes which are usually neatly lined up at the foot of the bed. Darren asked Marianne if they were now in the position she'd left them in, but she said no. When she had last tidied up Robert's room she had placed the shoes in a perfectly straight row with the toes just under the foot of the bed. Now, several of the pairs had been pushed further under the bed although the heels were still just visible.

While the other investigators were familiarising themselves with the room, Mike checked the toilet. He opened the door, peeked inside and then beckoned to another investigator to witness what he'd just found. The ceramic pig was again sitting merrily on top of the toilet seat. More photographs were taken before the investigators joined the rest of the team in Robert's room.

At 9.05pm the team decided to look in the recessed toy cupboard in Robert's room to both familiarise itself with the contents and also to have a look at the now-infamous doodle-boards. It was also important to take as many photographs as possible so that after a room was officially 'locked off' the location of the contents could be matched against the photographs to see if any changes had taken place, no matter how slight.

Inside the cupboard, on the top shelf, was a small, battery-operated toy. It was, in fact, a model of Scooby Doo, the ghost-hunting cartoon character so beloved by children. The toy, when switched on, will periodically 'speak' by uttering a number of humorous phrases. It had been switched off, but the polt had seemingly switched it back on. As Mike looked at the toy – but before he had touched it – it spoke.

'Peek-a-boo! I see you!'

It wasn't just the fact that the toy had been switched on that bothered Mike; it was the seemingly sinister appropriateness of the words. He wondered if the polt was sending a message to the team: *I can see you, even if you can't see me.*

Then again, it may just have been a coincidence. Or at least he thought so, until the toy spoke again.

'Let's solve a mystery!'

'That's really spooky', said one of the investigators behind Mike. 'It's almost as if it knows that that's what we're here for.'

Darren Olley turned the toy off, and Mike put it back on the shelf. He then checked the doodle-boards on the off-chance that the polt may have left them a friendly greeting. Both boards were blank. The investigators then made sure that all battery-operated toys in the cupboard were turned off before Mike finally closed the cupboard door.

Next, the investigators set about 'tidying' each room. Any objects placed randomly were set in easily remembered positions and 'squared off' at right-angles. Any objects balanced precariously on shelves, for example, were made secure to prevent 'accidental spillage' after the room had been locked-off. Nothing was left to chance. More photographs were taken before the rooms were finally secured. If anything moved, then the team would immediately be aware of it when they next entered.

At 9.27pm, the team eventually returned downstairs. However, after just three minutes the investigators heard a brief but distinct noise over the baby monitor extension. They decided to check.

When the cupboard door was opened in Robert's room, they were intrigued to see that the youngster's karaoke machine had been switched on once again. Disappointingly, Scooby Doo decided to remain silent.

Darren picked up the doodle-boards which seemed to be exactly where Mike had left them, face-to-face. When he turned them over, however, in full view of the other investigators, there were messages upon them from the polt.

On the first board were the words, *STOP IT NOW.* On the second was the instruction, GO *NOW.*

Mike, who was now getting really cranky with the polt because of its extended persecution of the family, decided to write a message back. After numerous photographs were taken of the messages, he wiped them off. He then chose one of the boards and wrote, *WE ARE <u>NOT</u> GOING!*

'There; that should piss it off!' he joked.

There were a few nervous giggles from behind him and some-one suggested that pissing off such a violent polt was maybe not an incredibly bright idea. Mike's response was that the gloves were well and truly off now and they didn't exactly owe the polt any favours.

At 9.50pm, the paint-ball gun belonging to Marc was found in the kitchen cupboard. It had previously been located elsewhere. It was photographed and a log entry made.

At 10.20pm, more cameras were strategically placed in Robert's room. Mike set his digital recorder to the 'record' position and the room was locked off once again. The team then retired to the kitchen for more coffee and a general chat about their feelings so far. The general impression was that something decidedly strange was indeed going on in this rather unassuming little terraced house.

The recording equipment was allowed to run for exactly one hour before the team did a check. Mike decided to bring his digital sound recorder downstairs and play it back to the investigators. On the recording, the investigators can be heard leaving the room. However, on the playback a succession of weird noises can be heard long after it was locked off. These included taps, bangs, thumps, scraping noises and other bizarre sounds. In contrast to the sound of the investigators' voices downstairs, which are faint and muffled, the anomalous noises are sharp, loud and clear. There was unanimous agreement from those listening to the recording that they had definitely come from within the room and in close proximity to the recorder.

At 11.30pm, everyone was back in the kitchen. Things had gone a little quiet, and both Marc and Marianne were beginning to relax. The presence of the investigators was a comfort to them, as they knew that, whatever happened, they were not alone. Someone cracked a joke and Marc laughed. Just then, however, there was a sharp, singular tap from somewhere behind him. He stiffened and then leant forward.

Darren said, 'Did you hear that? What *was* that?'

Marc looked uncomfortable and the colour drained from his face. 'I think it came from behind me.'

He stood up and turned around. On the seat of the chair behind him was a small, plastic figurine of a policeman, approximately 1cm in length. It was one of Robert's toys. This was a policeman with a difference, however, as his head had been ripped off. In addition, his feet and the base upon which they stood had been twisted and generally mangled. Marc's hands had been in full view all the time, and it was difficult to see how he could have faked this. If there were still any lingering doubts that Marc *was* faking everything, before the end of the evening they would be well and truly dispensed with. The polt was only getting started.

Darren Olley replayed film footage taken in Robert's room at the same time that Mike made his digital sound recording. Many of the noises recorded by Mike were on his footage, too, although others curiously seemed to be missing.

At 12 midnight, the team ventured upstairs once again. A plastic shuttlecock was found on the second step below the upper landing.

One of the more peculiar incidents that took place during the investigation – as if they all weren't peculiar – occurred at 12.15am on the Saturday morning.

Marianne received a text message from a friend, Kara★, who knew that the investigators were going to Lock Street to carry out their all-night vigil. She simply wanted to know how things were going.

In jest, Marianne sent Kara a text message saying that the polt had finished with her and was now coming for Kara. Marianne may have miscalculated Kara's reaction, and was worried that her friend may take it seriously. To rectify matters she immediately sent a second text apologising for the first, and reassuring Kara that she was only joking.

Marianne waited for a few minutes, hoping Kara would call. She didn't, and so Marianne rang her. Kara was fine, although she admitted being a little nervous after receiving Marianne's spoof text message. Marianne ended the conversation by telling Kara she'd ring her later in the day.

That should have been the end of the incident, but it was not. Minutes later Marianne received a terse text message from Kara which essentially said, 'Look, this has got beyond a joke. That last message really *wasn't* funny.'

Marianne looked baffled. She sent a reply text to Kara, asking her to forward on the last text which Marianne had supposedly sent her. When it arrived, Marianne almost went into a state of shock.

The message read, 'I *am going to kill you. I am coming soon.*'

The investigators sitting around the table were baffled too, as they were all witnesses to the fact that Marianne had *not* sent a second text message to Kara.

'Look, you were all with me . . . you *know* I didn't send my friend that text message!'

Marianne rang Kara again and emphatically tried to convince her that she hadn't sent her that last, chilling message. Kara didn't need convincing, and seemed to believe that Marianne was not the culprit. Mike didn't need convincing either, and was happy to believe that the polt was up to its old tricks.

Marianne asked Kara if she wanted to talk to one of the investigators, someone who would verify that she hadn't sent that last message. Kara said no, it was okay, but she was going to switch her phone off before going to sleep. She didn't want any more text messages coming in the middle of the night, particularly if they contained death threats.

After Marianne disconnected the call, she buried her head in her hands.

'I feel terrible now. If only I hadn't sent that first text as a joke ...'

'Look', said Mike, 'It wasn't your fault. *You* didn't send that last message, and that's what counts.'

'I know', said Marianne, 'but she sounds really scared. You could tell by her voice.'

'Yeah ... we could hear it too', said Darren.

There is a curious postscript to this incident. The following day Kara claimed that she hadn't actually received the death threat, and that she'd made it up as a joke. This struck Mike as odd. Would Kara really have tried to wind Marianne up like that when she knew what hell she was going through? True, Marianne had sent Kara a spoof text message as a joke, but then *immediately* contacted Kara and apologised. Kara had ostensibly sent her 'joke' text message to Marianne and then left her to sweat right throughout the next day.

And then there was the fear in her voice. Those close to Marianne as she talked to her friend could hear Kara's voice, and she really *did* sound scared.

Mike still isn't sure about the text message. True, Kara claimed it was a joke, but the contents were so similar to the 'genuine' messages sent by the polt that another possibility had to be considered. Was Kara simply claiming that she'd invented the death-threat message to protect Marianne from further worry and stress? Was she simply playing the matter down and distancing herself from the entire situation? By claiming that the whole thing was a joke, she would effectively render pointless any effort made by investigators to talk to her.

Maybe the threatening message sent to Kara was genuine; and maybe, as Kara claims, it was simply one joke following on the heels of another. The jury, Mike thinks, is still out.

As the investigators continually checked and re-checked both the rooms and their equipment, Mike, Darren and Danny took a short break.

'You know', said Darren, 'this *has* to end soon for Marianne and Marc. They can't sustain this level of stress indefinitely. We're going to have to do something.'

Mike thought for a moment and said, 'Well, I've told Marianne that I'd be happy to come back and smudge the entire house again. We know Marc is the focus, so that helps. At least we're no longer shooting in the dark.'

Suzanne McKay asked Mike whether he could actually carry out the smudging there and then. Danny, drawing thoughtfully on his cigarette, added that there was probably no time like the present. Mike agreed, particularly in light of the fact that Danny had actually accompanied him on the investigation. Danny, with his knowledge of Indian lore and culture, knew exactly what Mike was thinking. He also knew the dangers involved, and was fully prepared to step into the arena of combat with Mike.

Earlier in the evening, as they drove to Lock Street, Danny had handed Mike a plaited leather strap. It had been blessed by a man who possessed 'big medicine', as the Indians say.

'Keep this with you tonight. You might need it', Danny had said. His words would prove to be truly prophetic.

'Have you got your medicine bag with you, Mike?' Darren asked, 'You know; the one with your smudging equipment in?'

'No, but I don't need it. I can smudge with a cigarette. It's all the same.'

Suzanne was intrigued.

'So what exactly are you going to do?'

'We're going to smoke the bastard out from its hiding place. Let's see how *it* likes being scared shitless for a change.'

CHAPTER THIRTY

Fear No Evil

Even in one's darkest hour, when friends turn into enemies, for instance, or when so-called loyal companions commit gross acts of betrayal, solace can be found in the noble acts of others. Sometimes, it is the direst of circumstances that brings out the best in people. The Lock Street poltergeist investigation had certainly proved the point.

To Mike and Darren the true heroine of the hour was Marianne. The polt had plunged this undeserving young couple into the middle of a nightmare, but in some respects she had borne the brunt of the polt's vindictiveness. It was she who had watched it slash her partner's back to ribbons, she who had endured the horror of having the polt take her sleeping son from his bed and hide him from her. It was she, when other women would have run 'screaming into the night' as Danny articulately put it, who decided on a matter of principle that she was not going to be forced from her own home by this sadistic entity. Marianne had demonstrated a degree of guts and tenacity possessed by very few people indeed.

Marc, too had proved his worth. He had endured much of the attack upon his home with so much fortitude that it had actually made several of the investigators suspicious that he could be engineering the whole thing behind the scenes. They were

wrong. Marc would prove himself to be extremely brave, especially during the final hours of the evening's drama when the polt
would launch its most vicious attack of all.

Mike admired Darren, too. He had organised the investigation
with meticulous thoroughness and told Marianne and Marc that,
like Mike, he was now in this till the bitter end. No matter what
the polt did – no matter how bad it might get – he'd be there.

Danny would also prove his worth. As the final scene played
out, Mike would come to see the true value of friendship. Both
would end up locking horns with the entity that had invaded
the lives of others in the most obscene way. Both would end up
battling an invisible but malevolent ego whose heart was totally
and utterly dark. The enemy was a creature without conscience,
a personage devoid of pity. It lived to feed and fed to live. Its only
purpose was to survive, its only interest its own, miserable per-
petuation. It would punish with venom anyone who stood in its
way, destroy mentally and physically anyone who dared to defy it.
This, then, was the true nature of the beast. To their eternal credit,
every member of the North East Ghost Research Team counted
themselves in for the ride. They had come in on the tail-end of
the investigation, but had agreed to help.

'Now we're in, we're in', one of them said.

Mike looked at Marc and said, 'I know this sounds crazy, but I
need to borrow eight pebbles from your garden.'

As if this wasn't puzzling enough to the others, Danny then
broke open a cigarette and carefully removed the tobacco after
peeling back the paper.

Eight pebbles and one handful of tobacco later, Mike and
Danny knew that it was time.

'You should know', said Mike, 'that it is likely to attack someone, and it is likely to attack them very badly'.

'Who will it attack?' asked Darren.

'I can't say. It could be Danny, Marc or me. I don't think it will
be me because I'll be safe in the centre of what we call a 'medicine
wheel'. It may go for Danny, because he's outside of the wheel and
vulnerable. He's also helping me, which will not exactly endear
him to the polt. On the other hand, it may go for Marc. He's the

focus, and he's the one it wants to own. My bet is that it will make
a play for Marc, but I can't be sure.'

Darren asked Marc if he still wanted to go ahead. There was no
hesitation in his voice when he said yes.

'I just want this all to be over for us. I want us to have our lives
back ... back to normal.'

'Let's do it, then', said Danny.

The scene for the showdown was, predictably, Robert's bedroom. It was here where the polt had cunningly allowed the
toddler to develop a relationship with the discarnate 'Sammy' – a
seemingly naughty but essentially harmless quasi-corporeal companion – and then, slowly and subtly, masqueraded as Sammy in
an attempt to ingratiate himself with his next victim.

As everyone walked up the stairs, Mike and Marianne were last.
Mike stopped momentarily and looked at her.

'Marianne, my stomach and chest muscles are going very tight.
Something is going to happen. I know that it's up there, waiting.
I can *feel* it.'

'I know', said Marianne. 'I can feel it too.'

Upstairs, the investigators set up their recording equipment
once again. Then, as best they could, they sat or stood on the
outskirts of the room so that Danny and Mike had as much room
to work as possible.

Mike chose the wide chest of drawers upon the south wall
to use as a makeshift altar. In Indian tradition, the south is the
place of the past, the way things used to be. It is also the place of
new beginnings; a place of childhood, innocence and joy. Mike
wanted the purity of the south upon his altar. Upon it, he placed
an ashtray, and in the ashtray a handful of tobacco that Danny had
pressed into his palm earlier. As the tobacco fell into the ashtray,
Mike sensed a change in the room. A tension was building. The
polt was watching, and it was not happy.

A thought struck Mike, and, considering the circumstances, it
was an incredibly optimistic one. Earlier, when the polt had left two
messages upon the doodle-boards which read, *STOP IT NOW* and
GO NOW, Mike had interpreted them as threats. He had believed
the polt was saying, 'Get out now while you still can', in effect.

But there was something wrong with this interpretation. Why would the polt warn them to desist? It had never given any warnings before.

'When your enemy gives you a warning he is displaying mercy. After all, he could attack you by surprise.' An old Indian had said this, and it was true. But Mike knew that this polt had no mercy in its heart whatsoever. So, whatever the messages were, they were *not* warnings.

Then it struck Mike like a revelation. What if these brief missives from the polt were pleas *for* mercy? Could it just be possible that the polt was saying *please* go now? Could it, in fearful apprehension of the forthcoming ritual, be asking us *please* to stop it now? Mike had a funny feeling that, at long last, they were beginning to push the right buttons with this evil, psychic gangster. They were provoking it into reacting; creating a set of circumstances in which it just couldn't resist showing its nasty little hand.

'Mike said to Darren, 'You know, it's clever, that polt, but it's not *that* clever'.

When he was ready, Mike took the eight pebbles from his altar and faced north. He prayed to the Grandfathers to guide him in the immediate future, to aid him as both he and Danny grappled with the polt.

Mike then turned to the east, the home of the sun, and began to lay down the medicine wheel.

For those who don't know, the medicine wheel is probably the most potent spiritual tool employed by Indians. It consists of four stones placed at the cardinal directions – east, south, west and north, in that order – and four intersecting stones in between the first four. The wheel – sometimes referred to as a Sacred Hoop – is the place where all worlds meet. It is a roadmap of one's destiny, a guide to the spirit traveller and an instruction manual for the uncertain. It is the junction where worlds collide and dimensions intersect. Significantly, it is also the place where the Grandfathers will offer protection to those suffering harm.

When laying down a medicine wheel, one always starts in the east. To Indians, the east is the place of the sunrise. It signifies enlightenment and wisdom; both good tools to have when grappling with an enemy you can't see.

Mike placed the eastern stone, then the southern, then the western and finally the northern. One always travels clockwise on the medicine wheel. Mike tried to explain these protocols to those gathered as he proceeded. Finally, he placed the intersecting stones in place. Now all he had to do was smudge the wheel and offer the correct prayers.

Mike walked around the wheel clockwise; he was sensing, feeling, picking up on the subtle spiritual energies that were already starting to gather. Every time he passed a stone, he sprinkled it with tobacco. As he reached the north, he paused momentarily and offered a prayer, asking the Grandfather Spirits to guide his actions. He also asked for two animal spirits – the Bear and the Wolf to join him in his task.

He returned to his altar and picked up a cigarette. He lit it, and then proceeded on his journey. He continually inhaled and then exhaled forcefully, watching intently as the sacred smoke billowed around the circle.

Speaking to those gathered outside the circle, he said, 'You may find that the temperature in the room rises dramatically. Do not be alarmed at this. It is merely the sign of the Bear as it enters the wheel. You may then notice that it goes cold as the Wolf enters. This too is to be expected. First, though, you will feel the heat of the Bear.'

Suzanne gazed at Mike and said, Actually, it's getting very hot in here already; *very* hot'. Darren, Mike noticed, was already wiping beads of sweat from his forehead with a paper tissue.

Mike then turned to Marc, who was standing just outside the eastern aspect of the wheel.

'It is *you* that the entity will attack. Endure it as long as you can. Then, when you can endure it no longer, step into the wheel and you will be protected. Inside the wheel you will be safe.'

Danny had bent down and was now resting on one knee. His eyes were staring intently ahead of him, focusing on something unseen and yet obviously familiar to him. Every feature of his face was edged sharply with intensity, every muscle taut with anticipation of the battle ahead.

Finally, Mike sat down in the centre of the wheel and crossed his legs. He carefully placed his left hand in his lap and then covered his left wrist with the fingers of his right hand. Slowly he lowered his head and began to pray silently. He was, although the investigators on the outside of the wheel didn't know it, journeying to a place far, far away.

At that precise moment the polt – unable to help itself, consumed with its own, dark ego – made its move.

Marc jerked involuntarily.

'My body is stinging again . . . like it did last weekend. My skin is burning.'

'Lift up your shirt . . . *now'* ordered Mike.

Marc did as Mike asked, and there were gasps of incredulity from the investigators. Long, angry weal marks were already starting to appear on his torso.

'Jesus . . . look at that!' said one.

'Oh shit . . . *oh, fuck!'* said another.

Cameras flashed in rapid succession, capturing Marc's agony as evidence. Short, staccato sentences filled the air. Are you getting that?'

'Quick ... we need a camera over here . . .' 'There – just there – focus on his chest.' 'Look . . . they're starting on his back, now.' 'My God ... the heat in here is *incredible!'*

Danny stood up, allowing his gargantuan frame to dominate the proceedings. He grasped Marc's left hand and filed his palm with tobacco. Then he leant forward, whispering. Marc said later that he remembered Danny whispering to him, but he felt disorientated and could not recall the words.

'Don't worry', said Danny. 'I wasn't talking to you. I was talking to *it*.'

By now, Marc's entire body was vibrating, as if he was being electrocuted. Danny pushed him into the centre of the wheel. Mike quickly lit up another cigarette and faced Marc, who was facing north. Seven times he circled the besieged man, each time smudging him with the sacred smoke.

By now, Marc's frame was literally covered with welts and scratches.

Danny picked up a bottle of fruit juice that Mike had brought upstairs with him.

'Here', he said to Marc, 'you might need this.'

Marc was somewhere else and no longer seemed to comprehend. Mike took the bottle and removed the cap before giving the juice to Marc. Dazed, Marc sucked greedily from the bottle as Mike held up his shirt for him. It was soaked with perspiration and he was becoming dehydrated.

The Bear spirit and the Wolf spirit were doing their part, now. The polt was exceedingly angry, but it was on the outside of the circle and they would not let it in. In its demented state, it wanted to lash out, but it was becoming increasingly frustrated. The Grandfathers were looking after Danny, the wheel and the spirits within it were protecting Mike and Marc. No one else mattered to the polt, now. It wanted to feed, but was being made to starve. It wanted revenge, but was unable to mete it out.

'Keep it up, you dumb bastard', whispered Mike. 'Go on . . . burn yourself out.'

Outside of the wheel, the investigators were sitting in awed silence. Stunned at the drama unfolding before them, they could do nothing but watch and gasp.

Mike placed a hand on Marc's shoulder.

'It's okay. It can't harm you. Now you're in the wheel it can't get at you. It can't scratch you any more, and the scratches you've already got will soon begin to fade.'

Mike smudged Marc again, and slowly he stopped shaking. As Mike had predicted, the scratches began to lose their angry appearance. They didn't disappear completely, but they faded substantially. At this point, there was a distinct change of atmosphere in the room. It was, one investigator commented later, as if 'something had left'.

Mike wasn't sure that the polt had left, but it had certainly been dealt a body blow. Marc seemed to be recovering as Mike spoke to him.

'Marc, can you see this wheel of stones that has protected you? Well, I've created another one just for you with the sacred smoke.

Think of it as a portable medicine wheel, if you like. You can carry it with you wherever you go. It will protect you. If you want, you can step out of the circle now. You'll be okay.'

Marc was hesitant at first. Inside the sacred wheel, he felt safe, protected. Then he took his first, tentative step outside. Nothing bad happened.

Danny placed a reassuring hand on his shoulder.

'How do you feel?'

'Knackered', said Marc.

Mike offered a quick prayer of thanks before disassembling the wheel. Everyone then went downstairs for a much-needed cup of coffee.

For a while, everyone sat around the kitchen table in silence, hardly able to comprehend what they'd just seen. Now, no one had any doubts about the existence of the Lock Street polt – or its power. Mike uttered a word of caution when Marianne asked if it might have gone for good.

'Maybe, but you need to remember that the ritual was not really designed to get rid of it; only to smoke it out of its hiding place and to protect Marc. It may have burnt itself out completely, but I can't be sure.

'The good thing is that the atmosphere in the entire house has lifted considerably. If it hasn't gone, it's very, very weak. Now we know how to press the bastard's buttons. If it does return, we now have a much better idea how to deal with it. Let's just see what happens.'

Marc smiled.

'You know, this probably sounds strange, but ... well, it seems more *roomy* in here now. It's as if the place is bigger.'

'Well, in a way it is', said Darren. 'Remember, something heavy and oppressive has been lifted away, even if it does turn out to be temporary.'

One by one, the investigators started to open up. For the most part, they expressed their amazement at what they'd seen.

But the polt hadn't quite finished. Like the leopard that can't change its spots, and the scorpion that can't change its nature, a polt can't stop being a polt. As long as it exists, it will do what polts do. Mike was not surprised, therefore, when it started up again after an hour's lull.

After finishing their coffee, the investigators decided to venture back upstairs. Everything was completely normal, and Suzanne again remarked upon how much 'lighter' the atmosphere was.

Everyone relaxed and started chatting. How strange, Mike thought, that smiles and laughter filled a room that, less than an hour ago, had been inhabited by a demented poltergeist.

Just then, there was a shout from the upper landing outside the room. The polt had been at work in the toilet. It had taken one of Robert's large, plastic building blocks, turned it upside down and filled it with water. It had then placed it neatly against the skirting boards in the north-east corner. The team quickly swung into action, once again filling the air with the whirs and clicks of their cameras. Someone went downstairs and made a log entry.

Within the next few minutes, the polt had moved the ceramic pig which had been placed in the bathroom. It had then turned the African Lady ornament around on the hall shelf, but not relocated her to another place.

Despite the re-emergence of the polt, Mike still felt extremely relaxed. These new shenanigans had not poisoned the much-improved atmosphere, and he voiced the opinion that it may just be engaging in a last act of defiance before going away to wherever polts go away to when they either retire or are forcibly made redundant.

The building block full of water in the toilet had drawn the attention of the investigators, leaving Darren, Marc and Mike in Robert's bedroom.

Mike was stretched out on a bean-bag type chair, while Darren sat on Robert's bed. Marc was sitting on the chest of drawers that Mike had used as a makeshift altar earlier.

Suddenly the chest of drawers shuddered and Marc jumped into the centre of the room, shaking. On the top of the chest, near the wall, was a red, plastic toy hammer that, only moments earlier, had been sitting in a storage box adjacent to the chest.

Darren was the first to react.

'Bloody hell! I saw that hammer in the storage box just a moment ago!'

Crucially, both Mike and Darren had seen it in the box *after* Marc had sat down. There was no way he could have placed it there himself.

After the customary photographs were taken, everyone went back downstairs. Marianne, who had understandably hoped that the polt had gone forever, was now starting to feel uncomfortably tense again.

'Don't worry', urged Mike. 'Remember what I said earlier. It was never in the game plan to get rid of the polt when we did the ritual. We only wanted to smoke it out. If it comes back, we can deal with it.'

At 3.40am, some of the investigators went back upstairs. Mike, Darren, Danny and some of the others remained downstairs in the kitchen where, fortuitously, the baby monitor from the living room had been relocated. At 3.50am, a loud, menacing roar emanated from the monitor, stunning everyone sitting around the table.

Darren raced to the foot of the stairs and shouted up to the team members who were in Robert's room. None of them had heard a thing. The chilling noise had seemingly come from Robert's room, but was only audible to those in the kitchen.

Two minutes later, one of Robert's Power Ranger toys appeared in the middle of the floor of his room while several investigators were still present.

Exactly one minute later, everyone left the room except for Darren Olley and Marc. They decided to check the doodle-boards for messages before joining the rest downstairs. They opened the cupboard door and picked up the boards, but they were still blank. Then, behind them, they heard a *thud*. A pair of toy binoculars had been thrown to the floor.

At 4.10am, Marianne went upstairs with two of the investigators. Suddenly, she saw from the corner of her eye a white, amorphous cloud near the stairwell. It was similar to one that had appeared in Robert's room weeks earlier, and it clearly distressed her. Mike, who was in Robert's room, heard her shout out from the bottom of the stairwell.

At this point Danny made a suggestion. In an attempt to prevent the polt from becoming active again, he urged the team to 'shut the house down'.

'We need to turn the lights and all the electrical appliances off and, as best we can, settle down for the rest of the night. Actually, I think we need to do that right now.'

Darren hurriedly organised the team into small groups. Two would stay in the living room and two in the kitchen. Two would camp out on the middle landing of the stairwell, which left Mike, Danny, Marianne and Marc. Mike suggested that the couple should simply go to bed and try to get some sleep, but Marianne was too unnerved.

'I want to, but I'm scared.'

Mike suggested that he could stay in the master bedroom with them if it would make them feel better, and she agreed. Danny, who seemed to have drawn the short straw, would spend the rest of the night alone in Robert's room. He didn't seem fazed by this prospect in the least.

Gingerly, Marianne and Marc crawled into bed. Mike positioned himself by the door and turned on his digital sound recorder. He also removed his camera from its case and positioned the forefinger of his right hand over the 'on' button. If anything happened, he wanted to be able to turn the camera on and take pictures as soon as possible.

As the various teams settled down in the darkness, sleep started to overtake them one by one. Within minutes, Mike could hear Marianne sighing softly, while Marc engaged in some gentle but rhythmic snoring. Eventually, Mike himself fell asleep.

Even though the house was quiet for only a short while, to Mike it seemed an age. He awoke after little more that half an hour to the sound of footsteps coming up the stairwell. He could also hear the sound of faint whispering. Two male investigators – he wasn't sure whom – were talking to each other.

Suddenly, the door leading in to the master bedroom swung open gently. Mike could barely make out the shape of Mark Winter. Mark had left his position on the central landing to investigate what sounded like floorboards creaking further up the stairwell.

'Mike, was that you?'

'Was that me *what?*' Mike whispered, trying not to wake Marianne and Marc.

'Did you just open this door?'

'The door right here, leading into this room?'

'Yes'.

'No, I thought *you* just pushed it open because you wanted to talk to me.'

'I never touched it. I thought you had *pulled* it open from the inside.'

Just then, Darren Olley stepped forward. He'd been standing behind Mark on the landing, just out of Mike's line of sight.

'Mike, Mark never touched the door. I can vouch for that.'

If it was the polt, then this last small act of paranormality may well have been its swan-song. The term swan-song derives from an ancient belief that swans sing just before they die, and generally refers to the last act in a drama, the last action in an almost-ended life. Mike truly hoped that this *was* the swan-song of a dying polt.

Slowly, as dawn broke, the investigators began to rise. Marianne arose with them, while Marc, exhausted after his ordeal, slept on.

Marianne made coffee, and then an impromptu debriefing was held. Marianne said that she felt more optimistic now that she had in a long time. She wasn't sure why, but the change in the atmosphere of her home had somehow given her confidence that an end to the nightmare was, at long last, in sight.

Danny said that the experience had affected him deeply. He praised Marianne and Marc for their bravery in facing up to the horrors of the last few months without cracking up completely.

Suzanne said that she was quite simply stunned by the things she had witnessed. The experience had, she said, taken her to a whole new level of understanding regarding paranormal research.

Darren confessed to being 'gob-smacked'. Mike had already witnessed the polt engage in a slashing spree upon Marc's back the previous Saturday morning, but this was the first time Darren had seen such a thing with his own eyes. He confessed that it had given him a new respect for the spiritual beliefs of Native Americans.

Darren Olley, initially a little sceptical after his first visit to the household, was now a believer.

'What I saw was just amazing. What can I say? I *saw* it.'

Claire, Glenn and Julie were of like mind, too. They didn't say much, but then again they didn't have to. Their faces said it all.

Suzanne collected the detritus that the team members had left upon the kitchen table during the night and disposed of it. The rest of the team collected their equipment and stowed it away in their respective vehicles. Eventually the time came for goodbyes to be said. It was an emotional moment.

Marianne thanked the team for everything. Mike said he'd ring her the following day to see how things were, but if the couple needed him, they only had to pick up the phone.

It was fully light by the time Danny dropped Mike off at his home, and Jackie was just rising. He had a hot bath and then, mercifully, dropped off to sleep while sitting on the sofa.

Had the polt gone for good? Only time would tell. If Marianne, Marc and Robert could get through the next few days without incident then there may just be grounds for optimism.

CHAPTER THIRTY-ONE

Afterwards

Two days after the vigil had concluded, on the morning of Monday 4 September, Mike rang Marianne. She sounded buoyant, upbeat. Nothing at all had happened since the team left the house.

'Nothing at all?'

Absolutely nothing; not a single thing.'

'Let's hope it stays that way. It's early days yet, but this has got to be a good sign.'

Mike said he'd ring the couple again in a day or two.

Both Darren and Mike had some serious thinking to do. Both had been forced to rethink the very nature of the poltergeist phenomenon, and both had a much-heightened respect for the awesome power that a polt could actually generate.

In some respects, it had been a test of their stamina as researchers. Neither of them had ever had to face anything remotely like this during their careers. During the debriefing, Danny had said he would be happy to come along on other vigils if the team needed a spare pair of hands.

Darren thanked Danny, but couldn't help laughing.

'Mate, after what we've seen here – and after what we saw you and Mike do last night – anything else would be a stroll in the park for you, believe me. They're *not* all like this!'

After Mike and Danny had carried out the Indian ceremony with Marc, the atmosphere in the house had lightened considerably. Marc felt much better, too. There was a feeling of optimism that the polt may, at last, have vacated the premises. Before long, however, those hopes were to be cruelly dashed.

CHAPTER THIRTY-TWO

I'm Back

On Monday 4 September, not long after Marianne had told Mike that everything had been quiet, she happened to venture into Robert's bedroom. The time was 10.15am. To her dismay, she found two cigarette lighters standing upright on a chest of drawers. Like two toy soldiers, standing guard over a wooden fort, they exuded a subtle but definite air of defiance. Marianne wanted to believe that Marc had left them there, or at least that there was a rational explanation for their presence. In her heart of hearts, however, she knew that there wasn't. Even if Marc had left the lighters in Robert's room – an extremely foolhardy thing to do, considering the child's age – why would he have stood them upright in such an odd fashion? Still, clinging to her hope, she decided to ask. Marc had no knowledge of the cigarette lighters or how they came to be there.

Marianne was dismayed. She really had hoped that the polt had finally drawn a curtain over its protracted and malignant stage show. Suddenly, she felt the need to urinate. With her mind in a whirl, she walked towards the toilet across the landing and opened the door. Tigger, the oh-so-inoffensive cuddly toy, was there to greet her. He was sitting on the seat, and in his hand he held a wicked-looking carving knife.

Somehow, Marianne managed to compose herself. She *wasn't* going to let this get to her. She remembered what Darren and Mike had said on numerous occasions; namely, that the polt was doing everything within its power to frighten her. If she could stop herself from becoming frightened, then she would have gained a small but significant victory. She returned Tigger to Robert's room, replaced the knife in the kitchen drawer and did her best to put the incident out of her mind.

For the next few days, the house in Lock Street was, essentially, polt-free. There were no noises, no objects thrown. No Tiggers in the toilet, no pennies on the stairs. Marianne, Marc and the researchers were keeping their fingers well and truly crossed that it had finally gone for good.

On Tuesday 12 September, Marc and Marianne arose and made breakfast. At 11am precisely he went into the hallway, which is not particularly well lit, even during the daytime. Almost on autopilot, he flicked the wall switch which turned on the ceiling light. Suddenly, he found himself being thrown backwards. His back connected with the wall adjacent to the kitchen door, and he sunk to the floor, stunned. When describing what happened to the authors, later, he simply said, 'I received a massive electric shock'.

There had never been any trouble with this light switch before. Later the couple had it checked out by an electrician who told them it was in perfect working order. He was also puzzled as to what had caused Marc to be electrocuted.

'It just shouldn't have happened. I can't understand it', he said.

Marc couldn't understand it, either. There were no burn or scorch marks on him, and neither were there any on the switch. It has worked perfectly ever since.

On Thursday 14 September, at 4.10pm, Marianne came in from work and found Tigger sitting in the blue plastic chair. The chair was not situated in Robert's room, and neither was it on the landing where the polt sometimes left it. It was in the dining area, downstairs, close to the patio doors.

Gingerly, Marianne went upstairs to check that the rest of the house was in order. It *was* in order, for the most part, except that one of Robert's Action Man figures was lying upon her bed. Marianne removed it and placed it back in her son's room.

At 4.10pm, Marianne started to descend the stairs. Just as she was about to step off the upper landing she heard a distinct rustling noise. It was, she testified later, 'just above and behind my head'. Instinctively she wheeled around and looked up, but there was nothing to be seen.

At 4.45pm, the polt took one of Marc's baseball caps from their bedroom and placed it in the bathroom. It then rested for a while.

At 6.40pm, it took the quilt from Robert's bed and placed it in the toilet. When she entered Robert's room with the quilt with the intention of replacing it on the bed, she found that the blue plastic chair had been moved from its normal position. Ten minutes later it turned its attention to the quad bike in the hallway and switched the headlight on.

Marc returned home shortly thereafter, and at 7.30pm the polt threw a toy camera belonging to Robert down the stairs. The camera bounced off Marc's back, causing him considerable pain.

At 5.30pm the following day, Marianne baked a pie. After it had cooled she placed it in the refrigerator. Nothing untoward took place for several hours, and the couple felt reasonably optimistic that the polt may have retired for the evening. They settled down on the sofa to watch TV

At 9pm, Marianne made a hot drink for both her and Marc. She opened the refrigerator and removed the milk, and later recalled seeing the pie. An hour later she again made a hot drink and, once more, removed the milk from the refrigerator shelf. This time, however, she noticed that the pie had disappeared. Marianne immediately saw that something was very odd about this situation. Firstly, neither she nor Marc had left the room for so much as a moment since she last made a drink. This meant that neither she nor Marc could have removed the pie. Anyway, she *knew* that she hadn't moved it. Robert was staying with his grandmother that night and wasn't even in the house, so he couldn't be the culprit. Besides, the pie had been near the top of the refrigerator, nearly 5ft off the ground; way beyond tiny Robert's reach. This left only Bounder the dog and Midnight the cat as suspects. The cat was removed from the frame immediately; too small, too weak. Bounder possessed the strength to open the refrigerator door, but not the dexterity.

Marianne started to search for the pie. It was nowhere to be seen, but what she did find was a tell-tale pile of crumbs on Bounder's blanket. The dog had *eaten* the pie, but what disturbed Marianne was the fact that the dog could not have *taken* the pie. Even though she knew that Marc hadn't left the living room, she had to double-check. This is human nature at work. We ask people if they did something, even though we know they couldn't have, for the same reason that we check our doors are locked even though we know we checked them just thirty minutes ago.

Marc was puzzled.

'Marianne . . . I've been in here with you all the time, watching TV. Anyway, why would I want to give Bounder your entire pie?'

Could Bounder have opened the refrigerator door – somehow – and pulled the pie from the shelf? Absolutely not, and for at least two irrefutable reasons. The pie was sitting on the second shelf of the refrigerator, nestling between two wire platforms. There is no way that the dog – even if he had managed to open the door; something he'd never done before – could have manoeuvred the pie out of its narrow resting place. Furthermore, even had he managed to do so, the pie dish would simply have crashed to the floor and broken. Not only was the pie dish not broken, it was still sitting in its original position *inside* the refrigerator. Even if Bounder had, through the process of some miracle, managed to remove the pie from the refrigerator, how did the dog then return the empty pie dish to the refrigerator shelf? Further, how did it get the pie from the fridge to its blanket without dropping so much as a crumb on the floor? There was only one explanation: The polt had removed the pie, but left the *pie dish* in place. It had then seemingly fed the pie to the no-doubt exceedingly appreciative dog.

For nearly two hours, the polt rested. Then, as the couple ascended the stairwell to go to bed, Marianne's mobile phone was found near the upper landing. Perhaps this was a warning that it was not going to let them sleep easily that night, no matter how hopeful they might have been.

At 11.50pm, the polt threw a small plastic toy at the couple as they lay in bed. It ricocheted off Marianne's shoulder before hitting Marc on the head. Five minutes later, a five pence piece was thrown across the room. As the couple sat bolt upright in bed, it yanked the quilt which covered them sharply, depositing it near the door.

Marc got out of bed and replaced the quilt. With not much hope of success, the couple again tried to get some sleep. For over ten minutes the polt held back, waiting patiently until the couple were lulled into a false sense of security. Then, deftly, it struck again.

At 12.05am, the couple heard noises coming from outside their bedroom door. There was no doubt in their minds what they were hearing; it was the sound of someone walking up the stairs.

Despite everything that Marc and Marianne had been through, one can imagine the thoughts that ran through their heads. They had heard the sound of the polt walking around their house many, many times. However, there was just a possibility that an intruder had broken in and, brazenly, was walking up the stairwell to rob them. Marc leaped out of bed, closely followed by Marianne. They opened the bedroom door and looked down the stairwell. The footfalls had silenced, now. There was nothing to be seen; nothing, that is, except three ornamental candles which had been removed from the window-ledge on the central landing and placed on the stairs. Oh, and the African Lady figurine. She had been placed on the stairs, too.

Wearily, as Marianne watched, Marc descended the stairs and put everything back in its proper place. Then, mercifully, the polt let the couple sleep – if only fitfully.

After dawn, Marianne and Marc rose. Nothing happened during the morning. The couple, who were thankfully not at work that day, simply rested. They were both physically and emotionally exhausted, and would have been quite happy just to spend the day in front of the TV. The polt, however, had made other plans.

At 12.10pm, it moved the ornamental candles back onto the stairs. At least, it moved *two* of them onto the stairs; the third one was missing. Marianne replaced the two candles she could see back on the window-ledge, and then went upstairs to see if she could find what the polt had done with the third. She entered her own bedroom, and was immediately hit with the odour of melted wax. The polt had been burning the candle – or at least, *a* candle. She searched the room and found nothing. Still, the smell persisted.

Next she checked Robert's room. No smell of wax in there, but Marianne noticed that the bedclothes had been moved. She went to straighten them up, but as she did so her hand collided with something hard beneath the quilt. She pulled back the bedclothes and stared. There was the missing candle. It was intact, but warm. It had recently been lit.

At 12.15pm, Marc ascended the stairs at Marianne's behest. She showed him the candle lying in Robert's bed, just where she'd found it. Then, suddenly, they heard a sharp ricochet. Marianne, out of the corner of her eye, saw an object bounce off the toilet door. She made to walk out of Robert's room to see what the polt had thrown, but was stopped in her tracks. Something slowly floated out of the bathroom at head height, from right to left. It was the African Lady. Gently bobbing up and down she sailed through the air before coming to land on the stairs. It was, Marianne said later, as if the figurine – or maybe the person it represented, who knows – had taken on a life of its own. Marianne was starting to dislike the figurine intensely – or at least, what the polt was doing with it.

Five minutes later, the couple found themselves standing at the foot of the stairs. Marc placed the African Lady back on the hall shelf, at which point a tearful Marianne started to voice her feelings about how much more of this insanity she could take. The polt had well and truly stuck the knife in. Now all it had to do was give it a little twist.

A thunderous bang came from Robert's room. Terrified yet curious, the couple went back upstairs. They tried to open the door to Robert's room but were prevented. The trash can had been placed up against the door from the inside. Marc poked his arm through the narrow gap, grabbed hold of the edge of the can and manoeuvred it out of the way. On inspection, the room looked normal. This meant that the couple had no reason to stay in the room any longer than necessary, so they left. As they shut the door behind them, the polt angrily tipped over the blue plastic chair. Perhaps not receiving the reaction it desired, the polt then hurled a ceramic mug full of fruit juice – left there by Robert – against the inside of the door as they closed it.

When the couple entered the kitchen, Marc noticed that his phone had received a text message. Again the polt announced, *I'm back.*

As if he needed to be told. Marianne, for her part, just dissolved into a pool of her own tears.

For two days the polt left them alone. It was not being merciful; the notion that it had any compassion for the family at all had long since been abandoned. The entity was now timing things to perfection, acting with clinical precision. It had become a master in the art of striking at the very second when its actions would have the maximum effect.

CHAPTER THIRTY-THREE

Roll Cameras

From the outset, Darren and Mike realised that the poltergeist infestation at Lock Street was very special indeed. The poltergeist phenomenon is real, make no mistake about it. For those who are forced to endure it – and believe us, no one would subject themselves to this sort of thing willingly – the experience is nothing short of a living nightmare. To some degree, though, all poltergeist cases are special. They are *all* upsetting, *all* confusing and *all* surrounded by inexplicable phenomena. Generally, the differences -on a case-by-case basis – can be measured both by the length of the infestation and the intensity of the symptoms. Some polt cases are brief and little more than annoying. Others, like the case at Lock Street, can come perilously close to destroying lives. A polt who hides your car keys in the bread bin is one thing; one that cuts your flesh to ribbons and sends you death threats is quite another.

From time to time, a case comes along which attracts international attention. The 'Enfield case', the Amherst case' and the 'Cock Lane case' are still discussed by researchers the world over, even though the infestations themselves have long since ceased.

What makes these cases so special? Firstly, the number of witnesses. When one person says, 'Something is opening and shutting my living room door during the night', then the response may be little more than a raised eyebrow. When fifteen people claim to have seen furniture sailing through the air, and the witnesses perhaps include a brace of police officers, a seasoned newspaper reporter and, say, a physicist from a nearby university, people will definitely sit up and start to take notice.

Another factor in 'special' cases is the nature of the symptoms. Mild symptoms, like the occasional moving of small objects, will only be of interest to the media if they can actually catch them moving on camera. More dramatic effects, such as physical attacks, throwing knives around and threatening to kill you by mobile phone text messages, make better headlines. Although one wouldn't like to think that the media are only interested in dramatic headlines, we all know that it's true. On the positive side, dramatic headlines at least attract attention to a case and give poltergeist research the oxygen of publicity.

A third factor that makes a polt case special is the duration.

Let us imagine that, tomorrow, you the reader suddenly found your home invaded by a polt. Let us also imagine that, for a space of twenty-four hours, you were subjected to the most intense symptoms of polt infestation imaginable: the moving of objects (large and small), noises, raps, disembodied voices, death threats, cold and hot spots, pools of urine appearing on floors, the breaking of crockery, physical attacks upon your person, the damaging of electrical equipment; the list goes on ad *infinitum*.

Finally, imagine that, for that twenty-four hour period, you did nothing but chase round after the polt and cleaned up its mess. With Herculean effort, you might just be able to keep up with the entity and rectify the damage. Then, when it was all over, you'd surely want to tell a close friend or two about your terrifying ordeal, right? But stop and think; although you've probably endured more poltergeistry in a day than most people have to put up with in a lifetime, where is your proof? The truth is that you *had* a polt, but you no longer *have* a polt. Researchers can no longer establish the veracity of your experience because, a) the evidence has been destroyed, and b) the polt has departed and cannot be studied 'in the now'. Bluntly, all you have is a single, subjective eyewitness testimony and pretty much nothing else.

Sadly, the majority of cases are like this: They are of short duration, transient, and normally consigned to nothing more than memory before researchers have a chance to get in on the act. In special cases, a protracted infestation allows investigators to study the phenomenon and draw some conclusions about its nature.

Finally, the average polt is extremely choosy about whom it mixes with. Polts are the world's greatest experts at wreaking havoc and yet leaving no trace of their presence. Some North American Indian tribes have a saying which goes, 'Walk the earth, but leave no footprints.' This maxim could have been tailor-made for the poltergeist phenomenon. An experient may be plagued by a polt to the point of distraction, and yet, every time an investigator tries to ascertain hard proof, the entity will fade into the ether and allow no one other than the experient to know of its existence. Unfortunately, in many cases the only people provided with abundant proof that their polt is real are the experients, and no one else may be inclined to believe them.

Despite the risk, involving the media in a case can have certain benefits. First and foremost, it can make a cheating 'experient' think twice before engaging in trickery. Fraudsters may not be so keen to carry out their fun and games if they thought that they might be exposed on national TV, or emblazoned across the front page of a newspaper.

Some researchers claim to be wary of the media and state forcefully that they would never work with them. On examination, however, their claims almost always ring hollow. For example, if it wasn't for the media, the poltergeist phenomenon would only be known to a relatively small cabal of experients, few of whom may even know of each other's existence. No books would have been published on the subject, no newspaper articles printed informing the nation of ongoing cases and investigations. Even the much-slated sensationalist Hollywood 'B' movies, which have often portrayed the polt phenomenon in a hideously inaccurate manner, have at least brought the subject to the attention of a curious public. If there were no media involvement, there would never have been any TV documentaries made on the subject.

Researchers who are opposed to dealing with the media often forget that it is media coverage of polt cases and investigations – and *only* media coverage – that has enabled them to take an interest in the subject themselves and learn their craft.

Some media-shy researchers are simply jealous of the handful of investigators whose own work receives public recognition. 'It should have been me on there/up there/ getting that', they whisper to their supporters.

To the authors, another positive side to media involvement is much understated.

For months on end, the principal investigators had to watch as a close, loving family unit was victimised, bullied, threatened, physically attacked and psychologically terrorised by a powerful, cunning and invisible aggressor. At the outset, the authors told the couple, 'Look, you're not the only ones. There are many, many people – ordinary folk, like yourselves – who are going through this on a daily basis. What you're experiencing is not unique, but someday it may prove to be an inspiration to others who are enduring the agonies of poltergeist infestation.'

It goes without saying that the authors promised from the beginning that they would maintain the confidentiality of the Lock Street family if that is what they desired. Even when Darren and Mike considered the possibility of writing a book about the case, they agreed that the family would be given the choice of either going public or remaining completely invisible. The primary concern of the authors was to resolve the problem that the family was facing. If helping the family meant shelving the idea of writing a book, then the book would be consigned to oblivion, plain and simple.

What delighted the authors was the way that the couple, Marianne in particular, could so easily see the sense in going public. On numerous occasions, she told Darren and Mike, 'Look, if doing something like writing a book helps others going through the same thing, just do it'.

Writing the manuscript was a relatively easy task. Marianne had kept meticulous notes throughout the investigation, and the researchers had accumulated hundreds of still pictures and dozens of hours of film and audio footage. An entire history of the case had already been logged in written, picture, movie and audio format. All the authors had to do, essentially, was write up the entire affair in chronological order.

By October 2006, the bulk of the work on the book you are reading now had been completed. Mike and Darren discussed the matter, and felt that the time was right to approach a publisher. Mike telephoned a colleague in the media industry and discussed matters with him. His advice was simple, clear and straight to the point.

'Look, the amount of evidence you've accumulated sounds impressive. When the story breaks, you're going to have the world's press beating a path to your door. You need to do this right, Mike.'

Mike was aware of this, of course. He runs his own media business and deals with the press on a daily basis. One mistake in the media world, and you get crucified.

'Oh, and don't forget the TV side of things. You need to get the TV rights sorted out first, even before the book. Things might go pear-shaped, otherwise. I've seen it happen.'

Mike has two good friends in the media world; Bob and Marrisse Whittaker of Orion TV. Orion TV make documentaries for a number of television companies, and had engaged in discussions with Mike before about the possibility of making a magazine format series on unexplained phenomena, strange mysteries, etc. Mike had produced a feasibility report on the idea and sent it to Marrisse, and a 'taster' pilot show, about haunted public houses, was filmed in and around South Shields.

Marrisse happened to ring Mike in early September, and invited both he and his wife to a housewarming party at their new home on the north east coast, close to the Scottish border. Mike later took the opportunity to tell Marrisse about the Lock Street case, and wondered if Orion would be interested.

'It could be, Mike. Maybe we could do a one-off documentary on it. I must admit it sounds extremely exciting. Let me talk to Bob and I'll get back to you.'

Both Mike and Darren had refrained from discussing either the possibility of a book or TV exposure of the case with the family.

It wasn't that they'd tried to hide their intentions – quite the opposite, in fact. Mike had mentioned his and Darren's idea of a book to Marianne more than once, but the time had just never seemed right to sit down and discuss the matter in depth. The idea of sitting someone down as distressed as Marianne or Marc and engaging them in glib talk about books, newspapers and TV rights just seemed horribly mercenary, callous, even. This family was *suffering*.

The concept of a TV documentary appealed to Mike and Darren. Like a well-written book, it could provide researchers with invaluable insight and also help others going through the misery of polt infestation. First, though, they'd have to talk to the family. Writing a book and keeping the principal players anonymous is one thing, but keeping people anonymous in a visual medium such as TV is a far more complex challenge. Besides, Marianne particularly hadn't seemed too bothered about her true identity being released in a forthcoming book, so it was just possible that she might be perfectly happy to go public on TV!

In Mike's experience, trying to hide one's identity is fraught with problems. If the story is newsworthy enough, there are a number of tenacious investigators out there who will move heaven and earth to discover the principal characters involved. Even years later, you may still be in their sights. Indeed, exposing the identity of newsworthy-but-anonymous persons is a lucrative sideline for reporters. Whenever you see the word EXPOSED in a newspaper headline, you can bet your boots that there's a fat cheque in it for the hack who was camped outside someone's door two or three days ago. Going public voluntarily takes much of the heat out of the situation. It demonstrates to the world that you have nothing to hide, and allows you a much greater degree of control. You can plan your exposure instead of having it forcibly thrust upon you. True, when the story hits the headlines your phone will never stop for a few days, but such harassment is usually of very short duration.

Who in the press now looks for the guy who sat on the Queen's bed? Who now remembers the name of the woman who threw an egg at Edwina Currie? Which of the paparazzi still tries to take surreptitious snaps of the guy who coughed out answers to his mate during a televised game show? No one, that's who; for its *all* old *news*. And if perpetrators are soon forgotten, then victims will receive even less attention. Better to let the media have their little soiree, and then you can relax.

Marianne wasn't interested in the politics of dealing with the media. Magnanimous as always, she simply wanted to help others. Mike gently broached the possibility of making a documentary on the case, and she was more than willing. He told the couple that, if they wished, he would put all the resources of his media business at their disposal and make the initial flurry of interest in the case as painless as possible. Mike had done this for other clients, and the results had been spectacularly successful. By funnelling all media enquiries through his own business, he could essentially act as a filter, steering away from the family all unwelcome attention. The next day, he spoke to Marrisse Whittaker.

Orion TV arranged to visit the family on Monday 18 September. The arrangement was that Bob and Marrisse would take their cameras into the couple's home on the morning and conduct a number of interviews. Also, if the polt decided to play, they would try and film the entity in action. At any point in the proceedings, if either Marianne or Marc felt uncomfortable about continuing, the project would be drawn to a halt and any footage that could be used in evidence would be turned over to Mike and Darren.

That morning, Darren arrived at Mike's office and the authors held an in-depth meeting about where they'd go from that point onwards. Marrisse and Bob arrived later, and the investigators showed them some of the more spectacular bits of audio and video evidence. When everyone had been fully briefed, the four set off for Lock Street.

Bob and Marrisse are experienced journalists, but they are not hard-bitten or callous. In Mike's experience they always put the interests of people first, and would never sell their souls simply to get a good story. From the outset, Marianne liked them. They made her feel at ease, and assured her that they could be trusted.

For a while, nothing untoward happened. Marc was at work, and wouldn't be able to join them. That meant that only Robert and Marianne were at home with the researchers and the people from Orion. Experience had taught Mike and Darren that although the polt would still usually become active when Marc was absent, it tended not to be so boisterous. They couldn't give Orion any guarantees that it would make its presence felt when Marc was out of the house; they could only live in hope.

Over coffee, Bob and Marrisse asked Marianne to relate her story. She did so openly, and with candour. Satisfied, Bob and Marrisse then asked if they could have a look around Robert's room.

With the exception of leaving a coin on the upper landing, the polt did little else of note. Bob set up his camera, and Marrisse worked out the shooting script.

'I think we should interview Marianne first', said Marrisse. 'Maybe she could sit on that chest of drawers over there.'

Marianne obliged, and, although she later said she'd felt extremely nervous, she actually appeared very relaxed and confident.

Marrisse began by asking Marianne to relate, in her own words, when and how she'd first become aware that something was wrong.

Initially, the interview went fine. The only distraction was provided by little Robert, who insisted on jumping around the room, laughing and giggling. It wouldn't have been hard to conclude that, in terms of latent energy, he was far better equipped than the polt. This didn't faze either Bob or Marrisse at all. In fact, Robert's presence actually demonstrated what a happy little child he was, and how *normal* the house was apart from the presence of the entity. The authors found it quite touching to see how Robert repeatedly cuddled his mother as she tried to focus on the interview.

Although Robert's presence added a certain warmth to the interview, it eventually became apparent that it would be impossible to conduct it successfully while the child was still in the room. Little Robert, the loveable scamp, was just too boisterous. Bob Whittaker took matters in hand, and decided to take Robert downstairs where a large box of toys stood in the living room as a distraction.

As they descended the stairs, Robert suddenly paused. He turned and stared at Bob intensely. Bob later admitted that there was something chilling about this episode. He described Robert's face as 'solemn'. Quietly but firmly, Robert said, 'I used to have a boyfriend you know, but he died.'

Then, without so much as another word, the toddler raced down the stairs excitedly to play with his toys.

'There was something about the way he said that … it just made the hairs stand up on the back of my neck', Bob commented later.

What did Robert mean by this? Was he saying that he, Robert, had a young, male friend – Sammy, maybe – who had died? Or was something or someone speaking through Robert – the spirit of a dead female, maybe, whose boyfriend had died in unknown circumstances? A bizarre thought, but nothing seemed beyond possibility in that polt-infested house.

It was at this point, back in the bedroom, that the polt seemingly decided to introduce itself directly. Robert's Bob the Builder toy was lying on the beanbag chair in the corner. Marianne had switched it off earlier. The polt switched it back on, and then waited. Robert, restless, ran across the room at one point and fell upon the chair. He didn't collide with Bob the Builder, but he hit the beanbag with enough force to shake it slightly.

'Hello, team! Can you learn it?'

Marrisse turned and stared at the toy, slightly startled.

'Don't worry', said Marianne. 'It does that all the time.'

'I think Robert might have knocked it, and that's what made it speak' said Marrisse.

'Mmmm …' said Marianne, 'Except that I switched it off earlier.'

During the rest of the interview, Bob the Builder kept voicing his thoughts on various and sundry matters. As did Scooby Doo, and another unidentified plaything in the toy cupboard.

Marrisse recalls, 'The first time that the Bob the Builder toy spoke was when Marianne mentioned Robert disappearing and then turning up asleep in a wardrobe. I distinctly heard the toy say, 'Ha, ha! Can you find me?' Later I was certain it said, 'Ha, ha! Can you find me?' again. After the interview I checked to see if the toy said that as one of its recorded 'set pieces', but it didn't. And yet, that's clearly what it seemed to say to me.

'I know for certain that the toy was switched off throughout the interview, because straight after, I sat on the beanbag and picked it up – it had slid down the back between the wall – I pressed the buttons. Nothing happened, so I switched it on myself and it did a little welcome jingle. The welcome jingle wasn't the line I heard.'

After Marrisse concluded the interview with Marianne, Bob – Whittaker, not the Builder – prepared to interview Darren in the living room. Cameras rolling, he asked Darren for his professional perspective on the phenomenon. Meanwhile, upstairs, the other Bob kept chatting away.

Mike asked Marianne if it was possible for Bob the Builder to speak repeatedly in this manner without someone actually depressing buttons on the toy's keyboard.

'Once you turn on the toy, it won't speak automatically. However, once you've depressed that button there – she pointed – it will come out with some little witticism or question every thirty seconds or so'.

From the researchers' point of view, the interesting thing was that Marianne was adamant the toy had been turned *off*. Could Robert have turned the toy on at some point, when the adults had been distracted? No, because Bob the Builder would have been speaking regularly from the moment they entered the room, and he certainly hadn't turned it on *after* the researchers had entered the room. Even when Robert had fallen upon the bean-bag, he hadn't collided with the toy or made any physical contact with it.

Further, Marrisse Whittaker checked the toy after the interview was over and has confirmed unequivocally that the toy was *not* switched on.

Like so many other incidents, it was a mystery; unless one accepted that the polt was responsible, of course.

After a while, Bob Whittaker came back upstairs with Darren. He then interviewed Mike, and both he and Marrisse were quite happy with the results of the day's work.

Bob and Marrisse probably left the house at Lock Street thinking that that was the end of the matter, at least until they needed to return and shoot some more footage. The investigators were thinking along those lines too, but they had reckoned without considering the ingenuity of the polt.

During the entire investigation, the researchers had seen a small but steady accumulation of evidence that the entity was able to touch the lives of those who, although not at the centre of gravity of the case, were in some way connected with it.

The polt had sent text messages to Marianne while she was talking to Mike on her mobile phone, even though Mike was at his house and Marianne was at June's. It was as if the polt could extend its range of influence far beyond Lock Street when it wanted to. Of course, this wasn't surprising if, as the researchers believed, poltergeists were person-centred and not place-centred. The enigma was that neither Marianne nor Mike was the focus in this case.

On another occasion, the polt had surreptitiously introduced a nameless file into Mike's computer in his office. As Mike found out later, this wasn't the only occasion the entity had done something like this.

Early in the investigation, Marianne had received a message from the polt on one of Robert's doodle-boards. It simply said, DIE. Marianne had photographed the message with her phone, and then attached it to a text message which she forwarded to a relative. Intrigued, he downloaded the image onto his computer and opened it with a photo-imaging programme so that he could study it in more detail. His curiosity satisfied, he then deleted the file and forgot about it.

Weeks later, Marianne's relative heard a loud *bang* come from the vicinity of his computer and went to investigate. Nothing seemed to be amiss, but, to his amazement he found the previously-deleted file opened and displaying itself on his computer screen.

And then there was the incident with Daniel Jackson and his mobile phone. The polt had dialled Mike's phone from Danny's mobile phone at 2am, even though Danny hadn't touched it. Bizarrely, he was driving past Lock Street at the time.

Mike and Darren also recalled the occasion when a heavy tome had dislodged itself from a shelf in his office and slammed against the floor with a terrific thud.

Soon, Bob and Marrisse would see just how far the polt from Lock Street could reach.

CHAPTER THIRTY-FOUR

Go Bich Now to Your Mam

On Tuesday 19 September, the polt returned. At 12.45pm, it took the three ornamental candles from the window-ledge on the central landing and stacked them on top of each other. It then turned its attention to the African Lady and made her disappear. She was later found underneath a roll of carpet which was being stored temporarily in Marianne and Marc's bedroom. Marianne picked up the figurine and turned to leave the room. Tigger was sitting on top of her wardrobe, staring down at her. It was, she said later, as if it was observing her every move.

Marianne descended the stairs, wondering what the polt was going to do next. She didn't have to wait long to find out. The baby buggy in the hallway rattled and jumped about as she passed it, as if being shaken by unseen hands. She called out to Marc, who was in the dining area, to come and witness it. Marianne's partner quickly walked through the kitchen, turned left and opened the door leading into the hallway. With stunning accuracy, the polt hurled a plastic toy down the stairwell at precisely the right moment and caught him on the chest. It bounced upwards, and only missed Marianne's face because she instinctively ducked.

At 1.15pm, the couple heard noises emanating from upstairs. They decided to venture up and see what, if anything, the polt had done. Sometimes, you see, it wouldn't do anything. It would just *sound* as if it was doing something, which messed their heads up even more. On this occasion it seems that the polt didn't want them to go upstairs. As soon as they tried to ascend the stairwell it started to throw toys at them from up above. They took the hint and retreated back to the relative safety of the kitchen.

At 1.34pm precisely, they again tried to ascend the stairwell. Still seemingly wanting its privacy, the polt threw more toys at them. Marianne and Marc removed themselves from the line of fire and took shelter in the small recess by the door which led from the hallway into the living room. At 1.37pm, another toy came hurtling down the stairs and landed by the front door. At the same time they heard another large bang from upstairs and, bravely it must be said, took a decision to ascend the stairs no matter what the polt threw at them.

'I will *not* be stopped from going where I want in my own home, Marc!' shouted Marianne.

When they opened the door to Robert's room, they could see that the polt was in a somewhat artistic mood and had, as was its wont from time to time, engaged in a bit of impromptu sculpturing. Using a toy guitar, a plastic hammer and one or two other bits and pieces it had created its own little piece of polt-art right in the middle of the floor. Not quite sure what the polt was up to, or where this latest tactic was leading, they went back downstairs. At 1.50pm, however, they heard yet another loud bang. Marianne, by this time, couldn't face another confrontation with the polt. Marc, with great fortitude, ventured up the stairs alone. He placed his hand on the handle of the door which led into Robert's room and opened it, not sure what to expect. He stepped forward, only to be thrown back with great force. As his body slammed against the toilet door his lungs were totally evacuated. He lay there for a moment, stunned, breathless and whining faintly, as Marianne ran upstairs to help him.

Carefully – very carefully – the couple attempted to enter Robert's room. This time the polt let them, for it had something it wanted them to see. The door to Robert's toy cupboard was now open. Normally that meant only one thing; the polt had left a message for them. This time was no different.

Marc picked up the doodle-board and held it up for Marianne to see: I *AM GO NOW THANK*.

If the polt was, in its decidedly inarticulate way, promising to vacate 42 Lock Street, then it was lying. No surprises there, of course; it had lied many times before. The couple was back downstairs within five minutes, not wanting to spend a moment longer upstairs than was necessary. As they re-entered the kitchen, Marianne glanced over by the patio doors. Action Man was sitting there, keeping watch.

Less than five minutes passed before the polt struck again, stacking the candles on the window-ledge overlooking the central landing into a tower formation. As Marc and Marianne moved from the living room to the hallway, the polt entered the kitchen and, at 2.03pm, left a bullet-shaped sponge on the floor beside one of the dining chairs.

Marianne had her notebook with her, and was desperately trying to keep her event log up-to-date. The polt did not make it easy. Three minutes after it deposited the sponge in the dining area, it dropped a toy plastic screw on the floor behind them. The polt, perhaps exhausted and needing to feed, then went quiet.

But not for long. At 2.37pm, another *bang* upstairs ended the uneasy truce. As the couple walked through the kitchen to the hallway, a small badge belonging to Robert came shooting over their heads and landed in the ashtray on the table. At 3pm, Marianne found a red, plastic screw in the hood of her top. Another *bang* resonated down the stairwell. As the couple ascended to investigate, the polt gifted them three stickle-bricks on the central landing. As they neared the upper landing, Bob the Builder began to shout, 'Hello Team!' in eager anticipation.

At 3.10pm, while Marianne and Marc were sitting on their bed waiting for the polt's next move, they noticed the bedroom door opening ever so slightly. Both felt that the polt was watching them, but they stayed put for what must have seemed an eternity.

At 3.42pm, the couple decided to return downstairs. Marianne visited the toilet first, only for the polt to begin rap ping loudly on the door. As quickly as possible she rejoined Marc in the kitchen. There she found a toy microphone on a dining chair.

Eight minutes later and another *crash* came from upstairs. This time it was so loud the floor in the kitchen vibrated. As the weary couple yet again ascended the stairs, they noticed that the candles on the window-ledge had been rearranged once more.

At 4.25pm, Marianne decided to venture upstairs alone. Later, she said that she'd been desperate to prove to the polt that she wasn't going to be intimidated in her own home. This made little impression on the polt, who promptly turned the karaoke machine on in Robert's bedroom. Marianne opened the toy cupboard and switched it off. As she bent down to flip the off-switch, she noticed that the polt had scribbled over the doodle-board. No message this time, just a petulant, insane scratching. As Marianne went downstairs to rejoin Marc, the polt threw a stickle-brick at her, which glanced off her back.

At 4.30pm – before the couple had been able to draw breath – the polt yet again removed the three candles from the window-ledge and placed them in a triangular constellation on stairs. It then moved up the stairs into Robert's room and wreaked havoc within the space of a few seconds. Following closely behind it, the couple entered the room to witness the devastation. The polt, for its part, had already moved on. Chairs had been tipped over, the table was upside down and the bed had been moved into the centre of the room. Two chests of drawers were in the centre of the room adjacent to the table, and the plastic storage units had been pulled away from the radiator. Numerous toys were also scattered about, and both Bob the Builder and Scooby Doo were screeching with delight.

Marianne, accompanied by Marc, went back downstairs to get her mobile phone so that she could take a picture. As they passed the candles on the stairwell, they noticed that the polt had moved them yet again. As Marianne – phone in hand, at the ready – and Marc ascended the stairs, everything seemed quiet. They opened the door to Robert's room, only to find that the polt, in less than a minute, had returned everything to normal. Robert's room was once again in pristine condition.

As they descended the stairs, Marc noticed that another candle had gone missing from the window-ledge. They found it behind the door leading from the kitchen to the hall.

At 4.45pm, the couple heard the karaoke machine, which was upstairs in Robert's toy cupboard, burst into life. No matter how many times they would switch off the battery-operated toys, the polt would simply switch them back on again.

As they entered the room to switch it off, Scooby Doo greeted them warmly.

'Peek-a-boo! I see you!'

Marc tried to shut the door to the toy cupboard, but the polt wouldn't let him. Almost effortlessly, it matched his efforts pound for pound and determined that, no matter how hard he pushed and shoved, the door to the cupboard was going to stay wide open. As he walked over to the door to rejoin Marianne, the goldfish tank on the nearby chest of drawers moved slightly. No one had touched it.

At 4.50pm, as the couple left Robert's room, the toilet door swung open violently. Marc, who by this time was almost becoming immune to the incessant itinerary of polt behaviour, simply pushed it shut and walked down the stairs with Marianne close behind him. He paused only to pick the candles up from the central landing and replace them on the window-ledge.

For the next fifty minutes the polt rested again, and so did the couple. Then at 5.40pm, a faint but distinct thump reverberated down the stairwell. Exhausted, the couple still felt bound to investigate. Nothing was out of place, but it had left a message on the doodle-board for Marianne. *GO BICH NOW TO YOUR MAM.* Marianne politely declined the polt's invitation, and decided to stay put. The polt wasn't pleased, but waited until 8.30pm to voice its annoyance.

There is a recessed cupboard in the kitchen with a full-length wooden door. The couple keep the kitchen waste bin in there, as well as numerous tools belonging to Marc and other household items. In the past, the polt had messed around with the cupboard door, repeatedly opening and closing it. That had been terrific fun, so the polt decided to play the same trick again. The cupboard door swung open sharply. Marc shut it. The door swung open sharply again, so Marianne shut it. The sequence was repeated numerous times, so eventually Marc tried something new. There was a bolt on the door, but which was rarely used. He snapped the bolt shut, hoping that it would prevent the polt playing its tricks. No chance. The polt simply slid the bolt out and opened the door again, and continued to do so repeatedly until precisely 9pm.

By 9.30pm, the polt had seemingly become bored with opening the cupboard door and decided to mess around with the phones. It rang the landline downstairs from the landline upstairs no less than four times. On the first three occasions there was nothing but silence on the other end of the line. It was as if the polt was taunting them, but not willing to make direct contact. On the fourth occasion Marc answered the phone, and distinctly heard the distinctive sound of Robert's bedroom door opening. Marc ran upstairs, only to find Robert's door closed. Everything seemed in order.

The polt desisted for the night. Marc and Marianne tried to watch TV, but were unable to concentrate. Slowly, surely and systematically the polt was grinding them down, wearing them away.

CHAPTER THIRTY-FIVE

Footsteps in the Dark

On Wednesday, 20 September, both Marc and Marianne were at work. The house was empty, and so the polt could not feed. They both returned home late in the afternoon, but the polt did not begin work straight away. It waited patiently until they had both eaten and had had time to relax. Then, at precisely 8pm, it began.

Robert was watching TV with his mother and Marc. The baby monitor was switched on, which meant that any noises emanating from his bedroom could be heard by whoever happened to be in the living room. Of course, there should not have been any noises coming from Robert's room at all at least by conventional standards, as there was no one in there to make any.

But then the whispering began. Slow, faint breeze-like noises at first, quickly escalating into something distinctly akin to a voice. Tantalisingly, neither Marianne nor Marc could make out the words. But it *was* a voice, they concluded. As the flow of indecipherable word-like sounds continued, the tenor of the voice changed. At first it had possessed a feminine quality, but now it was becoming deeper, more guttural. Then the voice stopped.

Several times during the next forty minutes this scenario was repeated. Then, at 8.40pm, the polt tried something new. Firstly, it spoke into the monitor again. The words were still indecipherable, but nevertheless they attracted the attention of Marc and Marianne almost hypnotically. Then the sounds coming over the baby monitor ceased abruptly, only to be replaced by the sound of heavy, masculine footfalls on the floorboards upstairs. Whatever – or whoever – had been talking into the monitor was now walking around in Robert's room. The difference this time was that Robert was in bed. For a split second, the horror of the situation made them pause. Then, just as they both made a mad scramble for the stairwell, a thunderous crash echoed from above.

'My God! The *bairn!*' screamed Marianne.

At the top of the stairwell the couple peeked around the corner, almost terrified to look. It had moved the child before, remember. What if it had *stolen* Robert again?

The door to Robert's room was wide open, but before they could see whether the child was still in bed the polt slammed the door shut viciously. It was on the inside, presumably with Robert. They were on the outside, essentially helpless. Marc, using all his strength, forced the door open. Robert was standing there, rubbing his eyes, dazed.

'What's wrong?' he said.

Marianne and Marc did not want to stay in the room a moment more than was necessary. They scurried downstairs with Robert and retreated to the living room. Unfortunately, Marc had to leave the house for a few hours. This meant that Marianne and Robert would be left alone. He didn't feel good about this at all, but there was nothing he could do. Marianne put on a brave face and told him they would be okay. By 9pm, Marc had left the house.

For exactly one hour the polt lay dormant, allowing Marianne to assume that it may just have retired for the rest of the night. Then, on the stroke of 10pm, the TV switched itself off. It seems likely that the polt did this for a very good reason. The volume on the TV had been turned up quite high. The polt wasn't happy about this at all. How could dear, sweet Marianne hear its ominous footfalls upstairs if the sound of the TV was drowning them out? Off with the TV, then. Almost immediately, the footsteps began; slow, heavy, determined. The polt – or at least some manifestation of it – was pacing up and down, back and forth, in Robert's room.

For good measure it began to throw things around. A chest of drawers here, a table there – typical, polty behaviour without a trace of decorum or good manners. Marianne, terrified, began to cry. She then picked up the phone and began to press numbers on the keypad in quick succession.

Mike was in the bath when his mobile phone rang. Jackie, downstairs, took the call. Sensing that it may have been either Marianne or Marc, Mike got out of the bath and quickly rubbed himself dry with a towel. Jackie opened the bathroom door and handed the phone in.

'It's Marianne . . . she sounds upset.'

Mike said hello, and then told Marianne to take a deep breath and explain what was wrong. Marianne sucked in air, and then rapidly ran over the evening's events.

'But Mike, its still here. It's stomping around in Robert's room, knocking things over. It's getting angry, and I'm frightened. Marc's had to go out for a few hours . . . what should I do?'

Mike, who could clearly hear the polt pounding around in the background, told Marianne to stay with Robert in the living room, but to leave the patio door ajar so that if things got too bad they could get out quickly. He then ordered a taxi.

Mike asked Jackie, his wife, if she would come with him.

'Marianne is on her own apart from Robert, and I think it would be good if she had some moral support from another woman.'

Jackie was happy to accompany Mike, and they arrived at Lock Street just before 11pm. Marianne was clearly distressed, even though the polt had gone quiet. Just for now, its footsteps no longer echoed down the stairwell and the floorboards no longer creaked. The TV set, however, was switching itself on and off repeatedly.

Jackie had never met Marianne before, and immediately did her best to cheer her up. Robert heard the voices, and, rubbing the sleep from his eyes, toddled from the living room into the kitchen. As usual, he had a huge smile upon his face. Mike couldn't actually recall ever seeing Robert without his smile. It was angelic.

Mike asked Marianne if they could check upstairs, and, natu-rally, she was happy to oblige. Mike and Jackie ascended the stairs, and everything looked fine. The polt had placed the blue plastic chair on top of the matching table, but that was all.

'It will probably go quiet now that Jackie's come', said Marianne, but the polt had other ideas. For almost an hour, nothing happened. Then the unmistakable sound of a coin hitting the floor reverberated through the kitchen. It sounded as if it had landed near Jackie, but a thorough search of the surrounding area revealed nothing.

At 11.55pm, Mike suggested that they take another look upstairs. They reached the centre landing and Mike noticed that the candles had been moved. Marianne put them back in their correct positions, although past experience had taught them that such gestures were futile. The polt could – indeed, had – repeatedly move them back again within seconds.

A cursory examination of all the upper rooms revealed nothing out of place.

'Be thankful for small mercies', Mike said with a grin.

The polt didn't seem to think this was funny. As they walked down the last few steps to the hallway, it threw a six inch nail after them. It shot past Jackie's head and clattered to a stop in the hall.

Marianne flinched and let out a sharp yelp. 'Wow! Where did that come from?'

'I think it's a little token from our friend upstairs', replied Mike.

Marianne picked up the nail and handed it to Mike. It was not like any six inch nail he'd ever seen before.

'It was coated in some highly reflective substance . . . intense black, like polished jet. It was brand new, without a scratch or mark upon it. It was so shiny, perfectly formed ... it was like no nail I'd ever seen. I know this sounds bizarre, but it actually looked *expensive,* as if it was too good to be hit with a hammer. For some strange reason the thought went through my mind that this was the 'Rolex watch' of the nail world. I really don't know how to explain it other than to say that this nail looked expensive, classy, exclusive.'

Mike handed the nail back to Marianne. Just then he noticed a small pile of nails near the front door. These were short, stubby nails, like tacks. Later, after Marc returned, Mike would show him the nails. The smaller, silver-coloured nails with the matt finish Marc recognised.

'They were in the loft. I left them up there.'

Mike then showed Marc the shiny, 'expensive-looking' six-inch nail.

'That's weird. I haven't a clue where *that* came from.'

For the rest of the evening, the polt was relatively quiet. It threw the odd coin, made the odd thump or bang, but that was all. Until Marc returned, that is.

Almost as soon as he walked in the back door, the polt leapt into action. The TV switched itself on, and the most bizarre sounds started to come from over the baby monitor. At first, it sounded like static, but it quickly altered into a harsh, grating sound that had an unmistakable science-fiction quality about it. Mike removed his digital sound recorder from its holder, switched it on and pressed the record button. Instantly, the sound got louder and Mike wondered if it was being exacerbated by interference from the recorder itself. He immediately switched it off and stood back, but it made no difference; the weird, harsh noise just got worse, and the array of lights on top of the baby monitor started to flash red and green wildly. At one point, the mixture of light and sound reached such a crescendo that Mike wondered if the damn thing was going to explode.

Suddenly, the sound stopped as quickly as it started and the lights went out. An almost eerie silence filled the room, and then Mike went to check upstairs. He walked into Robert's room. Everything was in order, except that Scooby Doo, which had been switched off, was now chuckling wheezily from within the toy cupboard. Mike switched him off again, just as he asked, 'Do you wanna solve a mystery?'

Mike was in no mood for jokes, and went back downstairs.

Marianne was making tea and coffee, while Jackie was making every effort to lighten her spirits. It was working. Despite the events of the evening, Marianne seemed to have relaxed considerably.

As the four sat around the kitchen table, chatting, the polt suddenly lost centre ground. To re-establish its position it threw a small basketball onto the floor. It bounced crazily across the wooden planking till it was adjacent to Jackie, and continued to bounce up and down as if being patted by an invisible hand. Mike told everyone to ignore it. The polt, perhaps seeing that its party trick was not having the desired effect, let the ball be and it suddenly fell to the floor, motionless.

After a sufficient amount of time had passed without any polt activity, Mike and Jackie returned home. As ever, Mike reminded Marc and Marianne that he was only a phone call away if needed.

The polt did not resurface until 11.40am the following morning.

CHAPTER THIRTY-SIX

Another Vigil

On the morning of Thursday 21 September, Marianne and Marc were sitting in the living room watching TV. They were relaxed, happy even, as Darren, Mike and two other investigators were coming later in the day. They planned to stay overnight. Marianne and Marc always felt better when the researchers were there. It was as if someone was in control of the situation, giving the couple a welcome respite from the need to continually figure out how to handle the next instalment of the nightmare.

Suddenly, the door which led into the hallway opened without any human assistance. Momentarily distracted by this, the couple glanced at the door and then at each other. Then Marc pointed to the sofa opposite. The African Lady figurine was sitting there in full view, having mysteriously appeared there without the couple being aware of it.

Marc picked up the ornament and carried it into the hallway. He replaced it on the hall shelf, and just happened to glance up the stairs. From his vantage point he could see that the candles on the window-ledge of the central landing had been moved yet again. As he ascended the stairs to rearrange them, he heard a thump come from the direction of Robert's room. On entry, he found that the two chairs had been moved into the centre of the room.

Half an hour later, Marc was again going upstairs when he heard footsteps on or near the landing above. Robert's room had been trashed yet again. The bed was in the middle of the floor, the storage units had been dragged several feet from where they normally stood and the blue chair was standing on top of the matching table. This time however, the polt had done something different. It had opened the left-hand facing window wide, as if to give the room an airing.

Marc set to and began the thankless task of tidying up the room. By 12.50pm he had finished, and came back downstairs. The African Lady had evacuated herself from the hall shelf and now took pride of place in the centre of the kitchen table. Marc picked her up without comment and walked towards the hallway. The quad bike headlight was on.

Another *thump,* another investigation upstairs. This time, the polt had left Robert's room alone. For a change, it had decided to trash Marc and Marianne's room instead. The mattress was hanging crazily off the bed base, and the bedclothes were scattered across the floor. The pillows were stacked up against a chest of drawers. Unfortunately, as Marc started to put things back into place, the polt *did* move into Robert's room and, silently, started its fiendish work all over again.

Within minutes, Robert's bed had been moved. His trash can had been moved. The Peter Rabbit music box had started to play and a candle from the window-ledge on the central landing was now balanced on the top of Robert's door.

Marianne had had enough, and decided that the family should go to June's house for a break. As the three fugitives from peace walked down the path of the back garden, Robert turned and waved.

'Who are you waving at?' asked Marianne.

'I'm waving at Sammy', answered Robert, cheerfully. 'Look, he's waving at me from my bedroom window. Can't you see him?' Marianne looked up, but could see no one. Marianne thought long and hard, and decided that she would not be forced from her home. The family went back inside. It was only 1.06pm; just sixteen minutes had passed since the polt had begun to trash the rooms.

As soon as they re-entered the house, Marianne checked upstairs. The polt had stacked the candles up in a tower formation on the window-ledge

At 1.12pm, the karaoke machine in Robert's toy cupboard switched itself on. Scooby Doo was wheezing, while Bob the builder was cheerfully welcoming the Team. Children – invisible children – were laughing and giggling. Sinisterly, the polt seemed to be flooding the house with an aura of barely bridled insanity. At times like this, Marianne observed, their home was 'like a mad house'.

At 1.30pm, Marianne needed a pen so that she could catch up with her events log. The problem was that her pen was upstairs, and she felt distinctly uneasy about venturing there to retrieve it. Still, she ventured forth anyway. She could not resist the temptation to take a peek into Robert's room at the same time. True to form, the polt had been at work again. She found the microphone unit of the baby monitor inside the toy cupboard and the karaoke machine in the middle of the floor. Bob the Builder was shouting, 'Hello, team! Can you learn it?' Not to be outdone, 'Scooby Doo started shouting, 'Scooby dooby-doo!' even though he was switched off. On the verge of emotional collapse, Marianne retrieved her pen and plodded down the stairwell. She found that the baby monitor in the living room had been unplugged, and was now hidden under a cushion on the sofa.

At 2.05pm, Marianne, sitting downstairs in the kitchen, detected the faint but distinct aroma of burning candles. This troubled her, as neither she nor Marc had lit any. The couple ventured into the hall, where the smell of burning candles was even stronger. They guessed, correctly, that the aroma was drifting down the stairwell from one of the upstairs rooms.

In Robert's room, they found the source. An ornamental candle, in a decorative tin, had been placed on the blue plastic table. It was lit, its yellow flame flickering in the silence. Marianne, doing her best to maintain her composure, picked up her mobile phone and activated the camera facility. She tried several times to take pictures, but for no ostensible reason the camera failed to work. Frustrated, she then attempted to use the video facility.

This worked perfectly, and she was able to capture several seconds of footage.

No one expected what happened next. From right of camera, a small ball of yellow light – something akin to a miniature sun – drifted towards the candle and, seemingly, penetrated the tin it stood in. Four seconds later the light exited the candle holder at the same spot and flashed briefly before disappearing at high speed in the direction of the bedroom door.

On analysis of the footage later, one can clearly see the light ball leave a 'vapour trail' – or at least, some kind of wake, as it heads towards the candle.

Later, Marianne would say that she felt the polt didn't *want* her to photograph the candle. And yet, it let her take video footage. Why? Did the polt actually *want* Marianne to capture on film the weird ball of light, something that would almost certainly not have happened if she'd simply taken still pictures? We can only conjecture.

At 2.20pm, Marc suddenly realised that his employers' ID card was missing. Concerned, he began to search for it systematically On two occasions, Marianne checked a drawer in the kitchen. On the first occasion she took a cursory peek inside, but on the second she ransacked the drawer completely until she was absolutely satisfied that Marc's ID was not inside. Unbeknownst to Marianne, Marc had also searched the drawer thoroughly too. After thirty minutes of fruitless searching, the ID card appeared: in the drawer, sitting on top of all its other contents.

At 2.30pm, while the hunt for Marc's ID card was in full swing, Marianne's mobile phone rang. It was her landline, which was still supposed to be switched to 'incoming calls only'. As she accepted the call, the line went dead. Seven times over the next thirty minutes the same thing happened, and each time the line went dead as soon as Marianne answered.

Things seemed to quieten down for a little while after Marc had found his ID, but at 6.20pm, the polt left two pictures on the doodle-boards. The images were simple, childish faces. As the couple stared at the pictures, Bob the Builder burst into life. He repeatedly shouted, 'Hello, team!', as if Marianne and Marc had just walked into a family celebration.

At 7.30pm, Marc found a candle which had been removed from the landing window just outside the living room door. Shortly afterwards, Marianne found two more images on the doodle-boards. One was a cartoon-style depiction of the devil, the other a squiggle which bore an uncanny resemblance to Homer Simpson. As Marianne removed the doodle-boards from the toy cupboard and stared at them, Bob the Builder – right on cue – shouted 'Hello, team!' Then, Robert's toy drill switched itself on and begun to whirr incessantly.

At 8.15pm, Mike, Darren and Suzanne McKay arrived at 42 Lock Street. Marianne told the investigators that the polt had been quite busy, so hopes were high that the evening would provide more evidence. Mark Winter, the fourth investigator, joined the team later. As things turned out, it didn't take long for the polt to swing into action after their arrival. Just as they set foot through the door, it moved a plastic garden chair several inches across the kitchen floor.

For the next fifteen minutes or so, things were quiet. Every room in the house was checked, and everything seemed to be in order. Then, just after 8.30pm, Marianne found Robert's new money box – a traditional piggy-bank, purchased to replace the previous money box that the polt had broken – in the hallway just outside the door that led into the dining room. Mike took some pictures, while Darren and Suzanne made plans for how the rest of the evening would proceed. Worried about a recent rash of burglaries in the area, Marianne and Marc had gotten into the habit of keeping Robert's money box in the loft. The polt had seemingly found their hiding place and taken the money box from it.

Mike decided to take another quick look upstairs to check that the doodle-boards were blank, ready for the polt to use should it be in the mood to communicate. In actuality, Darren and Suzanne had checked them earlier; something of which Mike was unaware. Mike asked Marianne to accompany him, as investigation protocols insisted that no one should be allowed to wander around the house on their own. As they ascended the stairwell, Marianne noticed that two, small plastic figures belonging to Robert had been placed in a ceramic bowl which housed one of the ornamental candles on the window-ledge of the central landing. If the polt hadn't been behind this, Mike would have been tempted to call what he saw cute.

As Marianne and Mike entered Robert's room, everything seemed to be in order. Then Mike heard a faint whining noise coming from the toy cupboard. He opened the door.

'It's the toy drill again', said Marianne.

Sure enough, the toy drill which had been switched off earlier was now whirring away merrily. Mike picked up the doodle-boards while Marianne deactivated the drill. There were two messages; on one board was the word, *HI,* and on the other the word *YOU.*

'Were these here before?' asked Mike.

'No – Darren checked them, and the boards were blank.'

Mike took more pictures. As he did so, Scooby Doo, sitting on the shelf, wheezed and chuckled.

At 8.42pm, the researchers found a five pence piece in the hallway. Almost simultaneously, Marianne spotted a second one lying on the stairs. The coins were photographed and then retrieved. Everyone then gathered in the kitchen to discuss these new finds. The polt joined the meeting too, and made its presence obvious by dropping a twenty pence piece onto the dining table beside Marc. It rolled onto the floor with a clatter.

Three minutes later, at 8.50pm, a two pence piece came hurtling from the kitchen and struck Marc on the left shoulder. He winced visibly. Mike photographed the red weal that appeared almost instantaneously. The coin came to rest by the kitchen radiator next to Mike's seat. It too was photographed, and added to a ceramic pot on the table which contained the ever-growing assortment of coins that the polt was donating. Darren suggested counting it.

Marianne poured the contents of the pot onto the table, and announced that the total was no less than £1.53.

Five minutes later, at 8.55pm, another twenty pence piece landed on the kitchen floor next to Marc. The strange thing was that neither Marc nor Marianne could figure out where the coins were coming from. A bowl of loose change on a shelf in the kitchen had long since been removed in a futile attempt to reduce the polt's coin-related activity, and the money in Robert's piggy-bank was all intact.

At 9.01pm, Darren decided to try an experiment. He spoke directly to the polt, saying, 'Thank you very much for the money. You're so kind. Now, can you throw something else?'

The request received an instantaneous and positive response, as yet another twenty pence piece landed on the kitchen floor next to Marc's foot.

At 9.07pm, Darren and Suzanne went upstairs to perform a routine check. Marianne accompanied them. The bathroom door, which had been shut firmly on the last visit to the first floor, was now wide open. Marianne walked inside and was astonished to find that the decorative panel attached to the bath had detached itself. With some difficulty the researchers put the panel back in place. They then tried to remove it again by hand. This also proved difficult, and could not be accomplished without making a considerable amount of noise. A cursory check of the other rooms revealed nothing untoward, so the investigators returned to the kitchen.

On the back of one of the dining chairs was a hooded, casual top belonging to Marianne. She removed it – perhaps to wear, perhaps to put in her wardrobe, the authors cannot recall – and another twenty pence piece fell from the hood onto the floor.

At 9.43pm, yet another twenty pence piece was thrown from the kitchen area. It hit Marianne's right foot and came to rest under the kitchen table. Mike took a photograph of the coin before it was added to the collection on the table.

At 10pm, the researchers went to check the doodle-boards again. They were still blank. At 10.04pm, Mike wrote a message on one of the boards for the polt: THANK YOU FOR PLAYING. WHAT IS YOUR NAME? He placed the board on the red wooden chair beside the toy cupboard, but as he did so he noticed that the message deleted itself.

'Strange', muttered Mike, as he wrote the message a second time. He again replaced the board on the chair, only to watch incredulously as the message again faded away before his very eyes. Several more attempts were made to leave the message, but each time the words would simply fade away within seconds. He gave up.

Everyone sat down in Robert's room, hoping that a change of environment might provoke the polt into doing something. The researchers and the couple chatted about everything from football to finances, but the polt didn't react. At 10.24pm, they found out why. A faint *thump* was heard from the vicinity of the bathroom. Instantaneously, everyone stood up and went to investigate. Yet again, the bath panel had detached itself. Mike immediately started filming. At first, the panel appeared to be motionless, simply lying against the bath itself. Then Marianne shouted, 'It moved! It's *moving*!'

As the researchers focused on the panel they could see that Marianne was right. The path panel *was* moving. Exclamations such as, 'Jeez!' and 'Bloody hell!' filled the air. The upper edge of the dislodged panel was gently undulating, almost as if it was *breathing*. Darren, ever the professional, immediately asked if there could be a draught coming from underneath the bath. Perhaps a gentle rush of air was causing the panel to move. Later, thorough investigation proved that there was no draught whatsoever.

Suddenly, the panel fell still. Mike, wanting to see more, exclaimed, 'Come on ... do it again ... do it again . . . *please*!'

The polt obliged, and once more the panel began to undulate weirdly. Darren urged Mike to readjust the position of the camera so that it was pointing directly down at the edge of the panel from above.

As the panel continued to undulate bizarrely, Marianne gasped in amazement.

On the footage of the incident, Mike can be heard to comment, 'You know what the freaky thing is ...? It's so *slow* . . . look at *that*!'

It is very hard to articulate exactly what sort of movement the decorative panel was engaging in. Certainly, the camera footage doesn't do it justice. Someone who wasn't present at the time, merely watching the footage, would no doubt wonder why those present sounded so excited. All the researchers can say is that the upper edge of the bath panel was visibly undulating in the most incredible manner.

In Robert's room, Marianne was (and still is) in the habit of placing all of her son's trainers, slippers and shoes in a neat row. The toes of each pair are placed just under the foot of the bed, the heels protruding outward. Lined up like soldiers, it is very easy to spot when one or more of the shoes have been moved from their original position.

During the course of the evening, the researchers noticed that Robert's footwear *had* been moved on several occasions. Of course, there could have been a rational explanation for this. It was indeed possible that a researcher, or perhaps Marc or Marianne, may have kicked the shoes inadvertently when entering the room. To rule out this possibility, Darren and Mike took several photographs of the lined-up shoes just before the room was cleared and 'locked off.'

At 11.18pm, the investigators entered the room and immediately checked the footwear under the bed. Without doubt, a number of shoes had been moved without human intervention. During the course of the evening the footwear was checked and photographed numerous times, and, on at least three occasions, Robert's shoes were not in their original position when the room was re-entered.

In addition to moving the youngster's shoes, the polt had also developed a fascination with fish. Robert has a fish tank in his room, a number of small, plastic fish ornaments and, to boot, a large stuffed toy in the shape of a fish. On entering the room, the researchers noticed that all of the above items had been moved and/or knocked over.

At 11.20pm, as the researchers descended the stairwell, Suzanne noticed that one of the candles on the window-ledge had been moved.

As everyone entered the kitchen, Marianne noticed that the screen of Marc's mobile phone was lit up. She picked the phone up and stared at it. As she did so, her mouth dropped open and her eyes widened. The polt had, seemingly been in the process of writing a text message when, presumably, the researchers had disturbed it with their presence.

The message simply said, *THE FISH BICH*. Marc had been upstairs with the researchers all of the time. Further, his mobile phone has a backlight which cuts out if no digits on the keypad are touched within a few seconds. This meant that the last digit – the 'FT in 'BICH' – must have been depressed just as the researchers – along with Marc and Marianne – entered the room seconds earlier.

The event was duly logged, and then the sound of footsteps upstairs caught everyone's attention. At 11.24pm, everyone ascended the stairs to investigate. Once again, the candles on windowsill had been rearranged.

Nothing upstairs seemed to have been disturbed other than the candles. Mike then suggested that it may pay the investigators to have a quick look in the loft, as the polt had occasionally made mischief up there, including removing Robert's piggy-bank. At precisely 11.30pm, Mike ascended a pair of stepladders and lifted up the hatch. He shone his torch around, but everything seemed to be in order. He paused to take two photographs in the hope that something – anything – might manifest itself. Just as he was about to close the hatch, he heard what distinctly sounded like a woman's voice. He was unable to make out the words, but was in no doubt that he was listening to the sound of a young female speaking. Over the space of thirty seconds or so, the voice faded away. Just as he closed the hatch cover, the door to Marianne and Marc's bedroom opened sharply.

Mike descended the ladder and told the others about the voice. None of them had heard it. At precisely 11.35pm, as they stood chatting, Robert's bedroom door opened in similar manner. An electronic whirring noise was emanating from the toy cupboard. Mike opened it, and saw a vivid pink light staring at him from out of the darkness. The karaoke machine had switched itself on. Fascinated, everyone went back down to the kitchen to await the polt's next move.

CHAPTER THIRTY-SEVEN

Candles and Cuts

Marc had been under a lot of stress, much of it hidden from the investigators. In an effort to control it, he had, unknown to Darren and Mike, begun to engage in frequent bouts of meditation.

There was no surreptitiousness on his part here; he had simply not thought to tell the researchers in detail exactly what form of meditation he was practising. In conversation around the kitchen table, Marc explained that he would simply light some candles, turn out the lights, sit on the floor, close his eyes and 'let himself go'.

'In fact', he said, 'its time for me to do some meditation now. Would you mind if I just went next door into the living room for a while?'

Absolutely not', answered Darren. 'Hey, it's your house, remember?'

Marc stood up and went into the living room. Every few seconds there would be a flicker of light shining through the glass door, indicating to the researchers that another candle had been lit. At this juncture something rather strange happened to Mike: He had an overwhelming urge to meditate himself, right there and then. Without any warning, he closed his eyes and began to journey to a faraway place. After a few moments, he was suddenly catapulted back to the 'here and now' and opened his eyes. At that very moment, Marianne, who had her back to the living room door, turned to talk to one of the researchers who had walked into the kitchen area. This put the living-room door just within her field of vision. Suddenly there was a sharp *crack,* and a twenty pence piece landed on the floor of the living room. It was clearly visible through the glass panel on the door itself. Marianne was the first to speak.

Clearly shocked, she stammered, 'That . . . that *coin* ... it just came from the other door leading into the hall. I *saw* it! It came *through* that door!'

If one looks through the glass door that leads from the kitchen into the living room, one can clearly see the door which leads from the living room into the hall, as the second door lies adjacent to, but at a 90 degree angle to the first. According to Marianne, as she turned her head she had looked through the glass door which leads from the kitchen into the living room, and seen the coin pass through the door next to it from the hallway into the living room itself. Whatever had happened, there was now a twenty pence piece lying on the living room floor. Within seconds, Darren opened the door leading into the living room and saw an obviously shaken Marc, still sitting on the floor, staring at the coin. Darren apologised for disturbing his meditation, quickly photographed the coin and made to leave. Mike wanted to photograph the coin, too, and walked over to the living-room door. When he entered he was puzzled indeed.

Mike had never before seen Marc meditate. He had assumed that the candles, often used as an aid to both meditation and relaxation, would have been liberally distributed throughout the room but in no particular pattern or order. He was wrong. Marc had laid them out in a perfect circle. Not wanting to disturb Marc's meditation, he quickly photographed the coin and left. As he closed the door behind him, something troubled him. He just couldn't work out what it was. It was, he remarked later, 'akin to an itch you can't scratch'.

At 11.58pm, while Marc was still meditating, Darren and Mike decided to check upstairs. Darren entered Robert's room first, followed by Mike. Darren had left the door to the room wide open, and Mike had no need to touch it as he entered. However, as he walked towards Darren, who was standing by the toy cupboard, he noticed Darren's face take on a distinctly startled appearance.

'Hey!' said Darren. 'Did you touch that?'

'What?'

'The door! Did you touch it?'

Without answering, Mike turned around to see what all the fuss was about. The bedroom door had closed behind him, but not with his assistance.

The two researchers scanned the room, noting that the blue plastic table and chairs had been moved. On inspecting the cupboard they noticed that the doodle-boards had been moved too. They had been in the bottom of the cupboard. Now they were perched on the top shelf.

By 12.03am, Marc was still in the living room meditating. The researchers had noted that both Marc's and Marianne's mobile phones were on the kitchen table in full view. Literally seconds later, the phones had disappeared completely. Battle-hardened though the investigators were, they were startled by this. Just as the polt had placed the African Lady figurine on the couch right in front of the couple, but without them seeing it, it had now done the reverse and stolen two mobile phones from under the researchers' noses.

Everyone began to search in earnest for the phones, but with no success. Mike then suggested that he ring Marianne's mobile from his phone. If it rang, then all the researchers would have to do is follow the direction of the ring-tone and it would lead them to the phone. Mike punched in Marianne's number on his own phone and waited. Several seconds went by, and then the muffled sound of Marianne's phone ringing pierced the stillness. Marianne walked over to the kitchen workbench and lifted up one of Marc's baseball caps. The phones had been placed underneath it.

Just then, at 12.10pm, there was a stifled yell from within the living room. Marc was standing in the middle of the circle of candles, obviously in pain. He was holding his hand to his scalp. The polt had poured hot wax from one of the candleholders over his head. Perhaps wisely, he decided to take a short break.

At 12.15am, Mike heard voices coming through the baby monitor. Marc and Marianne had heard these voices on numerous occasions too, but – irritatingly – could never make out what the voice was saying. It sounded similar, but not identical, to the voice he'd heard in the loft. There was nothing the researchers could do but venture upstairs to check.

Again, everything seemed in place in Robert's bedroom. However, one of the doodle-boards had a message on it. Bizarrely the message was not from the polt, but the message previously written *for* the polt by Mike – the same message that repeatedly deleted itself almost as soon as it was written.

Things then went quiet for over two hours. During the welcome hiatus in polt-related activity, Marc decided to resume his meditation. At 2.20am, Marc had a nose-bleed for no apparent reason. Then, without warning, scratches started to appear on his back. Instantaneously the researchers switched on their cameras and began to film the cuts as they manifested themselves. They were not as severe as on the previous occasions, but they were bad enough.

All the while, in the candlelight, Mike stared at the circle of candles. Eventually, he realised just what was disturbing him so deeply.

The candles were all set in small, ceramic dishes. However, at the four quarters of the circle there were no candles; only larger ceramic pots. One contained earth, another what looked like ashes. Mike realised that this was not simply a circle of light; it was a *spiritual* circle of some kind, different from an Indian medicine wheel, but not *very* different. Later, Mike asked Marc where he'd learned to perform such a ritual.

'I did some research on the Internet, and downloaded a few pages of information. I've found it really useful when I meditate.'

'What type of ritual is it?'

'I don't know, exactly. I think it's Chinese.'

What disturbed Mike was the fact that the polt had attacked Marc *within* the circle, not outside of it. Normally, the creation of any sort of spiritual wheel, hoop or circle has built into the instructions a protective element that prevents harmful entities or energies from invading it.

'Do you follow the instructions you downloaded perfectly?'
'Most of the time. Sometimes I forget the odd thing or two.' 'Have you forgotten anything this time?' Marc thought for a moment.

'Well, maybe. You're supposed to use salt, and sometimes I forget.'
'Did you forget to use salt this time?'
'Yes.'

For Mike, things were now beginning to fall into place. In many cultures, salt is seen as a highly protective substance that is extremely effective in warding off negative elements. Mike suspected that Marc, by forgetting to use the salt when he created his circle, had engaged in a ritual that would conjure up very strong spiritual energies while leaving him totally unprotected against negative energies or spirits that may want to make mischief within the circle's perimeter.

There was something else that needed to be taken into consideration, too. The polt had a voracious appetite, and Mike suspected that it could well be feeding on the energies that Marc was drawing into the circle.

'How long have you been carrying out this ritual?'
'For a good few weeks'.
'How often do you do this?'
'Three times a day. I find it really helps me relax.'

It dawned on Mike that Marc had, three times a day, effectively been handing the polt a veritable banquet of energy upon which it could feed. This would explain at least partially why the polt had managed to last so long without burning itself out, as polts usually do.

Mike explained to Marc that, in future, he should carry out the ritual as meticulously as the instructions demanded, and not cut corners. Mike then took the unusual step of entering the circle that Marc had created. He sat down, facing north, and removed from his medicine bag a shell and some incense. He smudged, and then waited.

Slowly but surely, Mike felt the presence of another personality within the circle. It was powerful, and it was not pleasant. Was it the polt? He could not say, but it was definitely someone or something that Marc did *not* want to mess around with.

Mike removed a number of stones from his bag and placed them in front of him. This drew an instantaneous reaction from the entity, which vacated the circle. There were still questions to be both asked and answered, but at least one of the polt's potential energy sources had now been closed down.

The following morning, the investigators left. Mike was worried about Marianne. Until the point when the researchers departed, she had seemed upbeat, confident. Then, just as they made for the door, she suddenly appeared crestfallen. As the car pulled away, Mike voiced his concerns to the others. They too were worried about Marianne. Mike said he'd ring her later that day to make sure that she was okay

As things turned out, Marianne was okay. Her sudden change of mood had been precipitated by a mixture of tiredness and frustration. To be honest, the researchers couldn't blame her. How she had endured such an obscene disruption of her life for so long was a mystery. She deserved a medal.

The following day was essentially quiet, and the couple decided to have a night out. Happy and relaxed, they returned home at 11.30pm.

Both Marianne and Marc had gotten into the habit of checking the premises whenever they entered. This was partly to satisfy Darren and Mike's need for accurate data, but also to help themselves. Returning to a 'normal' house helped them relax, at least a little, until the polt next struck. They ventured up the stairs, and experienced a brief surge of optimism when an examination of the toilet, bathroom and master bedroom revealed nothing untoward. Then they entered Robert's room, and their optimism vanished like smoke in the wind.

Robert's bed had not been moved, but it had two new occupants. One was Tigger, the other the pig-shaped table lamp that normally resided on the chest of drawers.

As Marianne and Marc had returned home earlier, they had stopped briefly to chat to two friends, Graeme* and Betty*. The couple invited Graeme and Betty round for a drink, and, even though the hour was late, they accepted. Shortly after Marianne and Marc found Tigger in bed with the porcine table lamp, they knocked at the door.

What Graeme and Betty made of the ongoing situation at number 42 Lock Street is hard to say, but there may well have been a degree of scepticism. Not that they didn't believe what Marianne and Marc had told them; but, in cases such as this, direct observation of the phenomenon with one's own eyes is often the only thing that will awaken people to the reality of the situation.

The couple's friends didn't have to wait long before the polt gifted them with all the evidence they needed.

Graeme was curious. He wanted to know more about the polt and its shenanigans. Marc suggested that they both take a walk upstairs. Marianne and Betty remained in the kitchen, chatting.

Perhaps it was because the polt had a new playmate. Maybe it just wanted to show off. Whatever the reason, it greeted Graeme's presence with an unprecedented show of force. First, it threw one of Robert's small, plastic fish at him. Next it threw Action Man. Finally, in a spectacular finale, it picked up Robert's red, wooden chair and hurled it across the room. At this juncture, a stunned and somewhat chastened Graeme decided to vacate the room. Marc, perhaps quietly satisfied that a point had been proved, followed hard on his heels.

When the two men had ventured up the stairs, Marc had left his mobile phone on the kitchen table beside the two women. At some point, when they were distracted, the polt pinched the phone. The entity was good at this. Over the months it had become a master at the art of moving objects during nothing more than a split-second diversion.

As the two men quickly descended the stairs, neither of them was aware that the polt had Marc's phone. Graeme became aware of it first, when the polt hurled it down the stairwell and caught him plumb-centre in the middle of his back.

Just before midnight, a loud bang sounded over the baby monitor. The polt then created a veritable orchestra of sound by activating Peter Rabbit, Bob the Builder and Scooby Doo all at once. Marianne and Marc had, of course, seen all this before. Graeme and Betty hadn't, and were probably beginning to question the nature of life, the universe and everything. The polt, for its part, let the quartet catch their breath. Then, at precisely 1.20am, it dropped a toy ambulance from the kitchen ceiling.

Eight minutes later, the kitchen table moved. At 1.35am, a Power Ranger toy fell from the ceiling in the kitchen. At least the ambulance had company.

Graeme and Betty finished their drinks off and journeyed home.

Between 2am and 3am, Marc engaged in some impromptu meditation in another 'candle circle' in Robert's bedroom. The room was vacant, as Robert was staying with Marianne's mother, June, for the evening. It also has more available floor space than the master bedroom. As the meditation progressed, the polt became more active. The door to the toy cupboard repeatedly flew open, the baby monitor kept switching itself on and off and Robert's collection of battery-operated playthings incessantly whirred, clicked, whizzed, beeped, talked and sang. Robert's bed moved, then the bedside lamp switched itself off. Weird noises started to filter through the baby monitor, such as heavy breathing, indecipherable whispering, static and -bizarrely – the distinct sound of someone chewing on a crisp, crunchy apple.

Some might argue that the polt was getting stronger because Marc had engaged in the ritual, once more providing it with a rich food source. However, as Marc was now making great efforts to carry out the meditation ritual correctly, and not leave himself open to spiritual attack, Mike thinks that this is unlikely. More likely, he believes, is the possibility that the polt was doing everything in its power to *dissuade* Marc from carrying out his meditation. After all, what good is a relaxed, happy focus to a hungry polt?

CHAPTER THIRTY-EIGHT

Housewarming

On Sunday 24 September, Bob and Marrisse from Orion TV held their housewarming party. Mike and Jackie arrived in the delightful little coastal town where they lived at around 1pm. Guests were asked to arrive around 2pm, so the couple had an hour or so to spare. Mike took some photographs, and then they went into a local public house that had a legendary reputation for being haunted. They had a soft drink, chatted to the manager and then made their way to Bob and Marrisse's home, just two streets away.

Marrisse Whittaker had prepared a magnificent buffet, and before long their large house was thronging with media colleagues, friends, family and neighbours. The party was a huge success, and the time simply flew by. Before Mike had had the opportunity to talk to even half the people he had earmarked, the night was over. Marrisse showed Mike and Jackie to their room, on the second floor, which was spacious, cheerfully decorated and had an *en suite* toilet and shower. Before long, both Mike and Jackie were deeply asleep.

Mike woke up at 4am. Nevertheless, he felt refreshed and just lay in bed thinking about Lock Street. Suddenly, there was an enormous crash from the floor above. Jackie, who was just waking herself, despite the early hour, sat bolt upright in bed.

'What was *that?*'

'I don't know', replied Mike, 'but it frightened the living day-lights out of me.'

Jackie giggled, and said, 'Maybe Bob fell out of bed!'

At around 5.30am, Mike got up, dressed, took his laptop downstairs and decided to do some work on the book manu-script. He set up the computer on the large table in the dining room, plugged in his aerial for wireless internet access and tried to check his e-mail account. The connection failed, and he tried again. Still no connection. He checked Bob's router in the hall-way, and it was switched on and fully functional. He shrugged his shoulders and decided just to get on with the book. He could check his e-mails later.

At 7am, Jackie woke up and switched on the light in the bath-room. Suddenly, all the electrics on the second floor went off. She shouted down the stairs for Mike, but there was little he could do. He had no idea where the fuse box was, and he was a stranger in a very large house. Jackie managed as best she could, and then came downstairs to make a cup of tea for her and Mike.

Bob and Marrisse joined them shortly thereafter, and before long they were all digging into several rounds of toast. Jackie men-tioned the problem with the electrics, and Bob said he would check it out later.

'It's strange, actually', said Marrisse. 'During the night the lights in our room went on and off several times.'

And then there was that weird light . . .' said Bob.

'Oh, I forgot to mention that', Marrisse continued. 'During the night there was this really loud bang . . . '

'We know; we heard it' interjected Mike.

'Well, when we looked we saw this really weird, green light. It started on the wall and then hovered over the lamp. I've never seen anything like it. It was just hovering there, shining down . . .'

Later, Marrisse related to Mike some further recollections about that evening:

> The crash in the room was so loud, I thought that at the very least a gigantic wardrobe had fallen over, if not the chimney fallen in. The crash was very close and came quite clearly from

the side of the bed Bob sleeps on. It was weird, because it actually seemed to come from right next to my ear.

As you know we don't have any free-standing wardrobes in that room and nothing at all had fallen over. The bedroom is directly above the one you were sleeping in.

After that, Bob went back to sleep, but I was wide awake and facing the bedside light again on the side of the bed that Bob sleeps on, when this green light appeared. It appeared quickly, just as though a light had been switched on. It was like an intense, green beam of light shining out of the wall above the lamp.

The source was about two feet higher than the lamp on the wall and funnelled out, wider at the bottom. I would describe it as 'pea-soup green' in colour.

The thing is, there is absolutely no natural light source in that corner of the room. Also, there were no cars passing by or lights on across the road that could have caused it, and the blinds were down. The light stayed there for around a minute, or maybe a little less, and then it started to move up the wall. It moved upwards for a distance of three feet or so, and then stopped. Then it went out just as though someone had switched it off. Interestingly, the lights either side of our bed also blew when the first floor lights did.

Earlier in the investigation, Mike would have dismissed out of hand any idea that the polt could have extended its sphere of influence to such a degree. Had Marc been in the house, he could have understood it; after all, he had been the primary focus, and even if the polt had now disconnected itself from him and was roaming free, it still seemed to be at its most active when he was around. But Marc wasn't in the house. As on previous occasions, the poltergeist was once again flexing its muscles beyond the confines of 42 Lock Street.

CHAPTER THIRTY-NINE

Flushed with Blood

On Tuesday 26 September, the polt started work relatively early. After eating breakfast with Marianne, Marc decided to take a bath. As he relaxed in the warm water, meditating on the day ahead, he heard someone walk across the landing and enter the toilet. He knew that this couldn't have been Marianne, as she was downstairs watching Robert. Marc got out of the bath, wrapped a towel around himself and investigated. Everything looked completely normal. Before returning to the bathroom, however, he decided to take the opportunity to relieve himself in the toilet. Marc urinated into the bowl and then, never thinking for one moment how devastating his next action may be, depressed the flush mechanism. The flush worked perfectly, except that what came out of the cistern was not water, but something that looked very much like blood. Hardly able to believe the evidence of his eyes, he yelled for Marianne.

Marianne, alarmed at the frightened tone in Marc's voice, ran up the stairs as quickly as she could. To her credit, and despite the sight that met her, she managed to retain her composure. Marc, still stunned, walked into the bedroom and sat down.

'I need to get this on video for Darren and Mike', she shouted. 'I'll have to get my phone from downstairs.'

Instinctively, Marianne pulled the toilet door shut just before she descended the stairs to get her phone. Almost before her hand had let go of the door handle, the polt flushed the chain. She pulled open the door instantaneously, astonished to find that it had removed every trace of blood from the bowl and replaced it with clean, fresh water.

Even for the polt, this was reaching new heights of creativity. Never before had it put on such a spectacular display of theatrics. This was reminiscent of the best (or, if you like, the worst) Hollywood 'B' movies. What next? Green slime oozing from the walls? Vampire bats? Or how about a few giant, flesh-eating slugs that crawl up from the basement and devour everyone before taking over the planet?

And yet, it had happened.

While the couple tried to work out what their response should be to this latest intimidation tactic, Marc noticed that his mobile phone was missing. At 12.20pm precisely, he found it. It was lying in the middle of the floor in the master bedroom. The screen was lit, and when Marc picked the phone up he could see that the polt had seemingly been in the process of writing a text message. Whether the message was finished or not, we cannot say. To whom the polt would have sent it is now unknown, although the obvious recipient would have been Marianne. The message, in chilling simplicity, simply read, *RIP*.

Marc walked downstairs and showed Marianne the polt's latest piece of electronic penmanship. He then deleted the unfinished (or at least unsent) text, and placed his phone on the kitchen table. Within seconds the polt had filched it. Later, Marc would find it secreted away in the recess under the stairwell. At around the same time, Marianne decided to bring her event log up-to-date. Or she would have done, had she been able to find her notebook. Unfortunately, the polt had pinched that, too, although it did return it later.

Ten minutes later, at 12.40pm, the couple heard a large *bang* emanating from upstairs. They investigated, as usual, but found nothing out of place. Just before they were about to descend the stairs, however, Marianne's eye was caught by something on Robert's bedroom wall, just beside the door. To her horror, she saw that the polt had writ large the letters RIP with a blue ballpoint pen.

What disturbed Marianne about this more than anything was that this act had no precedent in the polt's previous behaviour. Up till that point, the polt had never done anything that would actually frighten young Robert. True, it was unlikely that the three-year-old would have understood the significance of the letters RIP, but it had taken another step closer to breaking what had become an almost unwritten rule; *Marianne and Marc were fair game, but the polt had to leave the child alone.* In the past, the polt had lifted Robert out of bed and, on one occasion, hidden him in Marc's wardrobe. This was frightening for the couple, but Robert himself had slept peacefully throughout the entire experience. Even though a multitude of strange phenomena had taken place in Robert's room – more than anywhere else in the house, in fact – the polt had been meticulously careful never to expose the child to anything frightening. All the truly sinister stuff – bunny rabbits with box-cutter blades, toy ducks getting their throat cut – had either taken place when Robert was out of the house or had been discovered by an adult before Robert could see it and become distressed. Now, however, by writing the letters 'RIP' on the child's wall, the polt had inched just that little bit closer. Marianne, deeply disturbed at this latest incident, telephoned Mike. He said he'd come straight over.

At 1.15pm, Marc and Marianne heard a *thump* emanating from upstairs. They ascended the stairwell cautiously. The toilet and bathroom were in order, as was the master bedroom. Robert's room seemed okay too, except that the door to the toy cupboard was slightly ajar.

'Marc, I'm sure you shut the cupboard door before we went downstairs the last time.'

'I *know* I did', Marc responded.

As he pulled open the cupboard door even wider, so that he could see inside, the first thing that caught his attention was a large, blue toy-box lid. This had gone missing weeks earlier, and despite searching the house – and loft – extensively, it had never been found. To be honest, the lid is so large it would be almost impossible to miss if one was really determined to find it. Nevertheless, the polt had hidden it successfully until that point.

Marc pushed the rediscovered box lid to one side so that he could see whether the doodle-boards had been written upon. They weren't there. Then, without warning, both boards came shooting off the top shelf of the cupboard where the polt had secreted them. They clattered to the floor unceremoniously. Both doodle-boards were blank, and one was now damaged.

Just as the doodle-boards were falling to earth, Marianne noticed something strange indeed about the lettering that had been scribed on the bedroom wall. It had changed. The letters were essentially the same – in exactly the same place, even – but now parts of them had been scored over with a sharp instrument. Perhaps the polt was making a point of some kind, but its terrifying, unpredictable dementia made it impossible to know what.

Marianne drew Marc's attention to the change in the graffiti. His curiosity piqued, Marc simply replaced the doodle-boards in the cupboard and walked over to where Marianne was standing.

After examining the scored-over letters, Marc then told Marianne that one of Robert's doodle-boards was now damaged. Marianne asked Marc to show her. Dutifully he walked over to the cupboard and pulled at the door handle, fully expecting the door to open. It didn't. Marc pulled at the door with all of his strength, but it would not budge. He even tried placing his foot on the frame to get extra leverage, but to no avail. Then, suddenly, the polt relented. The door flew open and Marc, caught off guard, flew back across the room and collided with a chest of drawers before finally sprawling over the floor.

As the door to the cupboard opened, and while Marc was pirouetting backwards, the two doodle-boards ejected themselves from the toy cupboard forcefully and followed Marc in his wake. They came to rest beside him, and in front of a horrified Marianne.

As Marc recovered his composure, the couple noticed that the doodle-boards had been utilised once more by the polt. On one was the now familiar acronym *RIP*. On the other was a neatly drawn pentangle in a circle. Both images distressed Marianne deeply. The letters 'RIP' for obvious reasons, the pentangle because Marianne believed it was some sort of 'satanic symbol'. Marianne photographed the two boards and then placed them back in the cupboard. The polt, however, was not finished with them.

At 1.50pm, the doodle-boards were wiped clear by the polt. Marianne and Marc found them lying outside of the cupboard. What the polt had being doing with them in the interim, no one knew. Marianne placed the doodle-boards in the bottom of the toy cupboard and shut the door.

Merely moments later, she heard a bang from within. With a mixture of both dread and anticipation, Marianne walked over to the cupboard and opened the door. The doodle-boards were now on the top shelf, and even though they had been wiped clean, the pentangle symbol had returned to the doodle-board that was still operable. For good measure, the polt had switched the karaoke machine on and activated Scooby Doo, who, as usual, asked Marianne if she wanted to solve a mystery. She declined to answer, switched Scooby off for the umpteenth time, replaced the doodle-boards in the bottom of the cupboard and went downstairs just as Mike arrived. It was precisely 2.10pm.

Almost as soon as Mike entered the kitchen via the patio doors, the polt started to play tricks, intimidate. Marianne had brought the baby monitor into the kitchen area so that while she was working she would be able to hear any untoward noises in Robert's room. As Mike removed his coat, Scooby greeted him over the monitor's speaker. Mike responded positively to Marianne's offer of a coffee, switched on his video camera and went straight up the stairwell – alone. As he ascended, Scooby shouted over the baby monitor, 'Mike!' Marc said later that Mike's name was spoken as an exclamation, in the way one would shout the name of a long-lost friend you hadn't seen in ages.

Before Mike had even reached the upper landing, his camera had switched itself off. He switched it on again, and resumed filming. The camera switched itself off again, and did so several times more even before Mike had managed to enter Robert's room. Eventually the polt relented, and allowed Mike to film. A faint, barely audible *thump* came from within the toy cupboard. Mike opened it. On examination of the footage later, the camera suddenly pans hard left as Mike instinctively wheeled away from the cupboard entrance. Without warning, the two doodle-boards shot out of the cupboard from the vicinity of the top shelf and hit Mike forcefully on the head. Then, their energy and trajectory spent, they simply fell to the floor. Mike carried on with his cursory investigation, and then went back downstairs to finish his coffee.

Mike was annoyed that his camera was playing up. He switched it on again, and the phrase, 'WARNING! BATTERIES EXHAUSTED!' flashed on the screen.

'Damn!' said Mike. 'I wonder if the polt's done that'. These batteries were fresh just this morning. I've only just put them in the camera.'

Marianne had another pair of AA batteries that had never been used and were still in their wrapping. Mike thanked her and inserted them in the camera.

'WARNING! BATTERIES EXHAUSTED!'

Mike couldn't believe it, and groaned in frustration.

Marianne had another idea.

'Mike, I've got a set of batteries in my Sky remote control. Why don't I take them out, and you can try them?'

Mike was glad to try anything. For the third time that day, he inserted a different pair of batteries into his camera.

'WARNING! BATTERIES EXHAUSTED!'

Mike was just about to give up, when he remembered that, several weeks earlier, he'd placed two batteries in a small, zipped pouch in his bag. He checked, and they were still there. He placed them in his camera, and they worked fine. The significance of this incident is something that we will return to later in this book.

At 2.35pm, Mike asked Marianne if she was still managing to keep her event log up to date. Marianne said that she had, but was worried as the polt had pinched her notebook earlier.

'I hope it brings it back', she said dejectedly.

Just then, there was a faint but distinct rustling noise in the kitchen, like a sheet of newspaper being crumpled up in one's hands. Marc looked at Mike and knotted his brow, as if to ask, 'What the hell is *that?*' Marc, who was sitting at the kitchen table opposite Mike, craned his neck and stared over towards the kitchen workbench. Without comment, he stood up and walked over. There, in full view, was Marianne's notebook. The polt – on command, or at least as requested – had given it back.

In the north-east of England, specifically on Tyneside and Wearside, people are passionate to the point of fanaticism about football. If you're Geordie you'll be a Newcastle United or 'Toon Army' supporter, but if you live on the banks of the River Wear you'll support Sunderland. In the county of Tyne & Wear, you're either black-and-white or red-and white, it's as simple as that, really. Those reading this volume should not underestimate the strength of feeling over this issue. There are Geordies from Tyneside and 'Mackems' from Wearside who laugh at the cultural differences and sporting rivalries between the two areas and don't take them too seriously. The worst they'll do is engage in a little teasing and light-hearted banter. With others, feelings run far, far deeper. On both sides of the fence there are people who hate their Geordie or Mackem 'enemies' and would rather die than set foot in each other's stomping ground, except when there's a derby match on of course. Marc, who hails from North Tyneside, is a dyed-in-the-wool Newcastle fan – always has been, always will be. Robert is a loyal Toon Army fan as well, despite being only three years of age. The first time the researchers met him, he was wearing a miniature version of the famous black-and-white Newcastle United top.

On the outside of Robert's bedroom door was a poster of the now-retired Newcastle United captain, Alan Shearer. Shearer, a solid family man who has never been embroiled in any of the scandals that attach themselves to many other players, is a perfect role model for kids; no drugs, no drunkenness, no wild parties and no debauchery. Shearer will almost certainly go down in history as England's greatest ever exponent of 'the beautiful game' and one of the nation's finest sporting ambassadors. Because Shearer played for Newcastle, of course, Geordies love him.

Maybe the polt was trying to make a statement of some kind – it's really hard to say; but at 2.50pm Marc was shocked to find that the poster of Alan Shearer on Robert's door had been defaced. Both Marianne and Mike were right behind him as he made the discovery. The polt had repeatedly scratched a sharp object of some kind back and forth across the poster, essentially severing the former Newcastle captain's head from his body. The polt had decapitated Alan Shearer, and the couple were furious.

Marianne was the first to articulate her thoughts.

'My God ... if that isn't sacrilege, what is?'

Mike, trying to take the edge off the situation, said, 'It wouldn't have been so bad if it had been a Sunderland player!'

But the deed had been done, and nothing could reduce the impact of the desecration. Marc looked angry enough to explode.

'God, I don't believe it. Not only have we got a poltergeist in our house, it's a *Mackem* to boot!'

If the almost religious reaction to the polt's actions strikes you as over the top, then try living in Tyne & Wear for a while. Only those who aren't Geordies will be able to invest any humour into the situation. Nevertheless, this was the first time that Mike had seen the desecration of a sporting icon used to create feelings of anger by a hungry polt. Mike checked inside Robert's room, shut the door and followed the couple down the stairs.

At 3.10pm, Marc and Marianne again ascended the stairs with Mike. The investigator tried to open the door to Robert's room, but could not. The polt had jammed the trash can up against the door from the inside. Mike had caught the incident on film, and was glad. As the three went downstairs yet again, Marc found a pebble on the upper landing.

Marianne made tea, and was clearly upset by the new lows to which the polt was sinking.

'Mike, I'm concerned about that pentangle thing it drew on the doodle-board. I honestly thought it was some sort of Satanic symbol.'

'Well, its not – although people have used it as such. The important thing is not so much what the symbol is or means, but rather *what you think* it is – or means.'

'I don't understand.'

'Remember; the polt is trying to frighten you. If it knows that you have bad feelings about that particular emblem, and that there are negative thoughts in your head about what it may represent, then it will use it against you. To be honest, if the polt could frighten you by drawing a picture of Casper the Ghost, it would. It's not what the symbol means that's important, but what you think it means and whether it frightens you. The polt is just trying to push your buttons again, Marianne.'

'So, if I hadn't have had negative feelings about the pentangle symbol, the poltergeist wouldn't have used it to try and frighten me?'

Almost certainly not; it wouldn't have worked, so there'd have been no point to the exercise.'

'Mmm ...' said Marianne, deep in thought. 'I see what you mean.'

After chatting for a while, the trio decided to have another check upstairs. They walked through the kitchen and turned left to enter the hallway, when, suddenly, Marianne let out a shout.

'Mike, look! There's a fifty pence piece on top of the kitchen door!'

And, sure enough, there was. The distinctive lip of the coin was poking over the horizontal edge of the door. It was balanced precariously, but Mike wanted to know if it was possible to shut the door fully without dislodging the coin. He closed the door completely, but the coin stayed put. There was just enough room between the door and the doorframe to accommodate the coin without knocking it off.

'It could have been there for ages, for all we know' said Mike.

Marianne retrieved the coin and followed Mike and Marc up the stairs, and almost instantaneously drew his attention to something.

'Here, Mike ... feel this.'

'Mike took the fifty pence coin from Marianne's hand and was amazed to find that it was really hot. This was nothing like the tiny amount of warmth that Marianne's hand would have generated in the few seconds she had held it before handing it over to Mike. This coin was *hot*.

For the next hour or so, the polt merely engaged in a few juvenile party tricks.

At 4pm, the polt dropped a red pencil from the kitchen ceiling. It clattered to the floor, making everyone jump. Almost at the same time, the polt pinched one of the batteries which Marianne had lent Mike from the kitchen table. It wasn't returned until later.

At 4.06pm, a stickle-brick was put in Marianne's coat pocket by the polt. Exactly two minutes later, Mike decided to do a final check upstairs before leaving. The polt had scribbled on the door of the master bedroom with a red pencil, presumably the one that it had sent careering to the kitchen floor earlier. It had also scribbled on the chest of drawers in Robert's room.

On leaving the upper landing and descending the stairwell, Mike, Marianne and Marc were amazed to see that the polt had been at work, quite literally behind their backs. Huge arcs of Marianne's lip-gloss had been smeared on the stairwell wall, and the broken remains of the lip-gloss container were lying on the central landing. The candles on the window-ledge had been moved again, too.

As they descended the stairs, the patio doors, which had been locked, suddenly unlocked themselves. The handle arced downwards, as if pushed invisibly, and the right-hand (facing) door flew outwards violently. Mike wondered if the polt was gently reminding him that, at least as far as *it* was concerned, he had outstayed his welcome.

CHAPTER FORTY

Visitors from Afar

On the morning of Thursday 28 September, Mike met Darren at the ferry landing in South Shields. It was Mike's turn to fork out for a Full English and two large mugs of tea.

Paranormal investigators will often say that the very nature of their profession seems to attract weird events to *them*. Mike swears this is true. Wherever he goes, strange experiences follow him and bizarre phenomena seem to leap out at every turn.

'I never have to hunt for stories for my column. I have a constant stream of them sent in by readers, and the rest I attract like a magnet while walking down the street.'

As Mike and Darren turned into Market Square and headed towards the Market cafe, Darren suddenly paused and stared, goggle-eyed, at the pavement.

'What the hell is *that?*' he shouted, pointing towards the ground. Then he stooped down, seized something betwixt forefinger and thumb and lifted it up. Initially, Mike thought that it was a rusty knife blade. Then he noticed that there was a torpedo-shaped object on the other end.

Alright, Mike conjectured, a knife blade stuck in a piece of cork or something, then.

But there was what looked like a *second* knife blade sticking out of the other side. As Mike's eyes adjusted in the bright autumn sun, he realised that they'd been deceiving him. What Darren had in his hand was not two knife blades stuck symmetrically in a piece of wood, but a giant moth (deceased, thank goodness) of a size hitherto never seen before by either of the authors. What Mike had thought were knife blades were actually huge wings. They promptly took the creature to the offices of the *Shields Gazette,* one of the papers Mike writes for, and photographs were taken. The story of the giant moth appeared several days later. This fine specimen was, it later turned out, a Privet Hawk Moth, the largest species indigenous to the United Kingdom.

As Darren and Mike left the offices of the *Gazette* and prepared to head off to Mike's office, Darren joked about the giant moth.

'You know, if that moth had been alive we could have sat on its back and *flown* to your place.'

Thirty minutes later, the authors were drinking tea at Mike's and planning for the day ahead.

Some time earlier, Darren had taken part in an investigation with a couple called Dave Wood and Nicky Sewell. Dave and Nicky are founding members of PSI – *Paranormal Site Investigators* – and come with excellent credentials. Darren had told them about the Lock Street case, and they said that they would like to carry out some observations of their own, in situ, if possible. While the authors were tucking into their Full English breakfast at the Market Cafe, Dave and Nicky were already well into their 300-mile journey north. That afternoon, they would have the opportunity to experience the polt for themselves.

Darren and Mike had a generous cauliflower and broccoli curry for lunch, which they really shouldn't have, considering the size of the breakfast they'd ingested a short time earlier.

Dave and Nicky joined them an hour or so later, and Mike played them a short sample of some of the extraordinary footage that had been taken at Lock Street. They watched with obvious interest, but made no impromptu judgements.

Mike and Darren explained in more detail what they had been able to determine about both the origins and nature of the Lock Street polt, and then the team headed out for the house itself.

Marc wasn't there when they first arrived, but Marianne gave them a warm welcome. Everyone was supplied with tea and coffee, and then, ensconced around the kitchen table, Dave and Nicky asked her to tell them, in her own words, everything about her experience.

As time wore on, Mike occasionally checked upstairs. On one occasion he accompanied Marianne to the toilet, in keeping with investigation protocols. As they ascended the stairwell from the centre landing, Mike noticed a coin lying on the floor. It was a two pence piece. Darren, Nicky and Dave came to look as Mike took pictures, and the couple from PSI was intrigued, although they could hardly view the appearance of a single coin as evidential. For all they knew, it could have been dropped there accidentally or even placed there deliberately before they arrived.

Later there were a number of minor incidents. The decorative candles on the window-ledge of the central landing were moved around once or twice, and the odd knock, thump or bang occasionally drifted into the kitchen, although it was hard to tell where from. Mike and Darren were hoping that the investigators hadn't travelled all the way from Swindon, only for the polt to declare a no-show. They should have had more faith, bless them.

Marc arrived home, and was introduced to Dave and Nicky. He made a coffee, and then sat and chatted. Dave and Nicky asked him for his perspective on the entire Lock Street phenomenon. As best as he was able, he told them.

By 5.20pm, Marc was still chatting. Mike was watching his arms and hands constantly. It wasn't that he no longer trusted Marc, he did; but coin-falls had a habit of taking place in Marc's presence. If one happened to fall when Dave and Nicky were there, then Mike wanted to be able to say, 'I was watching him all the time; he wasn't responsible.'

As the four investigators and the couple sat and talked, a two pence piece flew out of somewhere – or perhaps nowhere – and landed under the kitchen table with a sharp crack. Marc's hands had been in view all of the time. Nicky took some specialist equipment from a large, metal case and attempted to take some readings.

At 5.30pm, a distinct *tap* was heard from the vicinity of the lower staircase while everyone was still gathered in the kitchen. A cursory inspection revealed another coin that had not been there previously. At 6.00pm, the polt deposited yet another coin outside the toilet, demonstrating that being mean-spirited doesn't necessarily dictate that you're just plain old mean. Financially, the polt could be an extremely good benefactor, at least in the small change department.

At 6.30pm, Marc left to meet with some friends, but he didn't stay out too long. Mike had to leave at 7.45pm, as he had a meeting to attend. Darren suggested that he return after the meeting was over, but Mike had to decline. He had a doctor's appointment early the next morning, and needed some sleep.

After Mike left, the polt took a break until 10pm. At that time, Darren and Dave ventured upstairs and installed a set of motion sensors in Robert's room. If anything – anything at all – should move during their absence, then an alarm should activate immediately. Dave Wood set up some motion sensors, too. However, it was Dave who noticed that while his own sensors were dormant, the activation light on the receiver of Darren's sensors was already flashing.

The investigators deduced that Darren's sensors were calibrated differently to Dave's, as Dave's set does not flash when activated. The crucial factor in this little vignette was not the mystery concerning why Darren's sensors flashed and Dave's didn't. A quick examination of the facts cleared up that little mystery almost in an instant. The important point is that we know that Darren's motion sensors were definitely operating and *switched on* at that juncture, as both investigators saw them flashing. Later, they found that the switch which activates the receiver had been deliberately moved from the *on* to the *off* position, thereby making useless Darren's equipment. As neither Darren nor Dave had disabled the sensors – obviously – the suspicion must be that the polt did it. Why? Was it simply being mischievous, or did it want to prevent Darren and Dave detecting its presence as it moved around Robert's room?

Later in the evening, Marc once again began to feel the burning sensations and itching that normally preceded the 'cutting' incidents when the poltergeist physically attacked him. Sure enough, when he lifted up his top up a number of welts and scratches were already starting to appear. Within a short space of time, they were visible all over his torso, including his shoulders, under his arms, his sides, and the back of his neck. This was all documented on video camera.

At 11.45pm, after Marc had recovered, the investigators and the couple engaged in a protracted discussion about the evening's events. Numerous times during the conversation, Nicky Sewell could hear the sound of breathing and footsteps, as though someone was running around downstairs. Robert and the family dog, Bounder, were downstairs at this time, but an immediate investigation showed that the youngster was fast asleep on the settee in the living room, and the dog was asleep at the far end of the kitchen.

'We were down there within seconds', said Darren. 'Whatever was responsible must have been paranormal in origin.'

At 12.30am, Dave and Nicky left the house and began the journey to their hotel in Newcastle. Darren, Marianne and Marc talked for a while, and then, at 2.00am, everyone retired for the night. Marc and Marianne slept in their bed, as normal, while Darren went to sleep on the sofa. Or at least, he tried to. The polt still wanted to play, and kept him awake most of the night by making 'thumping' noises and generating the sound of footsteps from upstairs. The footfalls, he admitted later, could have been made by Marianne and Marc, but the other sounds remained a mystery.

Eventually, Darren drifted off to sleep. However, at about 4.30am, he woke to find the quilt that Marianne had given him being pulled unceremoniously from him with considerable force. He was forced to pull the quilt back on top of him, and could feel considerable resistance while doing so. This happened on two occasions within the space of sixty seconds. Darren eventually fell asleep again, and woke up to find the house both quiet and peaceful.

At 10.30am, that morning, Darren inspected the house one final time and, to his satisfaction, found everything in order. He then bade the couple farewell and left for home.

CHAPTER FORTY-ONE

The Need to Feed

Mike and Darren have a friend called Stephen Swales, who lectures in information technology at a nearby university. Stephen is a Druid, and apart from his rather unorthodox spirituality, also has a deep and abiding interest in the paranormal.

On Friday 29 September, Stephen visited Mike to discuss some business. During that afternoon, Mike related to him the details of the Lock Street infestation and asked for his opinion. Although Mike had enjoyed many a conversation with Stephen on paranormal matters, he couldn't remember ever discussing the subject of poltergeistry with him and wanted to hear his opinion.

Stephen swallowed a mouthful of coffee and then leaned back into the sofa. He paused for a moment, stared thoughtfully at the floor and then asked Mike a question.

'Does the polt ever pinch mobile phones?'

'Yes, all the time.'

Then he asked another question which intrigued Mike even more.

'When it pinches the phones . . . does it take them upstairs?' Almost always'.

Stephen stared at the floor again, thinking.

'Do they have any electrical equipment in the affected rooms?'

'They do, yes. There's a TV and music centre in the master bedroom, and in Robert's room there's a TV and DVD player. Robert's room is also filled with battery-operated toys.'

'Does it ever mess around with the electrics, Mike?'

'Sometimes. On Tuesday it drained the power out of three sets of batteries before I could get my camera going. Luckily, the fourth set worked.'

'Let me guess; the first three sets of batteries were ordinary alkaline batteries, but the last two were rechargeable batteries, right?'

Now Mike was really intrigued. 'How did you know that?'

Stephen went on to relate to Mike some theories he holds about poltergeist activity. As well as feeding on the fear-energy that polts seem to crave, Stephen also believes that they can feed off electricity. It was for this reason that he wanted to know about the amount of electrical equipment in the bedrooms upstairs, which seemed to be the floor in the house where the polt seemed most 'at home'.

'Mike, do you know whether the couple switch their electrical equipment off completely at night, or merely leave it on standby'?

'They leave their TVs, music centres and other things on standby; why do you ask?'

'It seems to me that the polt could be feeding on the electricity held latently by the equipment upstairs. It would be interesting to know whether the poltergeist activity started when they first purchased the equipment and installed it.'

Just then, perfectly on cue, Marianne happened to ring Mike on his mobile phone to give him an update on how things were progressing. During the call, Mike asked Marianne when she'd purchased the TVs and other equipment that was now in use upstairs in their home.

'Do you know, that's strange. We bought those things at almost exactly the same time as we started having the trouble. In fact, I think it was the same week.'

Stephen interrupted the conversation at this point.

'Mike, tell her to switch off all the electrical equipment in the house tonight before she goes to bed, and not to switch it on again until tomorrow morning. Tell her to keep doing that every night for the foreseeable future. Then, let's see what happens.'

Mike relayed Stephen's instructions to Marianne, who said that she'd definitely give it a try. She would, in fact, try anything that might help. Mike, at that time, recalled that Daniel Jackson had also urged the couple to turn off all their electrical equipment before they and the investigators retired for the night on the evening of Grim Saturday. Perhaps there was something in this theory after all, then.

After the conversation with Marianne ended, Mike and Stephen took up where they left off.

'You see, that's also why I asked about the mobile phones. Are there any mobile phone masts near the house?'

'I could be wrong, but I think there are', replied Mike. 'Quite a few, in fact, on top of a nearby building'.

'You know', said Stephen, 'people don't realise how much power runs through those things, and they are actually *linked* to mobile phones. My guess is that poltergeists can feed off that power, just as they can off a domestic supply. That's why the poltergeist in that house keeps pinching the phones and taking them upstairs.'

And what about the batteries? How did you know that the last batteries I tried in my camera were rechargeable, while the rest were simply ordinary alkaline ones?'

'Rechargeable batteries are different, and poltergeists don't seem to like feeding off them.'

Stephen went on to explain the technical reasons behind his theory, but they went right over Mike's head. Nevertheless, Stephen seemed to know what he was talking about, and that was good enough for Mike.

Stephen's ideas were unusual, but Mike was impressed by the way he'd accurately predicted the type of batteries that worked in his camera, the fact that the polt kept pinching the mobile phones and taking them upstairs, the installation of new entertainment equipment upstairs at the same time the polt surfaced and, last but not least, the presence of mobile phone masts near the house. Now, all they could do was wait and see whether turning off all the electrical equipment at night – effectively cutting off the polt from a major food supply – worked.

CHAPTER FORTY-TWO

Body Count

On Saturday 30 September, Mike received a phone call from Marc informing him that he had captured some startling activities of the poltergeist using the video facility on his mobile phone. Mike was free that afternoon, except for the fact that he'd already made an arrangement for Jackie, and he had go to a local supermarket with his father.

Mike rang his father and asked if they could make a slight detour to Marianne and Marc's house before they went shopping. His father told him this was no problem.

At around 4pm, Mike's dad parked his car outside the rear of Marianne and Marc's house. All Mike intended to do was get Marc to transfer the footage from his phone to his own before the polt had a chance to delete it. Then he could upload the footage onto his PC later and study it.

Mike told his wife and his father that he wouldn't be long, so they both just sat in the car while Mike opened the back gate and walked up the path. An exuberant Bounder did his canine best to knock Mike over until Marianne scolded him.

What happened next must be explained in perfect detail so that its importance and significance can be recognised.

As detailed earlier, the entire rear face of the dining area of Marianne and Marc's house is fronted by large, transparent patio doors. The dining area and kitchen are, therefore, perfectly visible from the road outside if one looks through the gaps in the fence at the bottom of the garden. The importance of this fact will become clear presently.

Mike was dressed in a white shirt, black denims and a black, sleeveless jacket. Marianne was wearing blue denims, a blouse and a black, padded jacket. Marc was also wearing denims and a white T-shirt with a broad, blue hoop across the chest. As Mike entered the dining area through the patio doors, both Marianne and Marc were standing directly in front of him. Marianne was the closer of the two, while Marc stood slightly behind her near the door that leads into the living room.

Mike explained that he didn't have much time, and asked Marc if he could 'bluetooth' the two pieces of footage to Mike's mobile phone. Marc said he would, but asked Mike if he could show him the footage first. Mike agreed.

The first piece of footage had been taken in a corridor in a building that Marc visited on a regular basis. It was not, however, the family home. As the film played out, Mike could see a door at the end of the corridor that was in the open position. The hinges were on the right-hand side (facing) as Mike looked at the screen on Marc's mobile phone. Suddenly, the door moved. At first it looked as if it had been caught by a gust of wind. It swung on its hinges a distance of approximately six inches, and then swung back to its original position. Then it swung violently and slammed shut with a distinctive thud. Marc can be heard sucking in air sharply at this point, obviously startled. The film then ended.

Mike asked Marc what had prompted him to take the footage. How could he have known that the door was going to slam shut like that? The explanation was simple. The door had, that morning, moved seemingly of its own accord on several occasions when Marc was approaching it. On the third occasion Marc decided to have his phone camera ready just in case it repeated the exercise. It did.

The second piece of footage focused on a shelf bearing several ornaments. The small screen made it impossible to see exactly what these ornaments were, but one appeared to be a figurine of some kind. What riveted Mike's attention was the fact that the ornament was moving. Slowly but steadily, it was sliding back and forth along the shelf; three or four inches to the right, then three or four inches to the left. Then it would repeat the exercise. Mike would need to examine the footage at his office, of course, but his immediate thought was that the films looked impressive.

Mike activated the bluetooth facility on his phone, and then Marc proceeded to beam the footage to it.

Mike accepted the files and saved them on his phones in the 'Video Clips' folder. The three chatted for a few moments, and then Mike said he'd have to go. He said goodbye to Marianne and Marc and promised he'd give them a ring after he'd managed to analyse the footage.

As he walked down the path towards the garden gate, Mike accessed the Video Clips folder on his phone, intending to replay the footage. Just as he reached his father's car, he became aware that the Video Clips folder was empty. Thinking that he'd maybe stored them in his 'Images' folder by mistake – although he was sure he hadn't – he checked that folder too. They weren't there. Baffled, he returned to the house and told Marc and Marianne. Marc immediately said he'd send the two pieces of footage again. However, when he tried to access them on his phone Marc found that *his* Video Clips folder was empty too. The polt had deleted both files, and they were now lost forever. Angry, Mike said goodbye to the couple for a second time and, once more, headed for the car.

Both Jackie and Mike's dad, Peter, could see that Mike was upset about something, and asked him what was wrong. Mike explained what had happened, and cursed the polt ferociously.

As Mike's dad pulled away from the rear of the house, Jackie asked Mike who the other person had been in the dining room.

'What other person?' he replied.

'The man . . . the one trying to talk to you, Marc and Marianne.'

'*What* man? There was only Marc, Marianne and myself in the dining room. We were the only people in the house, actually, apart from Robert, who was in the living room the entire time watching TV.

At this point Mike's dad jumped in.

'Mike, *I* saw him. I could see you, Marianne – she was wearing a black jacket – and Marc. But there was another man, standing to your right.'

'Dad, there *wasn't* anyone else there in the house, I'm telling you.' Jackie proceeded to describe the person she'd seen:

'Mike, he was about your height, and he was wearing blue denims and a beige-coloured t-shirt. He had brown hair, maybe with a slight reddish tinge, and he needed a shave. He looked as if he had two or three days of facial growth.'

'That's exactly who I saw too', said Mike's dad.

Sensing that something peculiar may have happened, Mike asked them both what they remembered about the man apart from his dress.

'Well', said Jackie, 'he was standing to your right, in front of the dining table. And he kept stretching his arms and hands out, as if he was gesticulating. It looked as if he was talking to you, and trying to make a point. To be honest, he looked frustrated, as if you weren't listening.'

Mike's dad concurred, and said that this was his recollection, too.

The three went over the details several times during the journey to the supermarket, and both Jackie and Mike's dad, Peter, were adamant about what they'd seen.

Several questions posed themselves at this juncture. Who, or what, had they seen? And why hadn't Mike, Marianne or Marc seen this fourth person who was supposedly in the dining room standing right beside them?

Later, at home, Mike pondered over the conundrum and decided to ring Darren. After relating the substance of the incident, Mike said that he was reticent about telling the couple what had happened. The fact was that both Mike and Darren knew of a recently deceased person who was also known to the couple, and the possibility existed that Jackie and Peter had seen the spirit of this man in their home. Darren postulated that the reason why the spirit had remained invisible to those inside the house was that he hadn't *wanted* to be seen – perhaps so that neither Marc nor Marianne became upset. But what had he wanted?

'Maybe he was trying to protect them from the polt', thought Mike.

'Perhaps', said Darren in response. 'Or maybe he was trying to make himself visible to them and couldn't. Maybe that's why he looked so frustrated.'

So many questions, so many possible answers.

Several days later, Mike decided that he should tell Marianne and Marc what Jackie and Peter had seen. The couple were as mystified as everyone else, and no explanation ever did manifest itself. To this day, it remains a mystery.

CHAPTER FORTY-THREE

The Poltergeist – At Work

This following short, but vital chapter was written not long *after* the poltergeist at 42 Lock Street came to an end but was subsequently withdrawn from the original book due to reasons Marc and Marianne conveyed to us at that particular time. Because of the sensitive nature of the case, and the location of where this particular phenomenon occurred, it was decided to withhold the information. It was, however, subsequently released eight years later in a new publication detailing new and interesting cases post-South Shields along with highlighting some remarkable similarities between the cases.

The book (*Contagion: In The Shadow of the South Shields Poltergeist*, Ritson & Hallowell, The Limbury Press, 2014) also puts forward a number of ideas and theories about *potential* poltergeist infection that has been hitherto seldom debated, in the hope a seed may be planted, from which a large tree can grow. I (Darren W. Ritson) feel that the original deleted chapter that has now been subsequently re-edited and added to, should be included in this new updated and revised edition of the book bringing the remaining aspects of the account together under one metaphorical roof.

In William G. Rolls' book, *The Poltergeist* (Nelson Doubleday, 1972), he discusses a now-famous case that was investigated by

A.R.G Owen and subsequently written up in his own work, *Can We Explain the Poltergeist?* (Garret Publications, New York, 1964). The case became known as the Sauchie Poltergeist and is one of Scotland's best-known cases. It was said to have made its presence known between 22nd November and 2nd December 1960 and it centred around an eleven-year-old girl called Virginia Campbell. Roll states that poltergeists usually restrict themselves to a certain area – such as the person's home, which is normally the case – but not in the case at Sauchie, nor at South Shields, as we shall soon see. The poltergeist not only followed Virginia to her relatives' homes when she went to stay with them, it also made its presence known at her school too.

On one occasion on 25th November 1960, the poltergeist lifted the lid of Virginia's school desk three times while she sat at it. The teacher, Miss Stewart, had noticed the lid moving up and down and had at first presumed it was Virginia retrieving her belongings from within the desk. However, a closer inspection revealed that Virginia was actually pushing down hard on the lid in an effort to stop it from lifting up on its own. Fifteen minutes later, the teacher observed another school desk that was unoccupied at the time, rising from the floor and moving out of line with the other nearby desks. After searching for strings or trickery or some sort and finding nothing to account for the desk movement she was naturally bewildered by this seemingly impossible incident. This brings us nicely on to the events that transpired in 2006.

Towards the end of the investigation of the South Shields poltergeist, a series of incidents occurred which, like everything the poltergeist did, were both bizarre and intimidating. One of the residents of Lock Street, Marc, worked as a chef at a residential establishment in Newcastle upon Tyne. Coincidentally, his partner Marianne, the other resident of number 42, also worked at the same location but in a different capacity.

Marianne explained that, on one occasion, she'd entered the kitchen area where Marc worked and noticed that he'd placed a stack of dinner plates on a work surface. There was nothing at all unusual about this, and so she didn't give the matter a second thought. She then turned around and switched on the kettle before leaving the kitchen. As she made for the door, something caught her eye. The pile of dinner plates was now upside down. This startled her, as they had only been out of her line of sight for a matter of seconds. Something, it seemed, had apparently lifted up the entire stack and inverted it. She knew that no one had entered the kitchen area while she was there, and later stated categorically that due to her close proximity to the workbench it would have been impossible for someone to do this in absolute silence and without drawing her attention. It took her very little time to realise that her poltergeist was at work.

Over the next few days, other incidents took place of a similar nature. Plates, cups and saucers would be moved around — sometimes when neither Marianne nor Marc were present. On one occasion an entire collection of cutlery was removed from its normal resting place and deposited upon a work surface — again, whilst the witness's back was turned for mere seconds.

According to Marc and Marianne, it wasn't long before other members of staff began to report strange things happening. One worker kept shutting a window, only to find it open minutes later. This happened repeatedly within the space of an hour. Whether Marianne suggested to her colleagues that these bizarre phenomena may have been the work of a poltergeist or not we do not know, but she told Darren, on one occasion, every employee in the building had become sufficiently unnerved to the point where they all vacated the premises and stood outside one of the secondary entrances. As they huddled together discussing the situation, a pair of scissors plummeted from above and hit the ground with a clatter. The only place the scissors could have come from, the couple suggested, was an office window directly above where the workers were standing. Marianne knew that the office was not in use — something she substantiated when she immediately re-entered the building and checked.

Perhaps the most bizarre incidents that took place at that location were witnessed by Marc. On one occasion, he had been walking along a corridor when a door in front of him suddenly slammed shut. Several other times that morning the same thing happened — the door would either slam shut or at the very least move without any human assistance. Marc actually filmed the door moving with the camera facility on his mobile phone. On another occasion, he filmed a figurine on a shelf moving back and forth several inches – also without any human intervention. When these incidents occurred at Marc and Marianne's workplace, the poltergeist activity at their home had ceased. We were forced to consider the possibility that although our efforts to rid the family home of the poltergeist had been largely successful, the poltergeist was now seemingly focusing its attention on Marc and Marianne's workplace where it could carry out its activities relatively unhindered.

The thought crossed Darren's mind that the 'stand-by' electricity that the poltergeist had been seemingly utilising at the Lock Street house had been essentially cut off, thus forcing the poltergeist to find its energy source elsewhere – perhaps, he thought, at Marc and Marianne's workplace. This idea possibly reinforces the notion that most poltergeists, unlike ghosts, are person-centred as opposed to place-centred. Had the poltergeist simply followed the couple to work and become active there because we had made life difficult for it at Lock Street? It seemed a reasonable proposition; however, in cases like these, there are always more questions raised than any forthcoming answers.

For a few weeks then, the poltergeist brought about chaos at their workplace until eventually the symptoms of the infestation began to subside until it reached the point of non-existence – at work and at 42 Lock Street. The pressure and unease that Marc and Marianne were under at that particular time really was immense so it is no wonder they chose to keep the 'workplace polt activity' under wraps, at least until a later date; the thought had occurred to them that if their respective employers at that time thought for one moment that they had somehow brought paranormal activity to their place of employment, they could well have been ridiculed, or possibly even dismissed from their posts.

However, for all we know, Marc and Marianne's employer may have been more than understanding and fully sympathetic to their rather unusual plight and may have actually supported them – as Darren and Mike did – until the cessation of the activity;

understandably, they did not want to take that risk. Their jobs, their livelihood and their home was potentially at stake – so who can blame them?

After South Shields, Darren and Mike engaged in many debates and in-depth discussions about the preceding months, and re-evaluated their views on the poltergeist and its *possible* nature almost to the point of monotony. This was when the idea of the contagion aspect of the poltergeist phenomenon was largely discussed and given some considerable thought. During this process we stumbled across many questions that seriously needed addressing with even some attempts to answer them, or at least formulate theories. They became the basis of the follow up book previously mentioned – *Contagion*. Some might say that if Alexander Fleming had not been inquisitive about the interaction between mould and bacteria on a petri dish we may never have had penicillin. We believe that the same principles apply in poltergeist research. Questions must be asked and evidence, if collected, *must* be sifted and evaluated before any conclusions can be made. The re-asking of those questions and the re-evaluation of any evidence must be carried out before we can move forward.

No one has all the answers to the poltergeist phenomenon, yet. It remains one of the world's greatest mysteries. Perhaps the best we can hope for is that painstakingly, inch by inquisitive inch, we can move in the right direction and see the light get a little brighter with each passing year.

CHAPTER FORTY-FOUR

Conclusions

It had been a long, hard fight. In some respects, it had been a successful one. The researchers – and, of course, the couple – now had a much better understanding of this most bizarre phenomenon. Initially, the researchers had at least managed to introduce both Marc and Marianne to some coping mechanisms which had helped them survive their experiences, if not overcome them. To their delight – and the delight of Marianne and Marc, of course – the polt did not resurface at Lock Street after they began to switch off their electrical equipment at night. Stephen Swales had been right.

Mike, for his part, has had to modify his thoughts on the nature of the poltergeist phenomenon. He still believes that a poltergeist has its origin deep within the psyche of a highly-stressed person, but he now thinks that, once that stress is externalised, it can on rare occasions separate itself from its 'host' or 'focus' and begin to act independently. In essence, the polt can take on a life of its own. It no longer needs the presence of its host to be able to function. It is no longer 'person-centred' in the sense that it is attached to a specific individual. When the polt reaches this level of independence it can come and go as it pleases, feed on whom it likes.

This is what has happened to the polt at Lock Street, I believe, and I have my reasons for saying that. For example, in some respects the poltergeist mirrored Marc. Its handwriting was similar – at least most of the time – and never once throughout the entire experience has the polt harmed Robert. Although Marc isn't Robert's natural father, he dotes on the child.

On the other hand, the polt has developed an intense hatred of Marianne and became thoroughly sadistic in its treatment of her. There is nothing of Marc in *there,* for he dotes on Marianne too.

As the polt grew stronger it was able to separate itself from Marc. The aspects of his personality and character that it mirrored diminished, and its own personality developed.

In a weird way it's like a woman giving birth to a child. The child begins within the mother. After birth, it's still connected to the mother by the umbilical cord, so it is only partially separate but not independent. When the umbilical cord is cut, the baby is completely separate but still dependent for it has to feed from its mother. Eventually though, as the child gets older and stronger, all reliance on its mother ceases.

The relationship between a polt and its host goes through an identical series of stages. Fortunately, most polts die off before they become completely independent, which is a good thing, because by that stage they've become absolute monsters.

In the latter stages of the Lock Street infestation, it became clear that the entity was no longer following the normal conventions of polt behaviour. It would attack anyone and anything, feed anywhere. It was also clearly thinking for itself, aware of circumstances and events of which even Marc could have had no knowledge. Bluntly speaking, it just didn't need him any more.'

Perhaps the most chilling aspect of the entire investigation was the way in which the investigators were able to witness firsthand the raw, unbridled malevolence of a poltergeist at work. Darren and Mike have always accepted the existence of the phenomenon, but believe that only direct interaction can truly expose one to its true nature experientially.

'I don't want to seem narrow-minded', said Mike, 'but I never again want to hear anyone attempt to argue down the poltergeist phenomenon to the level of pure psychology. I think Darren probably feels the same way. Remember, we have dealt with a full-blown, cunning, vicious bastard of a polt *directly*. We, unlike many others, know whereof we speak. Those who pontificate about the nature of the polt without having experienced its power know nothing and, quite frankly, are not qualified to make lofty pronouncements.'

Another unanswered question concerned Sammy. At the beginning of the investigation, Darren felt that there might have been just one phenomenon present at Lock Street; the poltergeist and one or more 'accompanying apparitions'. Mike, for a long while, felt that there was a second entity living at Lock Street; a QCC or 'quasi-corporeal companion'. Slowly but surely, however, his confidence in this notion began to evaporate. The more Mike come to understand just how devious the polt could be, the more consideration he had to give to the idea that 'Sammy' may not have been a separate and distinct entity to the polt, but simply the polt manifesting itself in a guise that would fool Robert, the couple and the researchers.

One thing that led him to consider this disturbing possibility was the fact that, earlier in the investigation, 'Sammy' had left a message on one of the doodle-boards for Marianne. In it he had used the phrase, 'O.K. MAM'. This same phrase was also used by the polt when it sent an extremely sinister message to Marianne's phone.

Mike has not given up on the idea that Sammy may really have existed. Perhaps, as the authors have already speculated, the polt expelled Sammy from 42 Lock Street when it became powerful enough. Maybe, when the polt used the 'O.K. MAM' phrase in its sinister missive to Marianne it was simply imitating Sammy, *wanting* the couple and the researchers to think that Sammy and the polt were one and the same. The polt had proved that such devious tactics are not beyond its power.

Sammy — hopefully the *real* Sammy, if there is one-now only visits Robert infrequently. If the polt has disappeared altogether —

and it certainly seems to have — Sammy may return to the house on a more permanent basis, who knows.

So, what caused the polt's ultimate demise? Mike thinks that the smudging rituals played a part, and perhaps weakened the poltergeist, made life more difficult for it. The final blow seemed to have been when the couple began to turn off their electrical equipment at night. Did the polt 'die', then? Perhaps. For a short while it manifested itself at another location. Then, it simply disappeared altogether.

Perhaps not coincidentally, Marc at that time began to deal with his stress problem. For the record, the authors offered him a full and sincere apology for doubting him during the early stages of the investigation. Marc said he understood that their doubts were entertained simply because they were forced to consider trickery as a possible cause of the bizarre phenomena that were manifesting themselves in his home.

The researchers pray that the process continues. Marianne, Marc and little Robert deserve better — a happier, more contented life.

Just before the team left their house after the first overnight vigil, Daniel Jackson said something of profound importance to Marianne.

'You've both gone through a terrible ordeal, but think about it. You've come out of the fire as better, stronger people. Look at what you've gone through. How many people could have withstood the experiences *you've* been tested with? After this, nothing should ever faze you again.'

At the very outset, the authors made a promise to Marianne and Marc. They said, 'We will never walk away from you. No matter how bad it gets, we'll be there to help. You are not on your own in this fight, and we will not rest till you can enjoy the peace you both want and deserve.'

The authors now know what it is like to stare into the heart of darkness. Victims of the poltergeist phenomenon should also know that, tomorrow, there will always be another dawn.

Appendices

APPENDIX 1

The Society for Psychical Research Journal Review by Alan Murdie LLB

The South Shields poltergeist case of 2006 was quoted to have been the best attested and one of the most significant cases in over fifty years. Alan Murdie LLB, (Chairman of The Ghost Club of Great Britain, and Head of the Spontaneous Cases Committee for the Society for Psychical Research) carried out his own investigation into the case and studied much of the evidence that we had accumulated over the course of this year long investigation at 42 Lock Street. He subsequently published his findings in the *Journal of the Society for Psychical Research Vol 74.2 No. 899 April 2010 – P129–32*. With kind permission from Alan Murdie, Peter Johnson, and from the Incorporated Society for Psychical Research I will now publish verbatim his findings and his critique:

> *The South Shields Poltergeist* by Mike J. Hallowell and Darren Ritson tells the story of the authors personal investigation into one of the most extraordinary UK poltergeist cases in recent

years. The outbreak centred on a modest house at 42 Lock Street, South Shields, Tyneside during the summer of 2006, then occupied by a young couple in their twenties and their three-year-old son. The authors had the good fortune in being alerted to events at an early stage, and their account illustrates just how challenging and demanding a field investigation can become. According to their account in the book, numerous alleged paranormal incidents occurred, but with the South Shields poltergeist going far beyond the usual poltergeist repertoire of raps, object movements and levitations. Phenomena included physical assaults and scratches inflicted on one resident, and examples of matter-through- matter penetration. Most remarkable of all were apparent attempts in communication from the poltergeist, suggesting a rudimentary and malevolent intelligence at work.

In particular, the authors maintain the South Shields Poltergeist was adept at manipulating modern technology for its own ends, including the creation of bizarre and threatening text messages apparently left on mobile telephones. Crude messages were also scribbled upon a child's doodle board, seemingly in response to questions by the investigators. Other toys were moved and re-positioned in grotesque tableaux vivants, and two programme makers for Orion television who visited the house witnessed a speaking 'Bob the Builder' toy mysteriously croaking words out with which it had not been programmed.

Extraordinary as these incidents sound, they are not wholly without precedent in poltergeist literature. For instance, interference with telephones were a feature of the Rosenheim case in Germany in 1967 (Bender, 1969); similar claims of peculiar messages over the telephone also turn up in unpublished cases sent to the SPR as long ago as 1948 (Case File P55, 1948). Threatening scribbled messages have also been reported in a handful of historic cases.

For ease of reading, the authors present the details as an unfolding story documenting the progress of their involvement in events. This appears partly in emulation of Guy Playfair's

This House is Haunted (1980) on the Enfield Poltergeist, and
Guy Playfair has written a foreword for the book. This is both
a strength and a weakness. Whilst providing a readable account,
the chronology and precise dates of certain incidents is hard to
follow at times. Greater detail of certain incidents would also
be welcome, given the remarkable nature of the claimed events.
However, as with Enfield it is apparent that the authors were
dealing with a large volume of extraordinary and disturbing
phenomena. Descriptions of some of these incidents are inter-
spaced with theoretical discussions, reflecting the authors own
ideas and those of other researchers, with some conclusions
being questionable. Surprise may also be expressed at Mike
Hallowell's application of rituals derived from Native American
beliefs on site, in an attempt to quell the disturbances. Like most
poltergeists, the South Shields case was short-lived, and may
have ended in its own time. However, the authors remain open
minded in their account, and do not urge the reader to adopt
any particular viewpoint.

Of much greater significance are the authors own statements
that they witnessed a number of incidents for themselves in
situations which precluded fraud or any normal explanation.
Details of other witnesses and copies of their statements are
included in the book, so their claims are capable of a degree of
independent verification.

Given the remarkable nature of the South Shields case, it
has inevitably been subject to a good deal of discussion and
criticism from members of the SPR, and by other groups over
the internet. As a result, rather than be satisfied merely by the
account presented in the book, this reviewer elected to visit the
authors to see what further material they possessed. Both Mike
Hallowell and Darren Ritson were agreeable to meeting with
me, and on travelling up to Newcastle on October 11th 2009,
I was able to interview both of them for several hours. I was
also allowed the opportunity to examine their archives and files
of evidence, preserved at Mike Hallowell's home. Certainly, if
events happened as alleged, it was reasoned there would be a
considerable quantity of documentary, photographic and other

evidence available that would be consistent with the claims made in the book. This proved to be the case.

I was able to inspect over 450 original photographs, and make copies of many of them. Some of these provide a measure of corroboration to specific incidents in the book, such as the claimed distortion of a plastic table and its apparent restoration to its original shape. There are also films, documents and witness statements and far more material than is described in the book. The authors revealed in confidence a number of details and contacts not disclosed in their book, so the opportunity is available for further detailed study of this case.

As a consequence, I am of the opinion the South Shields poltergeist joins a small but significant collection of spontaneous cases where credible evidence has been obtained by investigators whilst disturbances were still occurring. Examples include Hannath Hall in 1957 (Cornell and Gauld, 1960), the Rosenheim Poltergeist (Bender 1969), the Miami Poltergeist (Roll, 1972) the Andover Poltergeist in 1974, (Colvin, 2008) Enfield Poltergeist case 1977-78 (Playfair, 1980), the Euston Square Poltergeist (Grosse and Barrington 2001). Furthermore, these well attested cases occur in context of over a thousand others reported since 1880 (Goss, 1979). Talking with the authors about defects alleged in their investigative approach, I was very much reminded of the famous dictum of American Judge Oliver Wendell Homes in (*Brown v United States* 256 U.S. 235 (1921)), that 'Detached reflection cannot be demanded in the presence of an uplifted knife'. When responding to a midnight telephone call from a highly distressed caller, there may be only time to snatch up one small camera before setting off, and certainly not an opportunity to deploy a whole range of technical gadgetry to try for recording manifestations. Indeed, the dynamics of a troubled family home may operate simply to thwart controlled experiments to laboratory standards, problems of equipment failure noted at many 'haunted' sites notwithstanding. A further ethical problem is the extent investigators should attempt to remain detached and merely observe phenomena, or actually help terrified occupiers bring manifestations to an end. As in other cases, the authors of *The South Shields Poltergeist* responded as best they could in very testing circumstances. In this respect, their book provides a cogent illustration of the problems that field investigators have to contend with and the on the spot decisions necessary.

It must also be noted that the authors have also been subject to a great deal of undeserved criticism for publishing their finds, much of it delivered indirectly from self-styled sceptics operating in the isolation of cyberspace. Some of these critics have eschewed reasoned argument altogether and simply engaged in personalised attacks, invective and libel against the authors. The result has been (as with original researchers in both the Rosenheim and Enfield cases) that Mike Hallowell and Darren Ritson have even been forced into threatening legal action to correct defamatory falsehoods being spread. It is perhaps inevitable that none of the console-based critics of this book have troubled themselves to directly inspect any of the original data and evidence on which it is based. Again, this mirrors the experience of the Enfield investigators (Playfair & Grosse, 1988).

This may be a lesson for future researchers, including further study of this case (the authors remain willing to share their data with the SPR). Thus, rather than expend time responding to fanciful criticisms or mere abuse, researchers would be better employed analysing the substantial quantities of poltergeist data already accumulated. Cluster analyses of such data, like as those conducted by Alan Gauld suggest patterns within poltergeist phenomena, which may potentially yield clues as to the nature of the forces at work (Gauld, 1979).

For example, as in the South Shields case, poltergeist activity frequently occurs within enclosed spaces, such as lofts and cellars and inside smaller domestic dwellings. They are much rarer in larger non-domestic buildings (for instance there are very few accounts of poltergeist phenomena inside churches) or the open air. Does this suggest that whatever energy which is behind poltergeists is encouraged by being contained within a relatively small physical space? Similarly, what can be deduced about the energy in disturbances, from the weight and trajectories of objects moved? Can the mathematics models of higher dimensions shed any light upon matter-through-matter penetration?

These are examples of the questions which researchers should be asking if the subject is to progress; *The South Shields Poltergeist* is a book which provides much significant data to analyse.

Alan Murdie

REFERENCES

Bender, Hans 'New Developments in Poltergeist Research' in Proceedings of the Parapsychological Association 6 (1969) 81-102.

Case File P55, premises in Brighton, 1948 SPR Archive, Cambridge University Library.

Colvin, Barrie 'The Andover Case: A responsive rapping poltergeist' in Jnl of the SPR (2008) Vol 72, 1-20.

Cornell, A.D. and Gauld, Alan 'A Fenland Poltergeist' Jnl SPR 40:705 Sept 1960, 343-358

Gauld, Alan & Cornell A.D. *Poltergeists* (1979)

Grosse, M and Barrington, M 'Report on Psychokinetic activity surrounding a seven-year-old boy' in Jnl SPR (2001) Vol 65 207-217.

Goss, Michael, (1979) Poltergeists: An annotated bibliography of Works in English, circa 1880-1975. Scarecrow Press, New York.

Playfair, Guy Lyon (1980) This House is Haunted

Playfair, Guy Lyon and Grosse, Maurice (1988) 'Enfield Revisited: The Evaporation of Positive Evidence" JSPR 1988-89 Vol 55 No 813 208-219

Roll, William The Poltergeist (1972) New York Signet Books

APPENDIX 2

Witness Statements

Statement of June Peterworth

I arrived at my daughter's home one evening, accompanied by my daughter Marianne, her partner Marc Karlsonn, my son Ian and my grandson Robert.

We all went up to Robert's room, and stayed there for about ten minutes.

While I was in Robert's bedroom I twice felt as if something cold had brushed past me. I dismissed this, and carried on talking to Robert. Robert then went into Marianne's bedroom to change into his pyjamas. I stood in the doorway and talked to him as he changed. Marianne was next to me, and Marc and Ian were in Robert's room.

When Robert had finished changing into his pyjamas we all went downstairs together to give Robert his supper. Ian was sitting in the living room watching TV, and talking to us.

After approximately twenty minutes, we all went back upstairs to take Robert to bed. Marianne said nothing seemed to have moved, but then Marc noticed that Robert's little blue chair was missing. We also noticed that the door to Marianne's bedroom had closed. Marc opened the door and found the chair in the bedroom.

None of us had been upstairs on our own, as we had all gone up and come down together. I had been the last one standing in the bedroom doorway, and had closed the door to Marianne's room when we went downstairs.

June Peterworth.

Statement of Suzanne McKay

When Darren Ritson asked myself and the rest of The *North East Ghost Research* Team along to Marianne's home, I felt rather apprehensive. However, I was glad that, finally, the team was able to go in and investigate with the objective of trying to help the family find some answers.

The night was unbelievable, and the activity that took place was very frightening. I now feel a sense of pride to have been associated with the family and have a great deal of admiration for them, particularly in the light of what they've gone through since the beginning of the year. Their strength has been remarkable.

The messages left on the child's doodle-boards were some of the first phenomena witnessed by everyone on the night. To be honest, I initially thought that the messages – scrawled in what seemed to be child-like writing – were threats directed towards the team. From this point onwards I knew that whatever was causing the activity had to be treated with the utmost respect.

For me, the pinnacle of the night came when Mike and Danny carried out the 'medicine wheel' ceremony, directly confronting 'the force' – whatever it was.

The appearance of the scratches on Marc's chest and arms was incredible, though very discomforting for him. We all stood in bewilderment and shock as these marks appeared from nowhere.

Darren Ritson, Darren Olley and I were standing as close to Marc as was physically possible, and we can vouch that at no time did Marc self-inflict the scratches that appeared on his body.

The appearance of other objects, which seemingly material-ised from nowhere, was one of the most perplexing phenomena I have ever witnessed. The other phenomena I witnessed on the night turned my thoughts and viewpoint upside down, quite frankly. I feel I have emerged a lot stronger from the experience, and am now 100 per cent confident that I have experienced real poltergeist phenomena. To coin a phrase, the night was 'mind-boggling'. I hope the family will soon have some well-deserved rest from this fearsome activity.

Suzanne McKay
Investigator with the North East Ghost Research Team
6 September, 2006.

Statement of Claire Smith

When I initially entered the house I didn't immediately feel 'on edge' in any way or sense any kind of atmosphere. I did have various hopes and expectations regarding what might happen: However, nothing could have prepared me for what I was to witness.

When we were shown around the house, various objects like ornaments, toys and clothing were seemingly out of place, and there was writing on both of the child's doodle-boards. Naturally, any investigator is going to initially question the value of this as actual evidence. As I had not seen the objects in their 'normal' locations before we actually arrived at the house, I was not sure whether anyone could have moved them prior to our arrival.

Throughout the night, several toys seemed to appear and drop from nowhere. I was very intrigued, but still not fully convinced. Naturally you have to consider every possibility. However, the toys were always dropped in a place where everyone was sitting. They were also *dropped* – not thrown across a room or kicked. They actually seemed to materialise from thin air, and I became increasingly intrigued.

Mike later suggested that if he performed a smudging ceremony it may provoke a reaction from the poltergeist. He said that this may adversely affect either himself, Danny or the male occupant [Marc]. We all went up to the child's bedroom, which seemed to be the focal point of the activity.

Almost as soon as Mike's 'circle' was complete, the male occupant said he felt a burning on his stomach. When he lifted up his shirt I could see scratch marks appearing on his body. When Darren Ritson lifted the back of Marc's T-shirt, I could see more defined scratches appearing. I was totally amazed and 'gob-smacked'. I was witnessing the most amazing paranormal activity I had ever seen, and was unable to come up with any kind of rational explanation.

When the pain was too severe, Marc stepped into the circle for protection. The scratches continued to appear; however, Mike explained that the scratches were the result of what had been inflicted upon the male occupant while he had been outside of the circle and that they would soon start to fade now he was inside the circle. Then, surely enough, the scratches began to fade and disappear. The fact that they disappeared so quickly also amazed me, because scratches like those would have marked anyone for a while, not just minutes.

I can only describe the experience in three words; phenomenal, amazing and scary.

Claire Smith
Investigator with the North East Ghost Research Team
6 September, 2006.

Statement of Glenn Hall

My account begins with the briefing which took place at Mike's house. After the team had been introduced to Mike, he briefed us on what had actually happened in the affected house. After he had shown us a short film of evidence collated from previous visits, we all travelled to the location.

During the journey I mentally absorbed the evidence Mike had shown us. One piece of footage in particular that had an impact on me was the film in which a bottle of water can be seen balancing unnaturally. This piece of evidence was actually caught on camera. I've never personally witnessed anything like the phenomenon shown on the footage, and was caught by surprise. It made me think, 'Glenn this is the *real deal;* this is what you have been investigating for.'

I couldn't contain my excitement, but also confess to having feelings of pure terror regarding what we might witness. Being quite sensitive to spirit I found it intriguing to be in this situation, but I was also scared.

Upon entering the house, we met the occupants and settled down to a nice cup of tea. The female occupant, Marianne, told the team that the night could well turn out to be quite busy, as she had experienced quite a lot of activity during that day.

During a sweep around the house, we found several objects out of their original position. A statuette was found at the foot of the first flight of stairs which originally stood on a shelf in the hall, and a porcelain pig that normally stood on a window-sill was found on top of the toilet seat.

When we entered the child's bedroom, both Darren Ritson and I felt our stomachs tighten. To me, this is always a sign of some sort of spiritual presence.

During our inspection of the room, the team found two doodle-boards with writing on them. One message said, 'Stop it now', and the other said 'Go now.' I was quite amazed at this but also felt a little suspicious. My honest opinion was that the phenomena recorded by Mike and Darren, and what I was seeing now, seemed too good to be true; so I *did* have some doubts.

During the night's investigation several other events took place. For example, a toy car was thrown or dropped outside onto the garden path, and a toy figure dropped from the ceiling – and was subsequently found. On closer inspection, the toy had had its head removed.

Neither of these events were closely witnessed by me, so I still felt sceptical. I wanted to believe these events were genuine, but until something happened in front of my own two eyes that evening I was still going to be stained with doubt.

The next event changed the way I see things in the world of paranormal research. Mike, who practices the spiritual ways of the Native Americans, briefed us on a ceremony called 'smudging'. Then we all gathered in the child's bedroom, outside a circle of stones, with our camcorders at the ready. The ceremony is a ritual that Mike thought may help evoke or entice the poltergeist into an outward manifestation. The male occupant, Marc, took part in this ceremony.

Mike and Darren Ritson had been led to believe from past investigations that Marc may well have been the poltergeist focus. The male occupant had been attacked by the poltergeist in the past, and it was deemed likely that this could happen again.

I had my camera fixed on the male occupant when the ceremony started, and during it he started to sweat and shake. On lifting up his T-shirt small scratches could be seen on his back and stomach.

When he actually removed his T-shirt, three large scratches appeared from nowhere on his back. This happened right in front of my eyes, and these initial scratches were followed by many more. I cannot explain where the scratches came from, and neither do I know why they disappeared from the male occupant when he entered the circle. I've only seen things like this in films, and never thought I would ever witness such a paranormal occurrence personally.

After this event I witnessed no further activity during our investigation. Upon close inspection of the male occupant's back half an hour later, no marks or scratches could be seen.

I'll never forget my night at this location. I've carried out over forty investigations in buildings as varied as old hotels and disused jails, and at locations as far apart as Scotland and the Cotswolds. Strange; all I had to do was go to a two-bedroom terraced house not far from home to get the answers I'd been seeking.

Glenn Hall
Investigator for the North East Ghost Research Team
6 September 2006.

Statement of Daniel Jackson

I would very much like to bear witness to the accuracy and truthfulness of the preceding account of the events that took place in my presence at the aforementioned address, at the specified time.

I attended the address given in the capacity of an interested amateur yet, as the narrative recounts, I was inexorably drawn into the unfolding events of 'Grim Saturday'.

I have learned throughout the last seven years of my life that most things of apparent 'meaning' that one encounters in this increasingly empirical life must initially be taken on faith to be re-examined later for real content once the white noise of modern 'society' is of lesser intensity.

Sometimes, however, the small, almost imperceptible bridges between the 'real' and the metaphysical can be wide enough to allow tangible access into the world between the ticks of the clock, to give intensely personal witness to a world governed by other, simpler lore. This was definitely one such instance.

Each one of us has the ability to derive real perspective in today's digitally-definite universe, if we can but 'tune out' the irrelevancies.

In this instance, a group of individuals came face to face with a set of circumstances which belie the modern world. They faced those circumstances in a measured, open-minded, but above all sensitive manner which engaged both my natural curiosity and my respect.

The family mentioned in this account have given me a new perspective of the way people actually are. They showed courage and determination in a situation where all 'current' scientific data suggests that this situation cannot occur. They showed a great amount of faith and character under extreme fear of an unknown danger, and taught all those who were present that each of us, when the occasion requires it, will still use their faith as their greatest defence.

The *Midewewin* way is an ancient, introspectively joyous creed for life born of a far simpler time. The practitioners of the way believe that prayer, meditation and a balanced approach to all life will come from the earth in revelation to be revealed in an intensely personal way.

It only remains for me to voice my appreciation to all involved for allowing me to be a small part of what transpired.

Daniel Jackson
September 12 2006.

Statement of Julie Olley

The night started with a visit to Mike's house, where we watched a DVD presentation of all the phenomena that the principal experients had been witnessing. It was quite amazing, but it must have been terrifying for them.

We got to the experients' house at approximately 8.30pm, introduced ourselves and had a cup of tea and a chat to find out what had been happening. As we were talking, we could hear bumps and bangs coming from upstairs. We went up to

have a look around. In the child's bedroom there is a cupboard
where all of his toys are kept, and when we looked at the two
doodle-boards, both of them contained messages. On one were
the words, 'Stop it now' and on the other 'Go now'. The boards
had been blank earlier on.

Marianne was clearly freaked out by this. We wiped the
boards and left a message on each one to see if anything would
appear, but to no avail.

Darren Ritson and Mike Hallowell tidied up a bit, and then
took photographic evidence of where everything was before
we all went downstairs. Later, a ceramic pig was found on the
toilet seat and a statuette was found on the stairs. When we were
all sitting in the dining room, a blue toy car seemed to fall from
the child's closed bedroom window and landed just outside the
open patio doors. This was witnessed by everyone present.

A shuttlecock was found on the second step down from the
landing, not long after Darren Olley and I had come downstairs
from collecting a locked-off video camera from the child's bedroom. Both Darren Olley and I were 100 per cent certain there
was no shuttlecock on the stairs when we came down.

Later, Marianne sent a text message from her mobile phone
to a friend. Marianne left her mobile phone on the table, and
we all went upstairs to see if anything had moved. After checking everything was okay, we all went downstairs again. Just
then, Marianne received a text message from her friend telling
Marianne not to send any more texts. Marianne phoned her
friend and told her she had not sent any additional text messages since the first one. Both Marianne and her friend seemed
freaked out by this, as Marianne had not touched her phone
since sending the last message. Marianne asked her friend to
forward her the last text she'd received back to her, which said
'I'm going to kill you, I'm coming soon' There are nine witnesses who know that Marianne did not touch her phone.

We were all sitting, having a cup of tea, when we heard
something hit Marc's chair. As he sat forward, a small figure
of a policeman could be seen. Its head was missing and it
was all twisted. We had a chat about the things that had been

happening, and Mike and Danny decided to do a smudging ceremony to try and provoke into the open whatever was in the house with us.

We all went upstairs into the child's bedroom, as that is where most of the activity was taking place. Mike started by placing some stones in a circle to form a medicine wheel and (I think) blessed the stones for protection with tobacco smoke. Marc had a small amount of tobacco in one hand and a bracelet of some sort in the other.

The temperature in the room rose significantly. Mike was inside the circle and Marc was outside. Suddenly, Marc started feeling a burning sensation on his chest and back. On lifting his T-shirt, we all witnessed scratch-marks appear on his torso. All of this has been documented on video tape and with photographs.

Marc then stood inside the circle for protection. The scratch-marks were still appearing on his chest, but quickly started to fade. By this time, the temperature had dropped again.

I don't think anyone in the room could believe what they were witnessing; actual bodily harm by an unseen force. I know *I* couldn't believe what I was witnessing. I still can't explain what I saw.

Later, some of us were in the kitchen and some were in the child's bedroom. Over the baby monitor the investigators in the kitchen, including myself, heard what we can only describe as a loud moan or sigh. The people in the child's bedroom heard nothing. Things then started to calm down a little, apart from a few bumps and bangs. Then, later, things started to materialise again.

Firstly, a green, upturned building block was found half-filled with water on the toilet floor. Then, a rubber hammer appeared from nowhere behind Marc in the child's bedroom, and another toy appeared on the floor in the same location. The statue on the hall shelf, which was flush against the wall (placed that way by Darren Ritson), had been moved to the centre of the shelf away from the wall, and the ceramic pig moved apparently on its own from the shelf in the toilet.

We then had another break, and each took a place in the house and turned out the lights. Danny stayed in the child's bedroom. Marc, Marianne and Mike were in the main bedroom. Darren Ritson and Suzanne McKay stayed in the living room. Glenn Hall and Claire Smith were in the kitchen, while Mark Winter, Darren Olley and I were stationed on the middle landing of the stairwell. All the lights were turned out, and at one point Darren, Mark and I heard what sounded like the creak of floorboards. Then we heard what we thought to be a footstep at the top of the stairs. Mark saw some light anomalies and captured them with his video camera – also at the top of the stairwell.

On going to investigate, the door to the main bedroom opened on its own. Both Darren and I saw that Marc could not have done this, as both hands and feet were well away from the door and Mike was lying behind the door in the main bedroom. Mike said he presumed that Marc had opened it. With that, the night came to a close.

An academic course I am currently undertaking covers poltergeist activity and, on reading some of the course material, I have come to the conclusion that what has been witnessed or experienced by Marianne, Marc, Robert, Mike, Danny and the *North East Ghost Research Team,* is PA:4 (Poltergeist Activity Level 4).

Disturbances at the house include: physical interaction/ marking/ manifestations/ apparitions/ amorphous shapes and lights/ levitation of objects/ object movement/ manipulation/ objects found stacked or arranged/ apportations/ asportations/ objects found unusually hot or warm to the touch/ disembodied voices or imitative sounds/ electrical or mechanical interference/ audible communication/ objects found that do not belong/ objects that go missing and turn up in odd places/ doors and windows opening or closing/ pets annoyed or upset/ strange drawings, writing, painting or pictures found/ audible disturbances such as hangings, knockings, rappings/ unusual smells and odours/ cold areas/ plasma effects, etc.

All of these phenomena have been witnessed by Marc, Marianne and an abundance of other witnesses.

I have carried out a few investigations at various places, but none has come close to what I experienced that night. The smudging ceremony was amazing. I went in with an open mind and was quite skeptical, but the things I saw that night I will probably never experience again. I will never forget the scratch-marks on Marc's torso. The memory of this investigation will remain with me for the rest of my life.

Julie Olley,
Investigator for the North East Ghost Research Team
14 September 2006

Statement of Mark Winter

On the night of September 1 2006, I was asked – as a member of The *North East Ghost Research Team* – to go to a private residence to corroborate some paranormal events that were alleged to have been taking place there by the occupants.

After our arrival, it wasn't long before things appeared to be happening. As we were checking the child's bedroom, one of the researchers noticed that two of the child's 'doodle – boards' had apparently been written on. The boards had been checked at the start of the investigation, and had been blank.

The messages read, 'Just go now' and 'Stop it now'.

I found this intriguing, as all persons in the house had been accounted for.

Later on in the night, we were having a discussion around the dining table when we all heard a tap on one of the chairs and, on checking, we discovered a small, toy policeman with its head missing and its legs mangled. The toy appeared to have come from nowhere.

After a short period of calm, we decided to try and provoke the 'spirit' into doing something. Mike Hallowell decided to do a Native American smudging ceremony, in which he would lay out a circle of stones called a medicine wheel and summon the 'wolf spirit' and the 'bear spirit'. Marc, another investigator and Mike stood in the middle of the room and conducted the ceremony. It wasn't long before Marc started complaining of a burning sensation in his back and chest. On inspecting Marc's torso, we were stunned to see scratches appearing from nowhere. Later on in the investigation, a child's building block appeared in the toilet, seemingly out of nowhere.

Later in the investigation, we decided to do separate vigils in different rooms with the lights turned off. Darren Olley, Julie Olley and I were situated on the stairwell and we heard what I thought was a footstep on the landing. I went up the stairs to investigate, and as I was standing on the landing one of the bedroom doors swung open without anyone touching it. I found this interesting to say the least, and could find no rational explanation as to why this had happened. I believe there is something unusual happening in the house, and would not be surprised if it is actually experiencing poltergeist activity.

Mark Winter
Investigator for the North East Ghost Research Team
September 14 2006

Statement of Darren Olley

The night we spent at 42 Lock Street will be a night I will never forget.

In fact, this was my second visit to the house. My first was fairly quiet – a few things moving about, but that was about it. On the second visit I expected to witness the same type and level of phenomena I had witnessed on the first, but I couldn't have been more wrong.

We arrived at the house at approximately 8.30pm. While we were sitting at the table talking about how we were going to proceed with the investigation, we could hear the odd bump and creak coming from upstairs. We went up to have a look around, and when we checked Robert's toy cupboard we were all amazed to find two message boards with writing on them; writing which Marc and Marianne both swore had not been there before. The messages read, 'STOP IT NOW' and 'GO NOW'. When Marianne saw these she screamed, and I have no doubt that she was genuinely terrified.

We went around the house and tidied everything we could away. Then we took photographs so we could check that everything was in the same place when we re-entered any given room. Among the phenomena that occurred within the first couple of hours was the movement of objects. A porcelain pig was found on the toilet seat, a statuette was found on the stairs and, later, a shuttlecock was discovered – again on the stairs. While we were sitting in the kitchen, a toy car fell from Robert's bedroom window When we checked, the window was locked and we were all downstairs at the time.

While we were sitting in the kitchen area, Marianne jokingly sent her friend a text message saying she was the poltergeist. She then apologised to her friend and left her phone on the kitchen table. A little later, Marianne received a text from her friend telling her to stop messing about; when Marianne contacted her friend she said she had received a text saying 'I'm going to kill you. I'm coming soon'. We all know that Marianne didn't touch her phone after sending the first text message. *[Authors' note: There was some dispute over the facts regarding this incident, as detailed in the main text of this volume].*

After all this occurred, Mike and Danny told us they wanted to do a 'smudging ceremony' which would either calm everything down or provoke a reaction from the poltergeist. The smudging started with Mike standing inside a 'medicine wheel' and Danny and Marc standing outside. During the ceremony, I was sitting down – facing Marc – and I could see his hand begin to twitch. Then his leg started to do the same. Just after I noticed this, Marc said his chest was burning; we lifted up his T-shirt and were amazed to see scratches appear; first on his chest, and then on his back. Marc said his back was burning and, again, when we looked there were scratches just appearing from nowhere -they had no apparent source. Eventually, it got too much for Marc and he had to enter the medicine wheel, where the burning sensation stopped.

After these events everything started to calm down; however, there were a few bumps and bangs and a few things found out of place, but nothing major.

The phenomena I've witnessed in this case are like nothing I have ever seen before. On my first visit I was very suspicious about the whole situation and didn't know whether to believe what I was hearing. However, after my second visit I now have no doubts that this case is a genuine one.

The scratches that appeared on Marc are the kind of things you expect to see in a horror film, but I can now say I have witnessed them in real life. I don't think I will ever get to experience anything like this again; this is a unique case, and it will be hard to return to other investigations and be happy with bumps and bangs after what happened at Lock Street.

Darren Olley
Investigator for the North East Ghost Research Team
September 23 2006

Statement of Jackie Hallowell

On Wednesday September 20 just after 10pm, I took a call from Marianne. I had never met her before, but knew of her because of Mike and Darren's investigation into the poltergeist phenomena at her home. She sounded very upset. I handed the phone to Mike and I heard him say that he'd go over to her house as soon as possible.

Mike asked me if I would go with him, as he felt that Marianne might be less frightened if there was another woman present. I agreed to go with Mike to Marianne's house. We arrived at the house just before 11pm.

As we entered the house the TV was switching itself off and on repeatedly. Marianne looked for the remote, but couldn't find it.

At one point we were sitting around the kitchen table drinking tea. Suddenly there was a loud sound, like a coin hitting the wooden floor in the dining room and then rolling. We were quite shocked. We all looked around in an effort to find the coin, but there was no sign of it.

Later we went upstairs to check if everything was okay in the bedrooms. Nothing seemed out of place. As we walked down the stairs towards the hallway, something shot past my head and clattered to the floor. It was a large, black nail. I have no idea where it came from, but I can say definitely that it did come from behind me as we walked down the stairs.

As we got to the bottom of the stairs, Mike noticed a pile of smaller nails near the front door. It is possible that they may have been there when we went up the stairs, but to be honest I really think we would have seen them.

After Marc returned home – just as he walked in the door, actually – the baby monitor in the living room started to make weird noises. It was a harsh sound, a bit like static, but very loud and rhythmic. I have never heard anything like it. The lights on the baby monitor were also flashing in a weird way, backwards and forwards. Mike recorded the sounds on his digital sound recorder. As he held the recorder next to the monitor the sounds seemed to get worse, and Mike thought that the recorder was maybe causing interference. He stepped away, thinking that this might make the sounds reduce, but it didn't. They just kept getting louder and louder. I remember Mike saying that the monitor sounded like it was going to explode.

Later we went into Robert's room to check, and there was a noise coming from the toy cupboard. Mike went over and opened the cupboard. The Scooby Doo toy was making laughing noises. I watched Mike switch the toy off and put it back on the shelf. Then I heard Scooby Doo say, 'Do you want to solve a mystery?' It was weird.

After we went downstairs Marianne made some more tea and we all sat around the table. Suddenly we heard a noise and when we looked we could see a plastic ball bouncing across the floor near the table. I have no idea where it came from. It bounced over towards me and kept bouncing up and down as if someone was patting it hard with their hand. It kept doing this for a while. Mike said we should just ignore it and we did. Eventually it stopped.

On Saturday 30 September I went with Mike and his dad, Peter, to Marc and Marianne's house. Mike said that Marc had some film on his phone of the poltergeist doing things, and that he wanted to copy it.

We got to the house late in the afternoon, and Mike went inside. I could see clearly the inside of the dining room through the patio doors. I could see Mike standing with his back to the patio doors. He was wearing a black jacket, black jeans and a white shirt. I could also see Marianne. She was wearing a black jacket and jeans. Marc was there too, and he was wearing a white T-shirt with blue on it and jeans. I could also see a fourth person. He was about the same height as Mike and Marc. He was standing to their right. He was wearing jeans and a T-shirt. I remember that the T-shirt was light brown or beige in colour. He had light brown hair that may have had a slightly ginger cast to it. The four were standing together and all looked to be talking, but I noticed that the man in the beige T-shirt seemed to be getting frustrated. He kept holding his hands out in front of him, as if he was trying to make a point but couldn't get it across.

When Mike came back to the car I asked him who the man in the beige T-shirt had been, and he said that there had been no such person in the room. Peter also was adamant that he'd seen the man standing in the dining room.

I have related here exactly what happened on these two occasions, and can say definitely that I can think of no rational explanation for what I witnessed.

Jackie Hallowell
4 October 2006.

Statement of Peter Hallowell

On Saturday 30 September my son Michael and I arranged to go to our local supermarket with his wife Jackie later in the afternoon. At lunchtime Mike rang me and asked if I would first take him to a house in South Shields where I was aware that he had been investigating a poltergeist case with his colleague Darren Ritson.

I cannot recall exactly when we set off, but I think we arrived at the house about 4pm. During the journey I recall Mike saying something about having to copy some film.

When we got to the house Mike left the car and went inside. After a while he came out. I remember that he was looking at his phone. He was just about to get in the car when he said that something wasn't right. He then went back in the house.

At some point I remember looking through the fence. I could see the inside of the house clearly. I remember seeing a man with short, fair hair. He was wearing a white T-shirt. I also recall seeing Marianne. She was wearing a black jacket. Marianne and the man in the white T-shirt were standing next to Mike. To the right I could see another man in a beige T-shirt. He seemed to be talking with the others.

After a short while Mike came back to the car. He was annoyed, and said that the film he wanted to copy had been lost, or words to that effect.

Jackie asked Mike who the man in the beige T-shirt was, but Mike said that there had been no one in the house dressed like that. I told Mike that I had seen him, but Mike was adamant that there had only been himself, Marianne and the man in the white T-shirt, whom he called Marc, in there at the time.

I can state categorically that I clearly saw the aforementioned man in the beige T-shirt standing with the others in the house.

Peter Hallowell,
4 October 2006

Statement of Jill Butler

On Friday 25 August, 2006, I went to the Market Cafe in South Shields and picked up Mike Hallowell, whom I have known for a number of years, and his colleague Darren Ritson. They had asked me to go to a house in South Shields that apparently had a poltergeist. Mike said that he would value my opinion about what was going on there. We got to the house about 11am.

When we got to the house, I was introduced to Marianne and Marc. Marianne told us about several incidents that had occurred since Darren and Mike had last visited.

I talked to both Marc and Marianne about their experiences. I could sense some negative emotions in the lounge, including unhappiness and anger. I felt that something had happened at this location, and that it had been very unpleasant. I also felt as if these emotions were connected with someone who had killed themselves under very sad circumstances.

After we had talked for a while, we went upstairs and walked into the bedroom of Robert, Marianne's young son. As they opened the door Marianne said something like, 'Oh my God, it's starting again'. She looked very upset and shaken.

In the middle of the bedroom floor I recall seeing a blue, plastic table. There were two stuffed toys on the table – a rabbit and a duck. The rabbit was sitting up and the duck was lying down. There was a large knife tucked under the right arm of the rabbit, and the blade was lying across the neck of the duck.

There was a shelf in the room with some toys on it. Also on the shelf was a frame, the sort that you would put a photograph in. Marianne pointed at it and said something like, 'Look, the prayer is the wrong way around'. She walked across the room and turned the frame around. It had a prayer inside, which she said had been given to Robert when he was Christened.

When I was in the room, despite the strange things I saw, I could not feel any negative presence or atmosphere. I asked Mike, and he said the same thing.

Mike and Darren seemed to be very sceptical about what they'd seen in the room, and said they'd have to talk to the couple about it.

Downstairs I sat with Mike and Darren as they talked to Marianne and Marc. At one point Marc went into the kitchen, and Darren followed him.

Not long after, I heard a clattering noise which came from outside the house. I heard young Robert, who was also in the garden, shout something like, 'What was that?'

We all went into the back garden, and I saw on the pathway two blue child's building blocks. Robert said that they'd come from the upstairs window.

Marianne said the blocks had definitely been in Robert's room, upstairs, and Mike agreed that he'd seen them.

When we came back inside, Darren found a large object, which I now know to be a paint-ball gun, behind the door leading into the kitchen. Marc said that the gun had definitely been upstairs in the bottom of his wardrobe.

While I was at the house, the phone kept ringing. Marianne kept picking up the receiver, but there was never anyone there. Every time she picked up the receiver the line just went dead.

After this happened several times, the phone rang again. Marianne retrieved the number and shouted something like, 'It's coming from your phone, Marc!'

Marc said his phone was in the kitchen. He went to get it but when he came back he said it was gone. Marianne suggested that Marc tried to ring his phone from her own mobile phone so that when they heard Marc's phone ringing they would know where it was. Marc tried to do this, but kept getting a busy signal as if his own phone was in use.

Not long after this the home phone rang again. There was a recorded message on it. An automated voice just kept saying the word 'Hi' over and over again.

During the rest of the morning, other automated voice messages saying different things kept coming.

To be honest I was staggered at the things I witnessed in the couple's house, and have no doubt that things were going on there that could well be termed paranormal, and for which there is no rational explanation.

Jill Butler
March 21 2007

Statement of Ian Peterworth

My name is Ian Peterworth. I am Marianne's brother and on numerous occasions when I have been at Marianne's home I have seen bizarre and frightening things happen.

On Wednesday 5 July, 2006, I was visiting my sister and her partner Marc. I happened to go up the stairs – I think it was to use the toilet – when I found Robert's rocking horse hanging from the loft hatch by its reins. I have no idea how it got there, but I'm sure no one in the house did it.

On another occasion, also at the top of the stairs, I found a large, stuffed rabbit belonging to Robert sitting in his blue, plastic chair on the landing. The rabbit had a blade from a work-knife in its hand or paw.

There was another time when I was using the toilet at Marianne's and Marianne happened to be in the bathroom. Suddenly there were loud bangs on the bathroom door, and then on the toilet door. I immediately opened the door, but no one was there.

On Friday 28 July 2006, I was at my sister's house when the investigators were there. We were all sitting in Robert's bedroom. Mike was sitting on the bed, and he suddenly shouted and pointed towards the wall opposite where the toy hammock was. He said, 'Look at that on the wall!'

When I looked I could see a small, black object about the size of a marble and it seemed to be floating down the wall slowly. It disappeared behind the chest of drawers. When the drawers were pulled away from the wall we found the object. It was a small piece from one of Robert's plastic toys. There was also some wood behind the drawers that had gone missing earlier.

I can say that the object had not simply dropped from the toy hammock. It was floating very slowly and I can't explain how it could have done this.

Later we were sitting in the kitchen with Mike when there was a loud noise, similar to a crack. We looked down on the floor and saw a penny lying there. Not long afterwards another coin appeared in the same way and I can say definitely that no one was moving at the time.

It was the same when the third coin dropped. It just seemed to come out of nowhere and fall to the floor.

After the coins appeared and fell to the floor something else happened which I can't explain.

Marianne's bag was in the middle of the kitchen table. I noticed that the strap on the bag was moving even though no one was touching it. It was very strange. It looked like someone was prodding it with their finger. Mike said that everyone should move away from the table. When we moved away the bag stopped moving, but then it started again.

At the same time as the bag was moving I noticed that a glass of water standing at the other end of the table was bubbling and shaking. It was weird. This got worse for a while, and then it stopped.

Darren Ritson and Darren Olley were upstairs when these things were happening. Afterwards, they came downstairs and sat around the table with us. Just then the table moved and bashed Darren on the leg. Marc moved the table back into its normal place.

On Monday 28 August, I was again at Marianne's house. Mike asked Marianne if she'd taken any notes. Marianne said that she had, and showed Mike her notepad which she had in her hand.

Just after this something strange happened. The freezer started to shake and Marc said that he'd seen something fall behind it. Nobody did anything at first. Then Marianne said she'd give Mike her notes. When she opened her notepad, a page of her notes had disappeared. I could not see how this could have happened, as they had definitely been in her pad minutes earlier when she'd showed them to Mike. I was standing next to her all the time, and the pad never left her hand.

Just then the freezer shook again and we pulled it away from the wall. From where she was sitting, Marianne saw something under the freezer as we pulled it away from the wall. She reached over and pulled it out, and it was the page of her notes that had disappeared from her notebook.

Later, after Mike had left, I went upstairs with Marianne and Marc to keep them company while they got some things together as they were going to stay at my mother's house. Because of the things that had happened they were afraid to stay in the house on their own. When we went into Robert's room, a large knife from the kitchen flew past us. We were frightened, and grabbed a few things and then went back downstairs. As we went down the stairs a yellow nut from one of Robert's toys came down the stairs after us and landed in the hall. We left it there and went into the living room, but it got thrown through the air again and landed in the room beside us.

I have seen a lot of things happen in my sister's house that I cannot explain, and they have been very frightening for members of my family.

Ian Peterworth
23 March 2007

Statement of Marrisse Whittaker

Working in the world of TV, one gets used to instant, would-be celebrities, touting outlandish stories to get their faces on to the screen. But what immediately struck us about Marianne was her obvious sincerity. She had agreed to our recorded interview, it seemed, as a last, desperate plea to someone who might possibly watch and who might finally be able to make her horrors go away. If anything, she was wary about publicity, particularly protective of her son Robert and at no time was any financial payment sought in return for talking to us.

What made her testimony most chilling, was the lack of sensational-ism in her telling of the truly out-of-this-world events happening in her home. She was weary, nervous about being left alone, at her wits' end. I would describe her as an intelligent and down to earth woman, not given to flights of fantasy. And afraid? Yes; very, very afraid.

While interviewing Marianne, a Bob the Builder toy kept bursting in to chattering sentences. I didn't want to stop the flow of the interview, so only checked out the toy when we'd finished. Such toys are, of course, prone to be trigger-happy, so I didn't for a moment expect anything sinister. But when I pressed one of the buttons, nothing happened. I discovered that the toy was not actually switched on and when I did switch it on and ran through the variety of sentences available, the words that I had heard repeated several times during the interview just didn't exist. I was quite clear what that sentence was, as it happened each time that Marianne mentioned incidents in which Robert had gone mysteriously missing and been found after a frantic search, asleep in unlikely places around the house.

The words I had heard loud and clear were 'Ha, ha, Can you find me, can you find me?'

Later, there were also some disturbing events that took place at our housewarming party.

I was wide awake when the crash shook the house, so I know I wasn't dreaming. It came suddenly, about an inch from my ear as I lay in bed and sounded like the biggest, heaviest wardrobe in the world had just toppled over and smashed to smithereens. Only we don't have any freestanding furniture in the bedroom, and as Bob and I leaped out of bed we found that absolutely nothing was amiss in the house.

I was still lying awake, heart beating, when ten minutes later, a peculiar light appeared from the wall above me. It came on suddenly, as if a torch had been switched on in the middle of the wall, pointing outwards. To have that shape, fanning out, there should have been a light source at that point. But there isn't, and the wall is at the back of the bedroom and three floors up. There were no cars outside that may have somehow flashed a light in the room and the houses across the road were all in total darkness.

I was still trying to figure it out, when the light started moving up. I couldn't take my eyes off it, not least, because it was the strangest pea-soup green in colour. It moved about a yard up the wall stayed still for a moment and then suddenly switched off – which is more than I did. Needless to say, I didn't get much sleep for the rest of that night.

Marrisse Whittaker
Orion TV

Statement of Bob Whittaker

One of the strangest things that happened when we interviewed Marianne, was an incident with Robert. Robert is an extremely bubbly, boisterous and happy child, not seemingly affected by the events in question. Playful and sweet, his very young age meant that his vocabulary never stretched further than a cheerful one word answer, a nod or giggle to questions.

During the interview with Marianne, he was particularly lively and a little distracting, so I led him out of the room in the direction of his toy box. Suddenly, walking down the stairs, he turned, looked straight at me and solemnly said. 'I used to have a boyfriend you know, but he died.' It made the hairs on the back of my neck stand on end. The next second, he raced away happily to play as though he had never spoken a word. It was disturbing. Not least because it was the only sentence I ever heard him speak.

My training is in journalism and what impresses you most about Mike Hallowell, is his painstaking, careful, evidence-based approach to investigating incidents such as this. He's not the sort of person to have the wool pulled over his eyes or to exaggerate events for greater effect. I know for a fact that he spends as much time explaining to people that their perceived psychic experiences are as much due to every-day, logically explained causes, as to unearthly ones. He takes the scary out of the supernatural, the panic away from the paranormal, turning fear of the unknown in to a fascinating journey of discovery.

Bob Whittaker
Orion TV

APPENDIX 3

Statement of Dave Wood and Nicky Sewell from PSI

We were called to observe an alleged poltergeist case in South Shields, Tyne and Wear, on Thursday 28 September, 2006.

The case was discussed in advance with investigators Darren Ritson and Mike Hallowell. We were shown a DVD compilation of evidence from stills cameras, video cameras and mobile phone cameras.

A variety of unusual occurrences were described to us at this point by Darren and Mike – and by the family at 4pm – when we went to house concerned.

Mike and Darren will, we are sure, freely concur with our conclusions about this evidence. The occurrences that had taken place, primarily since December 2005, were subjectively convincing to the wide range of people who had experienced them. However from an objective and critical outsider's perspective the testimony thereto amounted to a rich amount of subjective experience and anecdotal evidence. None of the evidence provided the required level of objective proof needed to draw firm conclusions.

One conclusion we could reach easily was the possible sources of these ostensibly paranormal events. This incontrovertible conclusion was that these events were either the result of unknown paranormal processes or of fraud. Many series of events that are defined as 'hauntings' by families are the result of misattribution. That is to say, in a context of haunting expectation a series of normal but ambiguous events are, in effect, mistaken for paranormal events. Due to the intelligent and deliberate nature of events in the house, a possible cause of misattribution can be ruled out.

A number of unusual events took place in the period of eight-plus hours we spent in the house. These included various 'discoveries' and auditory events. However, as no one witnessed these events directly and the areas were not monitored, no conclusions can be drawn on the basis of these.

However, two unusual events did take place in our presence. At 1710hrs, all six adults in the house were sitting at the dining room table – the occupants of the house, Nicky, Mike, Darren and Dave. The location is home to one infant who was the only other individual in the house, in the adjoining living-room. In the middle of a group conversation, the group noted that a modern two pence piece landed loudly underneath the centre of the table. A surface thermometer was used repeatedly over the following minutes. The coin's surface temperature of 14.5 degrees Celsius remained unchanged. Unfortunately, no-one present saw the origin of the coin and no video cameras were set up in the area. Therefore, while we would not believe it of anyone present, the possibility of human intervention could not be ruled out.

At 2345 hours, five adults were seated in the infant's upstairs bedroom. The child itself was sleeping downstairs. A video camera had been recording the adult male resident for the previous five minutes. Nicky and investigator Darren's attention had been attracted by a noise from the ground floor of the house. Nicky and Darren took the video camera downstairs and returned within seconds. During this time, the two adult residents of the house and Dave had been sitting in conversation.

Seconds after Nicky and Darren's return, the adult male resident announced he was feeling discomfort on his torso. This had occurred in the past, followed by a series of scratches appearing on his body. Darren trained the video camera on the adult male resident and requested that he took his shirt off. Within seconds, observed by the video camera and all persons present, red marks appeared on the adult male resident's torso. The apparent scratch marks began on his under arms, followed by deeper marks across his stomach and chest. These marks appeared to draw tiny globules of blood. The apparent scratching then began on his back. Within two minutes the scratches began to fade but were still visible upon our departure from the house.

This evidence appears compelling because the apparent scratches rose while the group watched and were captured on video camera. However such evidence cannot, in itself, be considered robust. The video camera did leave the room for approximately one-minute and although Dave personally observed the adult male resident for that period it is unlikely, but conceivable, that scratching took place prior to reporting without his attention.

Before any conclusions are drawn from this event – or future events with a video camera present for the whole period – the advice of a medical professional should be sought. While we have no medical training it would be necessary to rule out these scratches taking place resulting from natural physiological processes.

In our view, this case represents a good opportunity for possible objective evidence of paranormal processes – as we believe paranormal events or fraud could only explain the case.

However, serious consideration should be given to an increase in human and equipment resources coupled with a robust and widely consulted methodology. Only if this were to take place would the case, in our view, transcend the status of compelling subjective and anecdotal evidence into objective evidence from which firm conclusions could be drawn.

Further Reading

Adams, Paul & Brazil, Eddie, *Extreme Hauntings: Britain's Most Terrifying Ghosts* (The History Press, 2013)

Ashford, Jenny, *The Unseen Hand* (Bleedred Book & CreateSpace, 2017)

Braddock, Joseph, *Haunted Houses* (B.T. Batsford Ltd, 1956)

Cooper, Callum E., *Telephone Call from The Dead* (Tricorn Books, 2012)

Crowe, Catherine, *The Night Side of Nature* (George Routledge & Sons, 1848)

Day, James Wentworth, *In Search of Ghosts* (Muller, 1969)

Fodor, Nandor, *On the Trail of the Poltergeist* (The Citadel Press, 1958)

Fraser, John, *Poltergeist: A New Investigation into Destructive Haunting* (Sixth Books/John Hunt Publishing, 2020)

Gauld, Alan & Cornell, Tony, *Poltergeists* (Routledge & Keegan Paul, 1979)

Hallowell, Michael J. & Ritson, Darren W. *The Haunting of Willington Mill* (The History Press, 2011)

Holder, Geoff, *Poltergeist Over Scotland* (The History Press, 2013)

Hole, Christina, *Haunted England* (Batsford, 1940)

MacKenzie, Andrew, *Hauntings and Apparitions* (Heinemann, 1982)

Maple, Eric, *Supernatural England* (Hale, 1977)

Maxwell-Stuart, P.G., *Poltergeists: A History of Violent Ghostly Phenomena* (Amberley Publishing, 2011)

Norman, Diana, *The Stately Ghosts of England* (Muller, 1963)

O'Donnell, Elliot, *Haunted Britain* (Rider, 1948)

Owen, A.R.G, *Can We Explain the Poltergeist* (Helix Press, New York, 1964)

Parsons, Steven T., *Ghostology: The Art of the Ghost Hunter* (White Crow
  Books, 2015)

Parsons, Steven T. & Cooper, Callum E., *Paracoustics: Sound and the
  Paranormal* (White Crow Books, 2015)

Parsons, Steven T., *Guidance Notes for Investigators of Spontaneous Cases:
  Apparitions, Hauntings, Poltergeists and Similar Phenomena* (Society for
  Psychical Research, 2018)

Playfair, Guy L., *This House is Haunted: An Investigation into
  The Enfield Poltergeist* (Souvenir Press, 1980)

Poole, Keith B., *Haunted Heritage* (Guild Publishing, 1988)

Price, Harry, *Poltergeist Over England* (Country Life, 1945)

Price, Harry, *The Most Haunted House in England: Ten Years Investigation of
  Borley Rectory* (Longmans, Green & Co., 1940)

Price, Harry, *The End of Borley Rectory* (Harrap & Co., 1946)

Ritson, Darren W., & Hallowell, Michael J., *Contagion: In the Shadow of the
  South Shields Poltergeist* (Limbury Press, 2014)

Roll, William G., *The Poltergeist* (Nelson Doubleday, 1972)

Spencer, John & Spencer, Anne, *The Poltergeist Phenomenon, An Investigation
  into Psychic Disturbance* (Headline Book Publishing, 1996)

Willin, Melvyn J., *The Enfield Poltergeist Tapes* (White Crow Books, 2019)

Wilson, Colin, *Poltergeist: A Study in Destructive Haunting* (Hodder &
  Stoughton Ltd, 1981)